# Interdisciplinary Studies
# in Business Behavior

Edited by

## Joseph W. McGuire

Professor, General Business and Its Environment

University of Washington, Seattle, Washington

## SOUTH-WESTERN PUBLISHING CO.

Cincinnati 27        Chicago 44        New Rochelle, N. Y.        Dallas 2
                        Burlingame, Calif.

G59

Library of Congress Catalog Card Number 62-12627

H266
**Printed in the United States of America**

# PREFACE

•

The central theme of this book is the theory of business behavior. Based upon one or more of the behavioral sciences and mathematics, each chapter is a variation upon this theme. Persons interested in business should be vitally concerned with this topic, for implicit to the entire study of business and its subdivisions is an underlying theoretical structure. This book is also addressed to all persons who have an interest in the changing nature of theoretical business studies. It is hoped, therefore, that this volume will stimulate further theorizing and empirical research in business.

This book grew out of a graduate seminar I have conducted for the past five years in the area of Business and Its Environment at the College of Business Administration of the University of Washington. Each of the authors at one time was a graduate student in this seminar in business behavior, and his chapter was originally a seminar paper. These chapters, therefore, are representative of many such papers which have been written (and in some cases published elsewhere) by the students in this seminar over the years. I wish to acknowledge the work of all these individuals; their interest in the subject of business behavior and their participation in past seminars have made a contribution to this volume. However, I wish to acknowledge in particular the cooperation of those former students who have written the essays for this book, for they have given a great deal of time and effort to make it possible.

*J. W. McGuire*

## EDITOR'S SERIES

We are proud to present in the Editor's Series books that we feel should be available to the profession.

Books in this series are selected and published because of their scholarly nature, their contribution to advanced thinking and research, or their general professional contribution to the improvement of business and economic education. Appropriate manuscripts will be considered on their merit.

Books of the Editor's Series are those that every professionally minded person will want to possess. They should be in every library. Most of them will be useful as supplemental readings for students.

# CONTENTS

# Chapter 1

# INTRODUCTION

Joseph W. McGuire

---

The keynote of American life is change, which goes on continually and unremittingly. During the past century the alterations in our society have occurred on a gigantic scale and have taken place so rapidly and permeated so widely that change itself has come to form the central core of our existence and is considered commonplace. We accept first white, then green, then striped toothpastes; changes are made from four-cylinder automobiles to cars with six, to cars with eight, and back again to four cylinders; and yes, even the advent of the nuclear age requires of most persons but brief and transitory adjustments. In this world of constant change perhaps no institution has been affected more vitally, or changed and yet brought about changes more rapidly, than the business firm.

The past one hundred years have witnessed widespread and significant changes in business conduct. Early in this period the Captain of Industry—that tycoon who, as Veblen once wrote, "started out to do something and ended up to do somebody" [1]—passed from the American business scene and was replaced by the corporate manager as the dominant business personality. During these years the typical small enterprise has been reduced to only an insecure handhold in the economic fabric and is permitted to exist only in those interstices which remain unfilled—through tolerance or lack of interest—by the handful of giant-sized corporate entities which now produce over half our national output. Ownership and control have been separated, and the stockholder has be-

---

[1] Max Lerner, editor, *The Portable Veblen* (New York: The Viking Press, 1948), p. 389.

1

come primarily an income recipient rather than an active participant in business policies. Business concerns have weathered such philosophical movements as social Darwinism, scientific management, human relations and organizationalism, and are currently inundated with the notions of social responsibilities. This list of changes basic to the very nature of business concerns could be extended, but the point would seem to be sufficiently illustrated: that fundamental business institution—the firm—has undergone far-reaching and significant changes during the past century. Finally, if one thing is certain in an uncertain world, it is that these changes in business will continue into the future.

With all these changes in business it might be expected that new explanations and fresh theories of business behavior have been continually evolving. It must be considered remarkable, therefore, to find that until very recently there was only one important theory of business behavior and that this theory was based essentially upon the hedonistic calculus of Jeremy Bentham, an English philosopher who died in 1832.[2] Thus, business operations which have rapidly changed have continued to be explained by a theory which has remained relatively static, and which, so some scholars claim, never has been founded in reality. This theory, whether it be considered as a description of the behavior of nonexistent business institutions, or as a prescription for business which can never be completely filled, sets forth the concept of the rational businessman moving with certainty toward the goal of profit maximization.

It is in the light of a rapidly changing business environment and a relatively constant theory of business behavior that this volume is written. In recent years the study of business also has begun to change. Concepts and methods, models and tools have been uncovered in such diverse disciplines as mathematics, sociology, psychology, anthropology, philosophy,

---

[2] The theory of the firm was perhaps first explicitly presented by A. A. Cournot, *Richerches sur les Principes Mathematiques de la Theorie des Richesses*, translated by N. T. Bacon (New York: The Macmillan Company, 1897), first published in 1838.

biology, engineering, and economics, and have been applied in new and exciting ways to the theory of business. The results of these interdisciplinary studies are located in widely scattered journals and books. This book, then, is written to draw together much of this material from other fields, and to focus what is relevant upon the area of business. However, each author not only sums up the pertinent literature on his subject; he also evaluates it, applies it to business, presents his conclusions, and in this process gives his own insights into the subject with which he is concerned. Thus, this book is more than a text, for it contains a good deal of original observation. It is written, moreover, with the awareness that much of the material it contains is exploratory. In this sense, it looks toward the future study of business rather than to the past, for in business as in politics, this is indeed an age of new frontiers.

## The Economic Theory of the Firm

The economic theory of the firm plays a central role in this book, although it is not treated specifically in any of the chapters that follow. Like the ghost in *Hamlet*, it is the catalyst for action, an ingredient essential to the plot, although it generally remains concealed from direct observation. Because of its importance, it is fitting, therefore, that we should examine this theory briefly here.

There is no one economic theory of the firm which is universally acceptable to all economists. There is, nevertheless, ample evidence in the form of articles and books to indicate that some economic consensus of opinion exists. Briefly, the "traditional" theory of the firm postulates a goal—maximum profits, and then describes how this objective may be attained through the process of marginal analysis.

The firm in economic theory is an entity operating in given environments which do not constantly change. The variables in the economic model, (*e.g.*, prices, inputs, products) may be altered, but the parameters of market structure are not varied. In the model of perfect competition, for example, firms are defined as price takers, and they cannot individually affect market conditions through their actions. In more imperfect market environments, firms do have some degree of control over prices. However, economists traditionally view market structures as discontinuous, and there are no well-known models in which the operations of firms are described as the market situation changes. Thus, we have few, if any, theoretical explanations of the phases a firm might pass through as its position oscillates over time from that of a price taker to a price maker. In one instance (at least), such a dynamic economic model would be useful, as when innovating firms, monopolists for an initial period, find themselves competing with imitators and lesser innovators. Generally, the economic model of the firm is static, and the environment in which the firm operates is rather rigidly defined.

We have noted that the firm in economic theory is an entity. By this we mean that the business concern is viewed as a single unit, or person, dealing with problems of marketing, pricing, and production. We really never observe the internal relationship of the firm in economic theory, but we do know that it acts rationally toward its prime goal of maximum profits. This notion of a "black box" with predictable actions but irrelevant mechanisms for action has led some economists to consider the firm as though it were, for theoretical purposes, a single person—the entrepreneur.[3] The firm (entrepreneur) is therefore looked upon as a transformation unit, taking in inputs and altering these in some way to outputs, with the limits of its activities set by a specific market situation and restrained by its goal of profit maximization.

The firm in economics is ordinarily described as efficient, or rational. Traditionally, it has been regarded as perfectly rational, although in recent years there has been considerable dissent from this view. Perfect rationality requires that the firm know all possible alternatives and their consequences so

---

[3] Cf., James H. Strauss, "The Entrepreneur: The Firm," *Journal of Political Economy*, Vol. 52 (June, 1944), pp. 112-127, and R. H. Coase, "The Nature of the Firm," *Economica*, New Series, Vol. 4 (November, 1937), pp. 386-405.

that it is enabled to move with certainty toward its clear-cut and single goal of maximum profits.[4]

In order to maximize profits, it is necessary that business concerns produce at those levels of output where the "gap" between revenues and costs is greatest, for at this point net revenues (or profits) will be as large as possible. It is evident, therefore, that two of the most vital factors in this theory are revenues and costs, which are ordinarily expressed in monetary terms. Both revenues and costs depend, in turn, upon two variables: the price and number of units involved. For example, gross revenue consists of the prices at which each unit of output is sold multiplied by the number of units sold; and total cost equals the prices of all inputs times the number of inputs.

The task of the entrepreneur, then, is twofold: (1) to minimize costs and, (2) to maximize revenues, and to do both in such a manner as to maximize net revenues. It is assumed that the entrepreneur is rational and that he possesses perfect knowledge of his costs and revenues so that he is enabled to accomplish these goals through the use of marginal analysis.

It is conventional to depict the firm in economic theory as confronted with a known demand schedule and known costs over a feasible range of inputs. The prime decision made by the firm, given these conditions, is to select that specific output which will maximize its profits. This decision involves others on the number and mix of inputs and outputs. The primary and all secondary decisions are made through an examination of pertinent variables at the "margin." The use of marginal analysis in the economic theory of the firm ordinarily involves the comparison (in money terms) of additions to more than one of the pertinent variables. Marginal cost, for example, consists of the cost of producing an additional unit of output, while marginal revenue is the income which is received from the sale of additional units of output. If the production of

---

[4] Of late, some economists have argued that it is more realistic to consider that firms have a number of goals (an ordered preference function) rather than one goal. Such arguments, unfortunately, destroy the simple predictability of the theory.

an additional item will return more additional revenue than it costs to produce, then entrepreneurs will increase output. On the other hand, should marginal costs exceed marginal revenue, production will not be expanded. The optimum profit, then, will be at that level of output where a further increase in production will add more to costs than to revenue, while a reduction in output will subtract more from revenue than from costs. In other words, profit will be maximized where marginal cost and marginal revenue are equal.

The entrepreneurial decisions on inputs are made in similar fashion. If the costs of hiring or buying additional inputs are less than their value to the firm, these units will be purchased or hired (as with labor) until their costs are equal to their value to the firm at the margin. In the same way, the ratios of the marginal values to the marginal costs of particular inputs will be equated to the similar ratios of other inputs. These conditions insure that the costs of production will be minimized.

This, then, is the skeleton of the economic theory of the firm, presented as simply as possible, which has been so violently attacked and so staunchly defended in recent years. In fact, between the attacks and the defense, the exact nature of the theory has become confused and its separate parts somewhat obscured. What began many years ago as a relatively simple blend of the goal of maximum profits and the means of marginal analysis has turned out to be considerably more complex. Among other questions to which conflicting answers have been given by economists are the following: Is the theory supposed to be a description of modern business behavior? Or is it a prescription for business operations? Or is it perhaps a description of how firms would act *if* they were rational and *if* they maximized profits? Affirmative answers to the first two questions raise so many further questions that they seem completely unpalatable to the authors of this volume. The last, which reduces the theory of the firm to a mere exercise in logic, is of little utility to serious students of business.

## Attacks on the Profit Motive

Emerson Hoogstraat, in Chapter 2, summarizes several of the problems inherent in the traditional economic model of the firm. One central difficulty, as he points out, is that the notion of maximum profits has never been defined in a manner acceptable to most economists. For example, time always has been a particularly vexing problem and is one which has not yet been resolved satisfactorily. In the short-period, profit maximization is a more quantifiable and definite amount than it is over a longer interval. Often businessmen do not charge what-the-traffic-will-bear in the short-period, however, for to do so would not maximize profits over a long time span. But, to state that firms do try to maximize their profits over long periods is so vague, and so permissive, that such a statement is meaningless.

In a business world dominated by management groups and notable for absentee and almost voiceless ownership, the differences between those who receive profits and those who make profits are steadily growing wider. The definition of profits to shareholders, who, for example, may not be especially concerned with the construction of an industrial empire, may differ substantially from that held by the executives of the firm. Yet, which concept of profit is valid, and which should prevail? Further, what kinds of profits are to be maximized? Tax laws, other governmental restrictions, and accounting practices have not made this an easy question to answer.

These are only a few of the questions raised by Emerson Hoogstraat. They are sufficient, nevertheless, to illustrate certain problems of importance in the traditional economic theory of the firm, and to point to the need for a fresh approach to the study of business behavior. If we assume, finally, that the economic theory of the firm does not do what we want it to do—to explain usefully significant aspects of business behavior and to help us to predict such behavior—then we must turn to alternative theories for these explanations.

## Alternative Theories of Business Behavior

Business situations are not necessarily unique. They do not stand, alone and apart, separated completely from the main stream of human activity. Behavior in business is fundamentally human behavior, and as such, those theories useful in social disciplines (sociology and psychology, for example) should retain a great deal of their utility in business situations. The discovery of this seemingly obvious fact has been—together with the simultaneous stress upon mathematics—responsible for much of the awakening that has taken place in the study of business in recent years. Theories originally applicable in alien situations, which were not meant specifically to be used to explain business activities, often have provided insights and explanations useful in business. If such "borrowed" theories—whatever their origin—prove useful in explaining or predicting business behavior, then, by all means, let us borrow them. If they must be twisted, altered, shifted, or modified to adapt them to business, and if they then assist us to understand business, these changes should be undertaken, for the pragmatic test of a theory is its utility.

It is in this vein that most of the following essays have been written. In Chapter 3, for example, Lee Burns comments upon Cannon's physiological theory of homeostasis, which is somewhat related to Weiner's concept of cybernetics, and upon viability theories. There is a great deal of evidence to indicate that that business "body," the firm, has a deeply rooted urge to survive which is even more basic than profit maximization. The desire to remain viable, plus the human tendency toward habitual behavior, makes attractive the rather plausible theory that businessmen strive toward established equilibrium positions set through experience, and to counter movements away from these positions. Unfortunately, although it is possible that mechanisms within the firm react to restore equilibrium, it is not clear how equilibrium is set, or whether it is static or dynamic.

Organization theory, as discussed by Charles Lee in Chapter 4, is an ever-growing field of study for business scholars.

As Lee observes, however, while this area has a common sociological framework, much of the research has been fragmented. Whether the purpose of organization theory is to establish "ideal" structures for efficient bureaucracies, to predict organizational success, or to describe and perhaps improve the operations of organizations is difficult to determine, and research in this area appears to be going off in all directions. At this stage of development, however, experimentation seems to be more desirable than cohesion, and in their efforts to uncover new evidence, organization theorists are evolving fragments that appear to be leading to exciting new theoretical structures.

## Interdisciplinary Approaches to Business Behavior

Business has sometimes been called a practice in search of a theory. It is not a science, it is said, because men in business fail to employ the scientific method. This may be true—business is probably more of an art than a science—but there are signs of an emerging methodology, in large part mathematical, which gives promise of a greater use in business of more scientific approaches to important operations. The role of mathematics in the construction of models of behavior has been encouraging, and it may well be that the use of high-speed computers will permit the manipulation of the large number of variables significant in the construction of a theory which will enable researchers to simulate and perhaps predict business behavior.

This book contains three chapters on the use of mathematics for exploring business theories. The first, Chapter 5 by Leo Spier, examines a new pseudo-mathematical tool, graph theory, which may prove to have considerable utility for business as a descriptive device. The rigor and preciseness potential of graph theory is illustrated by Spier's presentation of increasingly more complex models of bureaucracy. In Chapter 7 Richard Trainor discusses mathematical programming techniques, which are becoming more widely used in the solution of specific business problems. Of these, the most commonly employed is linear programming. Linear programming, as a method for finding a maximum, has certain advantages not possessed by marginal analysis. Businessmen have always been skeptical of the utility of marginal analysis, primarily because they have not been able to distinguish with precision the marginal variables which are considered important. With linear programming, on the other hand, they can evidently attain maxima in business situations where they have knowledge of the constraints involved. Unfortunately, linear programming may not be too helpful in developing the theory of the firm. As the name implies, linear programming utilizes functions described by straight lines, and much of economic theory, for example, is based upon functions which are nonlinear. Despite this weakness, linear programming has been useful to the theoretician, for it has concentrated attention upon internal output and cost restraints independent of market structures and demand, and in this way has contributed to our knowledge of an area somewhat neglected by traditional theory.

William Boore, in Chapter 8, discusses the relationships between the theory of games and the theory of business. In a game of chess, for example, the moves of each player are usually contingent upon the moves of the other and must be taken into account in planning future moves. In games, as in business, certain rules must be followed, and the actions of one firm often depend upon what other firms do, or what they are expected to do. If, to illustrate this point further, firm A wants to increase prices in an industry with only a few other competitors, it must not only foresee the consequences of this action *per se*, but must also predict the actions of its competitors, each of which might react differently. The complexity of business actions is enhanced in this environment, and the maximization of profits in the traditional sense may be difficult, if not impossible. In the real world, businessmen must take the reactions of others into account, and the theory of games establishes a framework (highly idealized, to be sure) wherein the behavior of "rational" businessmen is predictable. Normally, however, all of the rules of a game are established in advance, while in actual business practice all the rules are not predetermined, and may, in fact, never become completely clear.

It must be evident from several of these comments that businessmen actually operate in environments in which there is a great deal of uncertainty, so that they can never be sure that their choice of alternatives will result in desired outcomes. Bryce Orton, in Chapter 6, discusses the effects of uncertainty upon business behavior. If we do not know with certainty what the outcome of our action is going to be, how can we maximize, or try to maximize, anything? Or how can we behave rationally in an irrational world filled with uncertainty? These are questions which scholars from many disciplines have tried to answer, and several alternative schemes for dealing with uncertainty have been worked out. Orton analyzes a number of these models and evaluates their potential utility for business.

Two of the chapters contributed to this volume are concerned primarily with the interrelations between psychology and business. The first of these, Chapter 9 by Alvar Elbing, is confined to an examination of the investigations of psychologists in the broad areas of perception and motivation and the applicability of their results to behavior in business. After reading Chapter 9, one cannot but agree that these investigations have reached conclusions which should be taken into account in a general theory of business. Businessmen are not omniscient. They do not perceive all of the alternatives in a decision-making process, nor do they consider all the consequences of their decisions. Men in business—as men everywhere—have only limited perceptions of reality. Similarly, they move toward a variety of goals, some of which may be in conflict one with the other. Elbing contrasts these psychological concepts with the traditional theory of profit maximization and concludes that the former has a great deal to offer in the future construction of a realistic theory of the firm.

In Chapter 10 Mark Gibson attempts to tie together field theory, as developed primarily by the famous social-psychologist Kurt Lewin, and business behavior. Since Lewin constructed field theory to be sufficiently broad to encompass all kinds of behavior, it is not strange that it may be found useful in business. Furthermore, since Lewin employed a graphical method to describe behavior in a psychological environment, it should not be surprising that his methods may be of assistance in depicting the role of the businessman in his firm and for describing the interconnections between executives, firms, and industries. Gibson illustrates how field theory might provide us with new insights into behavior and discusses its applicability to business.

Valuable though psychology may be to students of business, it is evident that business behavior cannot be fully understood unless it is examined as a part of the over-all pattern of societal behavior. In Chapter 11 Jean Boddewyn surveys business theory from a variety of cultural approaches: the historical, cross-cultural, and subcultural. Each of these has its place in providing the broader setting in which business operates. As Boddewyn concludes, however, cultural theories are meaningless unless they are supplemented by socio-psychological theories of personality, for to attain a general theory of business behavior, both the actions and attitudes of the individual as well as the mores of society must be understood.

Modern man finds it difficult, if not impossible, to move outside of his culture without invoking certain societal sanctions. Businessmen, who after all are individuals within a culture, as are all men, must also conform to societal pressures. An important part of our western heritage, certainly, is the Judeo-Christian ethic to which our society subscribes. Richard Robinson, in Chapter 12, explores the relationships between our moral code and business actions as he searches for rules of conduct which will tell us how businessmen should behave. He finds that in our modern society codes of ethics and morals are so loosely defined they do not rigidly confine business (or nonbusiness) operations. The failure of businessmen to behave responsibly, however, may well be the fault of society and not of business.

In Chapter 13, the final chapter in this volume, David Huff presents a generalized approach to the theory of business. He employs a variety of disciplines (relying most heavily upon the sociological framework developed by Talcott Parsons) and attempts to synthesize these into a general theory of business. His model is useful in that it calls attention to the variables which he considers significant in a general theory. However, as Huff concludes, a great deal of work is still needed before truly predictable and general models of business behavior are constructed.

## Conclusions

In looking back over this introductory summary of the chapters to follow, one cannot but be impressed by the breadth and diversity of the current investigations into the theory of business behavior. The study of business in recent years has changed substantially, and there are signs, as set forth in this book, that it will be altered even more rapidly and more fundamentally in the future. Out of these chapters it is hoped one will catch the excitement and adventure of a field which is expanding vigorously and in which the opportunities for scholarship are tremendous.

Despite the variety of topics with which this volume deals, it contains a common theme: the search for parts to a general theory of business behavior. Each author has attempted to relate the subject matter of his chapter to the business structure. At this time it is not possible to draw all these fragments together into a unified theory. Nor is it reasonable, at this time, to discard all approaches but one. At this stage of development of business, theory experimentation is in order, and advances should take place on a broad front. Then, even if no general theory should be forthcoming, we have at least enriched and broadened the study of business.

# Chapter 2

# ATTACKS ON THE VALUE OF THE PROFIT MOTIVE IN THEORIES OF BUSINESS BEHAVIOR

Emerson E. Hoogstraat

## Introduction

Although economists generally realize that their simple model of firm behavior, constructed on the profit-maximization motive, does not explain such behavior adequately or predict market movements accurately, there remains a strong tendency to continue to use the profit-maximizing model as a theoretical device. Reluctance to abandon the classical model is understandable. It not only provides a very precise and easily understood explanation of firm behavior, but it also furnishes the base for a complete superstructure of production and distribution theory. If business firms are truly maximizing profits, we can not only determine how they will act under given sets of circumstances, but we can also explain why firms (and therefore their aggregation—the economy) utilize varying combinations of resources, why the providers of these resources receive the returns they do, why firms enter or leave certain industries, how firms determine their output and the prices of their products, and many other facets of economic activity.

We also find that if we combine the profit-maximizing model with certain other assumptions, such as the existence of pure competition, we not only arrive at an explanation for practically all economic phenomena, but find that the economic world so described is the best of all possible worlds. We find not just an orderly system, but a highly moral system, in which everyone will receive exactly in accordance with his contribution, and in which production and distribution automatically work out to the greatest benefit for the greatest number of people.

The hesitance of economists to tamper with the profit motive, even though they generally are aware that some revision would make it more realistic, is readily explained. To admit that firms may have motives other than profit maximization, or to admit that profit maximization may not be possible even when eagerly desired, is to admit that there may be serious flaws in the entire structure of traditional economic theory.

However, even though many economists claim that the inadequacies of the classical model are minor, and some steadfastly maintain that profit maximization is the unique goal of business activity, a growing group of writers have attacked it. They have discarded the ever profit-seeking economic man and have substituted in his place another species, the true character of which is subject to much debate.

## Attacks on What "Profit Motive"?

Despite the consensus that something else has either replaced or supplemented the profit motive as the determinant of business behavior, the consensus disappears when we attempt precisely to define "profit." For then we discover that different economists have different concepts of profit and profit maximization and that they lack agreement on which profits business firms attempt to maximize.

*Long-Run Versus Short-Run Profits.* Probably the best example of such a conflict of opinion is found in the concepts of short-term and long-term profits. Most economists will agree that business behavior fails to reflect either objective (actual) or subjective (intended) maximization of short-term profits, but will disagree heartily regarding the influence of subjective maximization of long-term profits on the policies of business firms.

Part and parcel of the short-term, long-term controversy is the confusion about the definition of long-term profits. Most economists probably would be satisfied with a definition that merely takes into consideration some sort of summation of future years' profits, perhaps discounted to the present with the use of some appropriate interest rate factor. If they happened to be among those who believed that firms did attempt to maximize long-term profits, they would assume that this is the figure that should be maximized. William Fellner, on the other hand, is of the opinion that, to the extent that firms attempt to maximize in a pecuniary sense in the long-run, they should attempt to maximize the present net worth of the firm, a figure determined by discounting to the present both future earnings *and* future capital gains. Maximization of such a figure as this, however, cannot be called *profit* maximization in the typical sense in which the word is used, according to Fellner.[1]

***What Kind of Profit?*** Entirely apart from the short-run, long-run confusion, we find that there is considerable confusion regarding the selection of the appropriate profit figure. Are those who defend the profit motive upholding the maximization of pure profits, accounting profits, gross profits, before-tax profits, after-tax profits, or what have you, as the goal of business activity? The advocates of the profit motive have not agreed on the solution to this problem and generally have failed to identify the profit they have in mind. Inasmuch as the proponents of the traditional theory generally have been careless in their definition of this vital part of their model, and have sometimes been in disagreement among themselves, we find that their antagonists, of necessity, have been vague in their definition of profits. However, it appears to the writer that if the reasons given by these antagonists for objecting to the unique validity of profit motives in the explanation of firm behavior are adequate under the assumption of any one profit concept, they are probably adequate for almost any other

---

[1] William Fellner, *Competition Among the Few* (New York: Alfred A. Knopf, Inc., 1949), pp. 164-166.

profit concepts. The question raised in this paragraph is probably an academic one, but it could be of significance in analyzing some of the attacks on the profit motive.

*Profits for Whom?* Whose profits are maximized, according to the defenders of the profit motive? Here again, we have a question by and large unanswered. Obviously, the profits to be maximized are those of the firm; but what does this mean? Objective profit maximization for the corporate entity very well may not mean objective profit maximization for the owners of the corporation because of the vagaries of the tax laws and the variety of tax situations in which the various shareholders find themselves. If we assume that objective maximization is not possible and that the most we can expect is subjective maximization, or intended maximization, the problem is complicated rather than simplified. For example, if corporate management acts in ways which it feels will subjectively maximize profit, but the owners of the business would have taken entirely different actions based on the same information, whose profits are being intendedly maximized—the corporation's or the owners'?

All of this might be classified as doing battle with an army of straw men. There may be nothing here to fight out at all. But these are thoughts which at least should be considered before attempting to analyze various attacks on the profit motive, whether we resolve the issues or not. Although differences in viewpoint on the matters discussed above probably will have little bearing on the arguments presented by the antagonists of profit maximization, a working hypothesis for the rest of this chapter will be that the profit we speak of is long-run profit, pure profit, and profit to the business entity as opposed to the profit to the owner of the business.

## Types of Objections to the Profit Motive

Classification of attacks on the profit motive is difficult because of the overlapping of views, regardless of the basis we choose for classification. A breakdown will be made, nonetheless, in order to facilitate an orderly presentation of the views of the various dissenters from the traditional doctrine. It must be recognized, however, that this is an arbitrary classification and that many writers' opinions will not fit neatly into any one class. The attacks on the profit motive will be grouped as follows:

1. Business motives in addition to the profit motive are present and perhaps dominant as guides to business behavior. The profit motive is not denied. It is merely removed from its unique position.

2. Personal motives of the management are present and perhaps dominant as guides to business behavior. Limited influence of the profit motive is not denied.

3. The profit motive is the dominant motivation in business behavior, whether other motives are present or not, but profit *maximization* is not a motivating factor.

4. Profit maximization is the sole or dominant motivation, but firms do not strive for it in a recognized manner because they do not use marginal analysis in decision making.

5. Profit maximization is the sole or dominant motivation, but firms cannot objectively achieve it because of uncertainty and lack of knowledge.

6. Profit maximization may be the dominant motive, but the decision-making function is so widely diffused that it is impossible of accomplishment.

## Other Business Motives

In objecting to the validity of the concept of profit maximization on the grounds that firms actually have several business or economic objectives, only one of which is profit maximization, economists are treading on slippery ground. To claim that the pursuit of objectives other than profit maximization is, *ipso facto*, non-profit maximizing behavior, is good sense *unless* it can be shown that the apparently non-profit maximizing behavior was actually enhancing long-range profits. Probably some of those who object to the concept of profit maximization on these grounds are not looking beyond the short-range. This makes these scholars right within their own frame of reference whether the apparently non-profit maximizing behavior which they point up contributes to long-range profits or not. But profit maximization in the short-run only would be such a ridiculous policy for the great majority of business firms that we hardly need consider objections to this kind of non-profit maximizing behavior; thus the working hypothesis stated earlier in this chapter that we would be concerned only with attacks on profit maximizing as a long-range goal. It is difficult to say to what extent the apparently non-profit maximizing behavior discussed in this section will or will not contribute to long-range profit maximization. Suffice it to say, such behavior will, in many cases if not in most cases, fail to maximize either short-run or long-run profits.

One classification of economic non-profit maximizing motives is found in a statement by R. A. Lester:

> A list of such goals might include the following: "satisfactory" or "reasonable" profits, maximum possible profits, security and convenience of the existing management, achievement and maintenance of sufficient liquidity to assure the firm's financial safety, and maintenance of the firm's market position or its established share of the industry's total sales.[2]

A colorful classification of some of these motives is found in George Leland Bach's *Economics*.

> A leading business executive recently described three of these non-profit objectives as: "Empire Building," "Ivory Tower Perfectionism," and "Maginot Line Building."
>
> The Empire Builders want to be big—leaders in their field. They want to keep chalking up one new sales record after another, or to swell their share of the market year after year, or to have the newest and biggest plant in the industry. The Perfectionists have their eyes glued on the goal of "efficiency," but sometimes on efficiency even at the expense of profits. . . . Traditional rules-of-thumb about "efficiency" are all too important for the Perfectionists. The Maginot Line Builders, on the other hand, pass up profits because they are afraid to take risks. Never willing to go out on a limb

---

[2] R. A. Lester, "Equilibrium of the Firm," *American Economic Review* (March, 1949), p. 483.

with a new product, they always keep cash and liquid assets at "conservative, safe levels." [3]

One needs little experience in business affairs to recognize many examples of these prototypes.

In these and other sources can be found repeated mention of the following non-profit maximizing business goals: (1) liquidity; (2) maintenance of a certain share of the market; [4] (3) maintenance of satisfactory "safety margins"; (4) expansion and growth; [5] (5) conservative financing; [6] (6) secure profits; and (7) efficiency. Three of these will be given special attention.

*Liquidity.* Joel Dean makes the following statement with regard to liquidity:

> Although liquidity position can logically be viewed as underlying maintenance of control, it is probably often an independent managerial comfort which blunts sheer profit maximization. As a consequence of balance-sheet considerations, executives sometimes deliberately choose a less profitable but more liquid alternative, when as is common the two pull in opposing directions. [7]

The quest for liquidity receives more attention as a non-profit maximizing goal than almost any other factor, as might be expected, considering the emphasis on liquidity by banks and other lenders and the strong sense of security which good liquidity positions give to business management. [8]

[3] George Leland Bach, *Economics: An Introduction to Analysis and Policy* (Englewood Cliffs, N. J.: Prentice-Hall, Inc., 1954), p. 339.

[4] Neil Chamberlain, *A General Theory of Economic Process* (New York: Harper & Brothers, 1955), pp. 217-250, and George Katona, *Psychological Analysis of Economic Behavior* (New York: McGraw-Hill Book Company, Inc., 1951), p. 203.

[5] *Ibid.*

[6] Joel Dean, *Managerial Economics* (Englewood Cliffs, N. J.: Prentice-Hall, Inc., 1951), pp. 580-582.

[7] *Ibid.*, p. 32.

[8] M. W. Reder, "A Reconstruction of the Marginal Productivity Theory," in R. V. Clemence, *Readings in Economic Analysis*, Volume II (Cambridge: Addison-Wesley Publishing Company, Inc., 1950), p. 259; R. A. Gordon, "Short-Period Price Determination in Theory and Practice," *American Economic Review* (June, 1948), pp. 265-288; Kenneth E. Boulding, "Implications for General Economics of More Realistic Theories of the Firm," *American Economic Review* (May, 1952), p. 40; and Bach, *op cit.*, p. 295.

*Safety Margins.* William Fellner poses the "safety margin" as a primary business objective. According to his concept, the safety margin is the difference between the sales price of a commodity and the average unit cost of producing the commodity. Because of uncertainty, business management will want to see this margin as large as possible so that unforeseen cost increases or price declines will have the least likelihood of wiping out the firm's profits. In any market situation other than pure or perfect competition, the level of output which will provide the maximum margin of safety will be smaller than the most profitable level of output. Consequently, to the extent the firm attempts to maximize margins of safety it fails to maximize profits. However, if the unfavorable cost and price changes are more than just feared—if they are actually anticipated—then the cost and revenue data on which the firm bases its output and pricing decisions will be changed correspondingly, and the level of output selected actually will be the most profitable level under the changed cost and revenue assumptions.[9]

*Secure Profits.* Very closely related to Fellner's concept of the safety margin as a distinctively recognizable goal apart from profit maximization is the goal of "secure" profits, as expressed by K. W. Rothschild.

> But there is another motive [other than profit maximization, in oligopoly] which cannot be so lightly dismissed, and which is probably of a similar order of magnitude as the desire for maximum profits: the desire for *secure* profits.[10]

Mr. Rothschild points out that profit security has failed to receive the attention it deserves because it is so easy to identify many actions designed to enhance the security of profits with the motive of long-range profit maximization. He objects to this confusion of goals, however, claiming, in the first place,

---

[9] Fellner, *op. cit.*, pp. 153-154, and William Fellner, "Average Cost Pricing and the Theory of Uncertainty," *Journal of Political Economy* (June, 1948), pp. 250-251.

[10] K. W. Rothschild, "Price Theory and Oligopoly," *Economic Journal* (September, 1947), pp. 308-309.

that *long-run* profit maximization is an impossible goal because of uncertainty about the future, and in the second place, that many actions taken for the sake of profit security are actually contradictory with the goal of profit maximization, citing as one example the reinvestment of earnings in the firm, when more profitable investment could have been made elsewhere.

### Personal Noneconomic Motives

Although there is a distinct possibility that many of the economic non-profit maximizing motives for business behavior discussed in the preceding section actually might contribute to long-run profit maximization, there is another group of non-profit maximizing motives for which long-range profit maximization hardly could be claimed, namely, the various personal, non-pecuniary motives of the management of the firm.[11] It is sometimes difficult completely to separate these motives from the economic ones, but it is probably advantageous to attempt to do so because of the significant difference in the way these two classes of motives can affect long-range profits.

The objections to the solely pecuniary considerations in the traditional profit motive model are well stated by Jim Reese.

> The traditional economist . . . makes two mistakes in assuming that the desire for money in itself is the whole motive force behind economic activity. In the first place, the satisfaction of human desires is not directly related to the amount of money the individual has, and in many cases additional funds do not bring additional satisfaction. In the second place, orthodox theory fails to consider that, even in the business world, satisfaction may be secured in ways other than by the acquisition of money.[12]

What, then, are these "human desires" which are not satisfied with money? One list is that given in a statement by John R. Meyer.

---

[11] Talcott Parsons, "The Motivation of Economic Activities," *The Canadian Journal of Economics and Political Science* (May, 1940), pp. 194-197, and Chamberlain, *op. cit.*, pp. 65-73.

[12] Jim Reese, *Our American Economy* (Boston: Houghton Mifflin Co., 1953), p. 125.

The suggestion is increasingly made that even those most economic of all men, the entrepreneurial types, do not simply maximize pecuniary profits but rather "utils" of satisfaction that encompass not only a recognized penchant for money but also a desire for job security, craftsmanship, financial flexibility, managerial independence, etc.[13]

E. Wight Bakke fills in some of the details in his pioneering work *Adaptive Human Behavior*. He poses the proposition that a firm, like all social organizations, is a "structure of living," in which each individual has a variety of goals. The managers of the firm are not only a part of the structure of living of that firm but are also a part of a structure of living of the social and professional group consisting of their acquaintances in other business firms. In both of these structures, the manager has a variety of goals which have been described by Bakke as *security* with respect to, *progress* toward, and *justice* in the midst of the following experiences: (1) respect of his fellows, (2) creature sufficiency, (3) control over his own affairs, (4) understanding of his environment, (5) capacity performance, and (6) integration with his environment.[14] It is certainly true that some of these goals can be attained through pursuit of the profit motive, but it is just as true that some of the goals can be furthered through non-profit maximizing behavior.

Benjamin Higgins specifically ties some of these personal goals (along with some economic goals) in with non-profit maximizing output policies. For example, the manager's desire for leisure will induce him to produce at levels lower than optimum, his desires for largeness itself and to avoid accusations of restricting output will cause him to produce at levels in excess of optimum, and his desires to conform to custom and habit, his unwillingness to experiment and his lack of knowledge of his revenue curves will induce him to

[13] John R. Meyer, discussion in "The Import of Some New Developments in Economic Theory: Exposition and Evaluation," *American Economic Review* (May, 1957), p. 336.

[14] E. Wight Bakke, *Adaptive Human Behavior* (New Haven: Yale University Labor Management Center, 1950), pp. 18-19.

stay put whether the output is above or below the optimum level.[15]

These and other writers emphasize a number of non-pecuniary aspirations of business managers which can be classified as follows: (1) desire for leisure, (2) desire to be one's own boss, (3) desire to be free from management worry, (4) reluctance to disturb routine,[16] (5) desire to retain control, and (6) desire to contribute to the public welfare. Some of these motives deserve additional comment.

*Leisure.* A fairly complete analysis of the effect of a desire for leisure on the part of management on the firm's profit maximizing behavior is given by T. Scitovsky and J. P. Nettl in separate articles. They use much the same analysis, showing that if an entrepreneur has a typical indifference as between increased profit and reduced entrepreneurial effort (leisure), the level of output he selects will be lower than his most profitable level of output. The only condition under which his indifference curves would result in the selection of a profit maximizing output would be where he has a constant marginal utility of profit—that is, where his desire for more profit would not be reduced as his profits rose.[17] Neither of the writers claim to know to what degree managers have a constant marginal utility of profit, but Scitovsky guesses that most businessmen have such a utility function.[18] Even so, this would leave a large number of managers who would readily forego additional profit for the sake of additional leisure.

Nettl makes the interesting comment that the manager is more likely to have a constant marginal utility of profit when profit earning is divorced from profit consumption (as in the case of the hired manager of a corporation) than when

---

[15] Benjamin Higgins, "Elements of Indeterminacy in the Theory of Non-Perfect Competition," *American Economic Review* (September, 1939), pp. 476-477.

[16] Reder, *op. cit.*, p. 253; Bach, *loc. cit.*; and Reese, *op. cit.*, p. 124.

[17] T. Scitovsky, "A Note on Profit Maximization and Its Implications," in American Economic Association, *Readings in Price Theory* (Homewood, Ill.: Richard D. Irwin, Inc., 1952), pp. 354-356, and J. P. Nettl, "A Note on Entrepreneurial Behavior," *Review of Economic Studies* (February, 1957), pp. 87-94.

[18] Scitovsky, *op. cit.*, pp. 357-358.

the manager is also the profit consumer (as in the case of a sole proprietorship or partnership).[19] Although this is certainly contrary to the widely accepted view that separation of ownership and control dulls the profit motive, Nettl receives at least limited support from some writers, such as George Katona, who says, "It appears . . . that the current widespread split between ownership and management functions does not provide valid arguments against the role assigned to the profit motive in our economy. As a rule, a salaried executive will strive for profits for his firm."[20]

That the desire for leisure will be particularly strong and its attainment particularly easy in monopolistic situations is the view held by J. R. Hicks:

> It seems not at all unlikely that people in monopolistic positions will very often be people with sharply rising subjective costs; if this is so, they are likely to exploit their advantage much more by not bothering to get very near the position of maximum profit, than by straining themselves to get very close to it. The best of all monopoly profits is a quiet life.[21]

As a final argument for the importance of the desire for leisure as a management goal, we have the following:

> A recent *Fortune* poll ["The Management Poll," *Fortune* (October 1946, p. 14)] asked this very pointed question of a number of business executives: "If you could double your income by working two or three more hours a day, would you do so?" Surprisingly, some 70 per cent of the corporate executives who were interviewed replied "no," that they would not be willing to work a few hours more in order to double their money income.[22]

***Being One's Own Boss.*** The abandonment of the profit motive or its relegation to a low priority is a typical accompaniment of a strong desire to be one's own boss—to operate a business of one's own choice in the way one chooses.

---

[19] Nettl, *loc. cit.*
[20] Katona, *ibid*, p. 197.
[21] J. R. Hicks, "Annual Survey of Economic Theory: The Theory of Monopoly," *Econometrica* (January, 1935), p. 8.
[22] Reese, *op. cit.*, p. 129.

The attraction of being at once president, vice-president, general manager, etc., of a firm, as well as the hope that conditions will improve, induces many small enterprisers to continue in business long after the more rational course would be to give up. There is a strong tendency for businesses which require little capital and experience to be overcrowded and chronically unprofitable for most firms.[23]

**Freedom from Worry.** Freedom from management worry and concern is certainly an important noneconomic goal of businessmen.[24] There are many ways in which this freedom can be increased. Joel Dean examines one of these, namely, the avoidance of long-term debt.

Debt financing puts an asymmetrical risk on management. The men who make the decisions rarely regard the profit prospects as adequate to offset the threat to their personal security from general reorganization in bankruptcy. In many corporations, management's share in the profits of successful ventures (in the form of dividends on the stock they own) is an insignificant source of income compared with their salaries, which show admirable stability over the business cycle.

*       *       *       *       *       *

Thus, despite stock-ownership and profit bonuses, the personal interest of executives is usually toward conservatism. Who is to condemn (or even know), if management turns down a risky venture that could cost them their jobs? [25]

**Retention of Control.** The desire on the part of the current managers of a firm to retain control of the firm in the future will affect the decisions they make, and very likely will result in some non-profit maximizing behavior.[26] For example, the planned rate of growth of the firm very well might be less than necessary to maximize profits.[27] An optimal growth rate might require the firm to obtain excessive amounts of funds from outsiders, thereby threatening the control of the incumbent management.

---

[23] Clark Allen, James Buchanan, and Marshall Colberg, *Prices, Income and Public Policy* (New York: McGraw-Hill Book Company, Inc., 1954), pp. 70-71.

[24] Reder, *loc. cit.*

[25] Dean, *op. cit.*, pp. 581-582.

[26] *Ibid.*, p. 32.

[27] Reder, *op. cit.*, pp. 256-258.

*Public Welfare.* There appears to be a growing tendency for business management to assume a goal of "public service," or "social responsibility." [28] It seems, however, that there is some difference of opinion as to whether this goal has taken a partial precedence over profit maximization, or a decline in the importance of profit maximization in the minds of businessmen has given them more room for this additional goal among their varied aspirations. Joel Dean evidently subscribes to the latter view.

> Possibly the inadequacy of hired management's incentives to maximize profits has also tended to make the "public service" aspects of business leadership more interesting to executives. There appears to be a growing preoccupation with the "social responsibilities of management," *i.e.*, increasing concern with the direct effects of management's decisions upon workers, consumers, and the business cycle. Whether such considerations deflect management's actions significantly from profit-making can probably never be determined, since retreat to "long-run" profitability defies analysis. [29]

## Profit But Not Profit Maximization

Perhaps this type of attack on the profit motive should not be honored with a separate classification. After all, probably all of the writers quoted in the two preceding sections of this chapter would subscribe to this particular attack. In a sense it can be considered as nothing more than the essential conclusion which must logically come out of their arguments that motives exist other than, and in many cases contrary to, the profit motive. It would be unrealistic to attribute to any of these writers the view that non-profit maximizing motives were the *only* motives for business behavior. Business firms must, if they are to remain in existence long enough to meet their first payroll, pursue the profit motive to at least a limited degree. The consensus of these economists must, then, be that the pursuit of profit is one of the several goals of business managers, albeit not the only one.

---

[28] P. L. Bernstein, "Profit Theory—Where Do We Go from Here?" *Quarterly Journal of Economics* (August, 1953), pp. 407-422.
[29] Dean, *op. cit.*, p. 33.

The classification stands apart, however, because some writers have made a special point of emphasizing that "satisfactory" profits rather than maximum profits represent a clearly definable goal of businessmen.[30] Although some economists merely make this statement without any specified reasons for doing so, two writers in particular have built up models of business or general organizational behavior which leave "satisfactory" profit (as opposed to maximum profit) as the only possible aspiration.

Kenneth Boulding supports his claim by developing a theory of the firm which uses *homeostasis* as the mechanism of decision making. Certain relationships within the business, balance sheet ratios for example, are somehow established as ideal, and the mechanism of the firm is so set up that significant deviations from these standard relationships will bring into play counteracting forces designed to pull the relationships back to normal. There is simply no room for a profit maximizing goal in such a model as this. Nothing is maximized. Variables, included among them profit itself, are simply restricted to certain ranges of fluctuation which are "satisfactory." Thus, the firm strives for "satisfactory" profits rather than maximum profits.[31]

Herbert Simon bases the rationality of his "satisficing" profits goal not on the force of mechanical organization but on lack of knowledge and what he calls "bounded rationality." "The replacement of the goal of *maximizing* with the goal of *satisficing*, of finding a course of action that is 'good enough' . . . is an essential step in the application of the principle of bounded rationality."[32]

## Failure Objectively to Strive for Profit Maximization

Economists who claim that firms do not objectively maximize profits because they do not use marginal analysis in the

---

[30] Paul A. Samuelson, *Economics: An Introductory Analysis*, Fourth Edition (New York: McGraw-Hill Book Company, Inc., 1958), p. 481, and Gordon, *loc. cit.*

[31] Boulding, *loc. cit.*

[32] Herbert A. Simon, *Models of Man* (New York: John Wiley & Sons, Inc., 1957), pp. 204-205.

proper way to determine optimum output and sales policies, generally rely on an analysis of the pricing policies of business firms to substantiate this contention. Prices based on formulae which do not utilize the economists' favorite marginal expressions or prices which remain stable over significant periods of time are considered to represent *prima-facie* evidence of failure to determine outputs and prices which will maximize profits.[33] Whether this presumption is true or not is probably determined by the individual circumstances. If failure to equate marginal revenue and marginal cost in making output policy and failure to charge what the traffic will bear at that level of output is solely the result of lack of alertness and willingness to make frequent changes, it probably represents non-profit maximizing behavior.[34]

On the other hand, if the establishment of output and pricing policies which do not meet with the economists' tests of optimization are soundly based on long-run profit maximizing concepts, such policies may hardly be considered violations of the profit motive. R. L. Hall and C. J. Hitch, in a survey of pricing policies, discovered that most firms used a "full-cost" pricing policy. That is, prices were determined by adding a reasonable profit margin to the costs of producing the goods. Most of the "full-cost" firms in the survey felt that they were following a policy which would at least vaguely maximize long-run profit, as indicated in the following responses:

> They do not charge more because experience teaches that if they do, the ground is likely to be cut under their feet by competitors. They do not charge less because competitors would cut if they did. When trade expanding, wise to change no more than cost to take advantage of expansion and not attract new-comers.[35]

> Frequent changes of price would alienate customers. They look on price cutting as a "slippery slope." [36]

---

[33] Reese, *op. cit.*, p. 121.
[34] H. M. Oliver, "Marginal Theory and Business Behavior," *American Economic Review* (June, 1947), pp. 375-382.
[35] R. L. Hall and C. J. Hitch, "Price Theory and Business Behavior," *Oxford Economic Papers* (May, 1939), p. 40.
[36] *Ibid.*, p. 38.

> They do not charge more because they aim at high long-run turnover. They never change a price unless there is a very large change in costs. Retailers dislike changes, particularly reductions, which reduce their margins. In any case, there are conventional prices and it would rarely pay to move to next lower or higher. They do not follow cuts by competitors because they sell against market in general.[37]

At least one firm in the survey failed to note a long-range advantage from "full-cost" pricing, or at least failed to say anything about it to the surveyors.

> They do not charge more because they do not go in for high profit: they could earn a much higher profit if they chose. No temptation to cut, as industry expanding.[38]

## Uncertainty and Lack of Knowledge

The claim that business firms cannot maximize profits because of uncertainty about future events and because of lack of knowledge about present circumstances is not truly an attack on the profit "motive" as such. The "motive" may still be very strong but simply thwarted in its complete realization—profit maximization. However, to this degree, it is certainly a legitimate objection to the traditional concept of the profit motive—a concept which assumes that if the profit motive is sufficiently strong, profit maximization will be the result.[39] Two quotations from writings on this subject will illustrate the nature of the argument.

> The information and calculability necessary for the management of a firm to move to its equilibrium profit-maximizing price-output combination are clearly not available. Uncertainty and ignorance are omnipresent. No matter how pleasing may be the prospects of an activity with the greatest possible profits, this choice for management is rarely on the agenda.[40]

---

[37] *Ibid.*, pp. 36-37.
[38] *Ibid.*, p. 35.
[39] A. A. Alchian, "Uncertainty, Evolution, and Economic Theory," *Journal of Political Economy* (June, 1950), pp. 211-221; S. Enke, "On Maximizing Profits," *American Economic Review* (September, 1951), pp. 566-578; and Gordon, *loc. cit.*
[40] Julius Margolis, "The Analysis of the Firm: Rationalism, Conventionalism, and Behaviorism," *Journal of Business* (July, 1958), p. 189, copyright 1958 by the University of Chicago.

In the absence of perfect knowledge and in the face of uncertainty, there is no objectively identifiable maximum. Uncertainty, as much as any other element, makes purposive maximization literally an impossible ideal. Because the future is unknown, because the present involves so complex a set of determining forces, no individual can operate with certain expectation of the consequences of the courses of action which are open to him. . . . Profit maximization thus serves as no guide to action.[41]

In line with his theory of homeostasis as the ruling mechanism in business behavior, Kenneth Boulding emphasises a special aspect of lack of knowledge. The homeostatic model is simply not constructed to provide management with the knowledge as to whether profit is or is not being maximized.[42] This approach emphasises a lack of internal information, whereas the writers quoted above seem to emphasize the lack of external information. Obviously, they are all right. Only a rank amateur in the world of business would pretend that he was aware of all of the factors which could influence his profit and that he knew how to act upon this knowledge.

## Diffusion in Decision Making

George Bach objects to the classical profit maximizing model on the grounds (among many others) that, regardless of the clearness of the goal and the completeness of the information available to the firm, there always will remain bureaucratic frustration to prevent full profit maximization.

Often top managers don't really make many decisions in large corporations. Instead, the various departments and units of the firm have their own existences, each pursuing partially the broad goals set by top management but each also interested in its own problems—looking good as a department, promoting its own interests against those of other departments, and so on. . . . Even on major, long-range issues, the decisions of top management may be pretty well determined by the actions of the various departments and by the information fed up to the top.[43]

---

[41] Chamberlain, *op. cit.*, pp. 240-241.
[42] Boulding, *op. cit.*, p. 36.
[43] Bach, *op. cit.*, p. 296.

With such a broad splitting of decision-making functions, it hardly could be expected that even the best laid plans could come to complete fruition.

## Conclusion

Economists have discovered many points of attack on the profit motive as a determinant of firm behavior. Business managers have other contradictory aspirations, they fail to understand and properly use acceptable methods to assure maximization of profits, they are plagued by confusion and uncertainty, and they have so diffused the decision-making processes that purposive coordination toward a profit-maximizing goal has become all but impossible.

Many of the attacks on the classical profit-maximizing model are found to be wanting when the firm is considered to be attempting to maximize long-range rather than short-range profits. Even more are found to be lacking in validity when we consider profit maximization as the *intent* of management rather than its accomplishment. But many of the attacks on the motive of profit maximization which have been presented in this chapter clearly overcome both of these qualifications.

All of this is not intended to mean that the profit motive, divorced from the goal of maximization, is not a very vital part of the motivational forces which guide business activity. Certainly there must be a fairly large measure of profit-seeking behavior if a firm is to survive. But the critical weakening of the profit motive has effectively destroyed the traditional model as a reliable predictive device. The classical model can throw a great deal of light on business activity, but cannot be relied upon as a consistent guide to business behavior.

The purpose of this chapter has been destructive. It has taken widely-held, seldom-criticized concepts and shown wherein they may be inappropriate, but has suggested very little to replace them. Reference has been made to certain motivations of business executives, such as the desire for leisure, the desire to avoid risks, the desire to be one's own boss, etc., but it was not part of the theme of this chapter to hypothesize regarding the significance of these elements in the complex of business motivations.

If the motive of profit maximization does not explain adequately the pattern of business behavior, it behooves the serious student of business motivation to look elsewhere. It might well be that the answers will be found in areas of knowledge remote from the field of the traditional economist. Sociologists, psychologists, anthropologists, philosophers, even theologians and mathematicians, lay claim to a special understanding of human motivation. Perhaps it is in one of these areas, or in a combination of all of them, that the answers ultimately will be found.

## BIBLIOGRAPHY

Alchian, Armen A. "Uncertainty, Evolution, and Economic Theory," *Journal of Political Economy* (June, 1950), pp. 211-221.

Allen, Clark; James Buchanan; and Marshall Colberg. *Prices, Income, and Public Policy.* New York: McGraw-Hill Book Company, Inc., 1954.

Bach, George Leland. *Economics: An Introduction to Analysis and Policy.* New York: Prentice-Hall, Inc., 1954.

Bakke, E. Wight. *Adaptive Human Behavior.* New Haven: Yale University Labor and Management Center, 1950.

Bernstein, P. L. "Profit Theory—Where Do We Go from Here?" *Quarterly Journal of Economics* (August, 1953), pp. 407-422.

Boulding, Kenneth E. "Implications for General Economics of More Realistic Theories of the Firm," *American Economic Review* (May, 1952), pp. 35-44.

Chamberlain, Neil W. *A General Theory of Economic Process*. New York: Harper & Brothers, 1955.

Dean, Joel. *Managerial Economics*. Englewood Cliffs: Prentice-Hall, Inc., 1951.

Enke, S. "On Maximizing Profits," *American Economic Review* (September, 1951), pp. 566-578.

Fellner, William. "Average Cost Pricing and the Theory of Uncertainty," *Journal of Political Economy* (June, 1948), pp. 249-252.

——————. *Competition Among the Few*. New York: Alfred A. Knopf, Inc., 1949.

Gordon, R. A. "Short-Period Price Determination in Theory and Practice," *American Economic Review* (June, 1948), pp. 265-288.

Hall, R. L., and C. J. Hitch. "Price Theory and Business Behavior," *Oxford Economic Papers* (May, 1939), pp. 12-45.

Harrod, R. F. "Price and Cost in Entrepreneurs' Policy," *Oxford Economic Papers* (May, 1939), pp. 1-11.

Hicks, J. R. "Annual Survey of Economic Theory: The Theory of Monoply," *Econometrica* (January, 1935), pp. 1-20.

Higgins, Benjamin. "Elements of Indeterminacy in the Theory of Non-Perfect Competition," *American Economic Review* (September, 1939), pp. 468-479.

Katona, George. *Psychological Analysis of Economic Behavior*. New York: McGraw-Hill Book Company, Inc., 1951.

——————. "Rational Behavior and Economic Behavior," *Psychological Review* (September, 1953), pp. 307-317.

Lester, Richard A. "Equilibrium of the Firm," *American Economic Review* (March, 1949), pp. 478-484.

——————. "Shortcomings of Marginal Analysis for Wage-Employment Problems," *American Economic Review* (March, 1946), pp. 63-82.

Margolis, Julius. "The Analysis of the Firm: Rationalism, Conventionalism, and Behaviorism," *Journal of Business* (July, 1958), pp. 187-199.

Meyer, John R. Discussion in "The Impact of Some New Developments in Economic Theory: Exposition and Evaluation," *American Economic Review* (May, 1957), pp. 335-338.

Nettl, J. P. "A Note on Entrepreneurial Behavior," *Review of Economic Studies* (February, 1957), pp. 87-94.

Nourse, Edwin G. *The Profit Motive and "Maximum" Profits.* Washington: The Brookings Institution, 1942.

Oliver, H. M. "Marginal Theory and Business Behavior," *American Economic Review* (June, 1947), pp. 375-382.

Parsons, Talcott. "The Motivation of Economic Activities," *The Canadian Journal of Economics and Political Science* (May, 1946), pp. 187-202.

Reder, M. W. "A Reconstruction of the Marginal Productivity Theory," in R. V. Clemence. *Readings in Economic Analysis*, Volume II. Cambridge: Addison-Wesley Publishing Company, Inc., 1950, pp. 251-259.

Reese, Jim. *Our American Economy.* Boston: Houghton Mifflin Co., 1953.

Rothschild, K. W. "Price Theory and Oligopoly," *Economic Journal* (September, 1947), pp. 299-320.

Samuelson, Paul A. *Economics: An Introductory Analysis*, Fourth Edition. New York: McGraw-Hill Book Company, Inc., 1958.

Saxton, C. Clive. *The Economics of Price Determination.* New York: Oxford University Press, 1942.

Scitovsky, T. "A Note on Profit Maximization and Its Implications," in American Economic Association, *Readings in Price Theory.* Homewood, Illinois: Richard D. Irwin, Inc., 1952, pp. 352-358.

Simon, Herbert A. *Models of Man.* New York: John Wiley & Sons, Inc., 1957.

Chapter **3**

# THEORIES OF BUSINESS BEHAVIOR FROM THE PHYSICAL SCIENCES*

Leland S. Burns

Much has been written in recent years concerning the inability of traditional economic theory to explain adequately the behavior of the business firm. Alternative theories of the firm have been developed, published, and attacked. At present we are in no position to predict the longevity of the new theories; however, they are worth considering, if only to raise a few doubts about the validity of (formerly?) accepted theory, which asserts that firms strive to maximize profits. We may, therefore, begin with the possibility that profit maximization *may not* be a realistic explanation of business behavior.

My purpose is to summarize what has been written about new approaches derived from other disciplines and applied to the firm and to formulate generalizations from this summary where possible. The focus is on explanations of firm behavior which rely on laws and theories evolved in the physical sciences; they are grouped under the broad topics of "viability" and "homeostasis."

Like other social scientists, the economist has been forced to develop principles, hypotheses, and theories which more often than not depend for their validity on foundations which are as unstable as human nature itself. Because the principles of human action are difficult to generalize, the economist has cast an envious eye on the work of the physical scientist,

* This chapter first appeared as an article, "Recent Theories of the Behavior of Business Firms," in the *University of Washington Business Review*, Vol. IXX (October, 1959), pp. 30-40.

who often can point to tangible and observable laboratory results as confirmation for his theory. A second reason for alluding to the physical sciences is merely to clarify an obscure theory, perhaps as a pedagogical device. In explaining an abstraction, it is not unusual for the instructor to employ the device of analogy. For example, Alfred Marshall explained the various and uncertain economic actions of men by reference to the laws of the tides.[1]

Marshall also observed the similarity between economics and biology; he compared the life of the firm to the rise and fall of trees.[2] In recent theories, two new analogies have been drawn from biology—*viability* and *homeostasis*. Both substantially modify traditional theory, the former emphasizing the long run, the latter the short run.

## Viability

What comparisons can be observed between firms and organisms? Like plants and animals, firms are small when they are born; they pass through recognizable stages of development as they mature; they reproduce offspring; and sooner or later they die. Most important, they are always "creatures of their environment." Occasionally they can rise above their environments—usually as the result of luck—but this is rare. Most often they exist in accordance with the established laws of nature, seldom at variance with them.[3]

It should be pointed out that the scholar who developed this reasonably sophisticated analogy admitted some time after its publication that its real purpose was only expository.[4] It was not intended that businessmen's actions be

---

[1] Alfred Marshall, *Principles of Economics*, Eighth Edition (London: The MacMillan Company, Ltd., 1920), p. 32.

[2] *Ibid.*, pp. 315-316.

[3] Armen A. Alchian, "Uncertainty, Evolution, and Economic Theory," *Journal of Political Economy*, Vol. LVIII (June, 1950), pp. 211-221, copyright 1950 by the University of Chicago; Armen A. Alchian, Edith T. Penrose, and Stephen Enke, "Biological Analogies in the Theory of the Firm: Comments and Rejoinder," *American Economic Review*, Vol. XLII (September, 1953), pp. 600-609; Kenneth E. Boulding, *A Reconstruction of Economics* (New York: John Wiley & Sons, Inc., 1950); Edith T. Penrose, "Biological Analogies in the Theory of the Firm," *American Economic Review*, Vol. XLII (December, 1952), pp. 804-819.

[4] Alchian, Penrose, and Enke, *op. cit.*

explained by studying the birds, plants, and flowers, as some suspected.[5] Attacks on the biological theory *per se* are thus irrelevant.

### *The Business Firm as a "Creature of Its Environment."*

Viability refers to the firm's ability to live, grow, develop, and prosper. In its narrowest sense, viability draws upon Darwin's principles of biological evolution and natural selection, which, in turn, are based on Malthus' well-known notions of population increase.

To survive, a firm must earn profits. A profitable firm has been "naturally selected" because it has been "adopted" [6] by the environment. Those unfortunate enough not to have been adopted have not been selected, and therefore do not earn profits. This unhappy circumstance is true whether the firm attempted to make profits or not; it is true whether the firm has attempted to adapt to the environment or not.

That the theory is derived from Darwin seems evident in this quotation from Alchian:

> Realized positive profits, not *maximum* profits, are the mark of success and viability. It does not matter through what process of reasoning or motivation such success was achieved. The fact of its accomplishment is sufficient. This is the criterion by which the economic system selects survivors: those who realize *positive profits* are the survivors; those who suffer losses disappear.[7]

Those firms which were adopted and profited did so because they were favored by their environment and responded appropriately, but an appropriate response is not necessarily rational. The appropriate action may be passive (for example, luck) or it may be active (such as the imitation of another successful firm). The theory perceives the firm as a creature of the environment in which it exists and any effort actively to maximize profits under these conditions might only meet with frustration.

---

[5] Penrose, *op. cit.*
[6] This is Alchian's terminology.
[7] Alchian, *op. cit.*, p. 213.

*Importance of Uncertainty and Risk.* The businessman thus apparently exists in the face of sizable odds. Because of uncertainty, he is unable to maximize profits. He is uncertain whether he will be selected by his environment to survive, although he may reduce this uncertainty by attempting to conform to those principles which he observes as having prompted the success of other firms. Still, a decision must be made with the realization that it may not result in the correct outcome.

> In the presence of uncertainty—a necessary condition for the existence of profits—there is no meaningful criterion for selecting the decision that will "maximize profits." The maximum-profit criterion is not meaningful as a basis *for selecting* the action which will, in fact, result in an outcome with higher profits than any other action would have, unless one assumes nonoverlapping potential outcome distributions.[8]

Thus we are told that the notion of profit maximization is distorted, complicated, and perhaps even destroyed by lack of certainty concerning the course of future events. Uncertainty may be measured by application of probability techniques using the Law of Large Numbers.[9] The unknown factor of uncertainty may be reduced to the probability of a future event's occurrence. Therefore, the businessman can make reasonably enlightened decision based on the probability that success will follow, or alternatively, that a particular risk has a certain probability of altering the decision's effect. Often the risk may be shifted, reduced, or neutralized. Even if it cannot be, knowledge of the risk and its probability of occurrence permits the businessman to pursue his intended course of action with a greater degree of certainty.

How is risk recognized? Businessmen must frequently decide among alternative courses of action. Decisions concerning the levels of output, price, inventory, wages, and marketing policy may be made daily. Each decision confronts the executive with distributions of possible outcomes, in a

---

[8] *Ibid.*, p. 212.
[9] Irving Pfeffer, *Insurance and Economic Theory* (Homewood, Illinois: Richard D. Irwin, Inc., 1957).

number equal to the alternative courses of action available. The result is complicated because outcome distributions overlap, causing the same outcome to result from several different courses of action.[10] For example, two simultaneous decisions to change a wage level and shift a price level may have in their distribution of potential outcome some of the same outcomes. Occasionally such overlapping causes either or both of the decisions to be unacceptable. It is necessary then to select another alternative and determine, if possible, whether this action includes among its distribution of possible outcomes maximum profit and/or maximum loss. If both outcomes are possible from this choice of action, the firm may be more prudent (and may find it more profitable) to select an alternative which would involve less risk combined with less profit. Given these conclusions, Chamberlain asserts that "profit maximization thus serves as no guide to action. One can only ask which course of action is preferable to the businessman, considering his subjective reaction to risk and uncertainty." [11]

But how important is risk in the context of viability? The only risk with which the businessman need be concerned is the chance of not being selected. If he is selected, he will prosper; if he is rejected, he will disappear. Thus "individual motivation and foresight, while sufficient, are not necessary." [12]

***Businessmen Can Control and Modify the Environment.*** Another view relies on the ability of businessmen to control and modify the environment, for they can exercise a measure of influence.[13] Personal contributions of each individual often bear upon the environment, altering it to a degree for himself and others. "Individual behavior cannot be explained without reference to the culture, and culture cannot be explained

    [10] Alchian, *op. cit.*, p. 216.
    [11] Neil W. Chamberlain, *A General Theory of Economic Process* (New York: Harper & Brothers, 1955), p. 241.
    [12] Alchian, *op. cit.*, p. 217.
    [13] Chamberlain, *op. cit.*, p. 5. As Chamberlain notes, Adam Smith fully recognized the importance of the culture over the individual but still believed that the relationship was bilateral.

without reference to the individual. Both views are correct, yet neither is complete without the other." [14] Philosopher Paul Weiss writes "we are neither free from all conditioning nor inexorably bound." [15]

Some supporters of this argument maintain that while it is difficult to alter natural resources, geographical factors, and government policies, businessmen can influence technology and the tastes of consumers, and it is in these areas they must operate to profit. The successful firm may, for example, rely on imitation or innovation transmitted by other firms.

To Chamberlain, the businessman's ability either to operate in spite of his environment or to operate so as to affect the environment to his advantage depends on his degree of bargaining power, defined as the "capacity to effect an agreement on one's own terms. . . ." [16] Such devices as breadth of line, product differentiation and innovation, and advertising and marketing practices are used to increase bargaining power.

To illustrate bargaining power, let us consider the line of products produced for the market. First, the broader the line, the less will total income be reduced by a decline in the price of any one product in the line. Furthermore, if the line is sufficiently diverse, demand may be supplementary, *i.e.*, a declining demand for Scotch may be offset by a rise in demand for bourbon.[17] Secondly, innovation will increase bargaining power by causing the line to be differentiated from any competing line of products. Finally, the broader the line available for production, the greater will be the possibility that management's choice of the correct combination will coincide with that choice which most closely approximates management's chosen aspiration level.

---

[14] *Ibid.*, p. 3.
[15] Paul Weiss, *Man's Freedom* (New Haven: Yale University Press, 1951), p. 63.
[16] Chamberlain, *op. cit.*, p. 81.
[17] Gin and vermouth would not suffice as illustrations since they are complementary, not supplementary.

If the entrepreneur can influence or determine the price at which goods are sold and the cost of the agents of production, and hence profits as well, he can more nearly approximate the desired balancing of cost and revenue factors which will allow him to achieve desired goals (or aspirations) regardless of whether the goal is profit maximization, market position, or another objective.[18]

The primary tool in management's kit for achieving the desired balance is the "projected balance." By definition, the projected balance tabulates all sources of funds arising from current receipts, borrowed funds, and other liability increases (based on expectations), and assets (the contributions of the past).[19] In other words, management seeks to balance inflows and outflows at a level regarded as satisfactory and consistent with its bargaining power in the market.

Failure to achieve projected conditions is tantamount to reducing bargaining power since the firm must be content with a less-than-satisfactory production level. The actual balance sheet may or may not agree with the projection. If the actual falls short of the projected, management derives a "preferred balance" in which it adjusts its bargaining power to achieve a performance superior to that which is being realized even if inferior to that originally planned.

The lesson to be learned is that profit maximization is a subordinate consideration inasmuch as management is concerned primarily with juggling its revenue and expenditure decisions in order to maintain favorable conditions for attaining the satisfactory norm defined as its "aspiration level." In this case, profits are a by-product of the interplay of market forces rather than the prime result of directed management decisions.

*Motives Other than Profit-Seeking.* Traditional economic theory assumes that the rational decision results in maximum profits. As soon as other factors (such as market position) assume equal or superior status to profit in the composite

---

[18] Further discussion of objectives other than profit maximization is found below.

[19] Chamberlain, *op. cit.*, p. 198.

aspiration level, maximum profits give way to "satisfactory" profits, *i.e.*, maximum profits less the dilution of any alternative goals.

P. W. S. Andrews [20] expands further the notion that businessmen are motivated by other-than-profit considerations and then develops his refutation of marginal analysis around the now classic paper by R. J. Hall and C. J. Hitch.[21] His idea centers around the businessman's setting of a price merely to cover average costs, thus making an output decision unnecessary. Under these conditions a marginal analysis is irrelevant to the decision, and, of course, there is no attempt to maximization whatsoever.

Therefore, there is a place—although perhaps an infrequent one—for profit maximization in the theories of those who maintain that man can influence his environment. But, as Chamberlain has suggested, there must also be room for motivations other than profit.

Knauth [22] points out that while trade position may depend on profits for this purpose, it is possible once a position is attained to increase profits by controlling price and costs to a greater degree than before.[23] He maintains further that the most important factor in determining superior position is research.

Those seeking position "have only one point in common: they all seek a refuge from the vagaries of the market place. They all attempt to modify or control the erratic confusion of automatic fluctuation, they all seek in the end to combine steady flow of demand with expansion of demand. . . ." [24] That is, they seek the stability of an equilibrium. This follows from "homeostasis," another possible explanation of firm behavior.

---

[20] P. W. S. Andrews, "A Reconsideration of the Theory of the Individual Business," *Oxford Economic Papers* (New Series), Vol. I, No. 1 (January, 1949).

[21] R. J. Hall and C. J. Hitch, "Price Theory and Business Behavior," *Oxford Economic Papers*, No. 2, May, 1939.

[22] O. Knauth, *Business Practices, Trade Position and Competition* (New York: Columbia University Press, 1956), Chapters 4-9.

[23] However, he is careful to point out that position is not synonomous with monopoly or competition.

[24] Knauth, *op. cit.*, p. 109.

**Homeostasis**

Borrowing again from a physical science—this time physiology—the economist finds in homeostasis a possible explanation of business firm behavior.

This term, coined by Walter B. Cannon,[25] refers to processes by which relative stability is maintained in an organism. Kenneth Boulding borrows the characteristics of homeostasis and modifies them for application to the business firm. As Boulding states, "there is some 'state' of the organism which it is organized to maintain, and any disturbance from this state sets in motion behavior on the part of the organism which tends to re-establish the desired state." [26]

Before recounting Boulding's application of the theory, let us consider an example of homeostasis and then its first social application as advanced by Cannon.

Knauth explains the physiological workings of homeostasis with the following example:

> If . . . a man encounters a grizzly bear on a forest trail, numerous complicated changes occur in his bodily mechanism. The rate of his breathing increases, the heart rate speeds up, the blood supply flows from the internal organs to the skeletal muscles, even the composition of the blood changes so that if he is scratched or wounded it will clot more rapidly. He is, in other words, physiologically prepared either to run away at top speed or to fight. Other situations call forth other sorts of adaptive changes in the body (and mind). The living creature is in homeostasis when these changes take place only in the presence of appropriate stimuli and disappear or are replaced by other changes when other sorts of stimuli appear. When, however, inappropriate responses appear in the body, or even appropriateness persists after the situation which calls them forth changes, then homeostasic equilibrium is disturbed. In other words, the man gets sick; he may even want to die. So with a business organization.[27]

---

[25] Walter B. Cannon, *The Wisdom of the Body* (New York: W. W. Norton & Company, Inc., 1932), p. 24.

[26] Boulding, *op. cit.*, pp. 26-27.

[27] Knauth, *op. cit.*, pp. 169-170.

*"Stability Is of Prime Importance."* After Cannon develops his theory of homeostasis [28] and applies it to the body and other physiological organisms, he proceeds to apply it to the environment and, in particular, to social and political organizations, to macroeconomics, and to marketing and communication theories. His simple conclusion is that "stability is of prime importance." [29] Because the organism often must use its extraordinary powers when its equilibrium (or homeostasis) is disturbed, it goes to extremes to avoid any occasion which would disrupt the status quo.[30]

Cannon's regard for traditional theory is apparent in the following extract:

> The organism suggests, furthermore, that the importance of stability warrants a specially organized control, invested by society itself with power to preserve the constancy of the fluid matrix, *i.e.*, the processes of commerce. Does not this imply that when there is prospect of social perturbation there should be power to limit the production of goods to a degree which would reasonably adjust the supply to the demand? power to lay aside stores of goods which could be released if crises arise? power to require the accumulation of wage reserves which could be used at times of temporary unemployment? power to arrange emergency employment or training for new types of labor skill? and power to accelerate or retard the routine processes of both the production of goods and their distribution, in accordance with desirable adaptations to internal or external disturbing factors? [31]

---

[28] Cannon, *op. cit.*, p. 38. Cannon credits Claude Bernard (*Les Phenomenes de la Vie*, Paris, 1878), a French physiologist, with first suggesting the idea. " 'It is the fixity of the *milieu interieur* which is the condition of free and independent life,' he (Bernard) wrote, and 'all the vital mechanisms, however varied they may be, have only one object, that of preserving constant the conditions of life in the internal environment.' " "No more pregnant sentence," in the opinion of J. S. Haldane (*Respiration*, New Haven, 1922) "was ever framed by a physiologist."

[29] Cannon, *op. cit.*, p. 317.

[30] *Ibid.*, p. 39. "There are oscillations, to be sure, but normally the oscillations are within narrow limits. If these limits are surpassed, very serious consequences may result. Ordinarily the variations from the mean position do not reach the dangerous extremes which impair the functions of the cells or threaten the existence of the organism. Before those extremes are reached, agencies are automatically called into service which act to bring back towards the mean position the state which has been disturbed."

[31] *Ibid.*, p. 318.

In sections which follow, Cannon suggests schemes for achieving commercial and industrial stability: control of credit, currency, production and wages, administered prices and other administrative controls, "and the assuring of the general public through governmental regulation that in any arrangements which are made, its interests will be protected." [32] He concludes:

> The projection of the schemes (above) is clear evidence that in the minds of thoughtful and responsible men, a belief exists that intelligence applied to social instability can lessen the hardships which result from technological advances, unlimited competition and the relatively free play of selfish interests.[33]

Needless to say, profit maximization (a "selfish interest") would find no place in such a theory.

*Application of Principle of Stability.* Boulding applies this theory to the balance sheet. "There is some desired quantity of all the various items in the balance sheet, and any disturbance of this structure immediately sets in motion forces which will restore the status quo." [34] A sale will register on the balance sheet as a decline in inventory and an increase in cash or receivables. To restore equilibrium, the firm must spend its new income to increase inventory to its former level. Thus, Boulding contends, "consumption 'causes' production in such a system, and, be it noticed, without any intervention of a price system or any assumption about maximizing profits or any other variable." [35]

Still, as in the cases of Chamberlain, Knauth, and some other contemporary theoreticians, profit maximization has a place in Boulding's analysis. But the place is a secondary one—this time equilibrium is of prime importance.

> It may well be that the great bulk of human behavior does not follow the patterns of sober, reflective maximization of advantage, but rather follows first the principle of inertia

---

[32] *Ibid.*, p. 321.
[33] *Ibid.*
[34] Boulding, *op cit.*, p. 27.
[35] *Ibid.*

(nobody does anything unless he has to!) and secondly the principle of least resistance (if you have to do anything, you do the thing that is easiest to do!). There is nothing which says that the line of least resistance is the same as the line of greatest advantage except the long, slow retribution of natural selection.[36]

Boulding's focus is the balance sheet, a regulator of production and position. Homeostasis requires the maintenance of a certain proportioning of balance sheet ingredients. When this proportion, termed the "preferred asset ratio," is not appropriate, self-correcting forces are energized which cause a return to the "optimum" balance. In short, the firm's goal is stability.

In summary, homeostasis assumes the following:

First, the firm operates under mechanistic conditions which are defined as ideal. The conditions may be determined by the environment or they may have been derived by the businessman either arbitrarily or analytically.

Second, such mechanistic conditions, if consciously derived, are considered desirable.

Third, at some deviation from the norm, a signal device will set into motion the control mechanism that restores equilibrium. Hence, once the mechanism is established and operating, business decisions are not necessary; the self-correcting mechanism takes over. Conscious deliberation has given way to nonpurposive action.

Establishing the original norm provides the only opportunity for a decision. But this decision may also be reduced to a mechanism; for the entrepreneur may merely copy a successful formula from another firm and apply it as his own norm. The norm may be as commonplace as a balance sheet ratio or a conventional markup. Whatever it is, the businessman reasons that this is the determinant of his associate's success and concludes that it may be his.

Finally, if (1) profit maximization is not regarded as a static concept but as dynamic and involving continual change

---

[36] *Ibid.*, p. 38.

to adapt price and output decisions to changing markets, and if (2) to keep abreast of the changing environment, the ingredients in the optimum mix must be changed, and if (3) "stability is of prime importance," then profit maximization is automatically relegated to a subordinate position.

*Chamberlain's Theory of Aspirations and Bargaining Power.* Although the terminology is different, Professor Chamberlain's theory closely follows that of homeostasis. The balance in his case is the equality or near-equality of revenue and budget decisions, the result being to maximize the satisfaction of a given level of individual aspirations. The satisfaction of aspirations is determined by several factors, each depending upon balance.

Each worker must balance at least two aspirations, *e.g.*, job aspirations and consumption aspirations. An optimization of consumption aspirations (*i.e.*, the aspiration to derive a sufficiently large income to satisfy the standard of living to which he aspired) could be achieved only at the expense of his job aspirations (*i.e.*, the satisfaction from working at a given job which pays more in amenities than in money wages). Maximization of both is impossible; therefore, a balance is required.

This also applies to profit maximization. If the individual has goals other than profits, in order to maximize profits he must of necessity forego nonprofit satisfactions. If nonprofit goals have a higher ranking, he is unwilling to forego them for maximum profit.

It is not difficult to think of business positions occupied by capable individuals who would not trade the nonpecuniary satisfactions of their present employments for higher paying positions. As Chamberlain points out, "the individual whose aspiration structure emphasizes job satisfaction will willingly sacrifice [money] income to achieve it." [37]

Furthermore,

> . . . in the case of management, job satisfaction may involve the creative satisfaction of developing a new or superior prod-

---

[37] *Ibid.*

uct or of building an enterprise, the competitive satisfaction of becoming the largest firm in the industry or the nation, the social satisfaction of being known as a fair employer or a leading citizen of the community, the political satisfaction of wielding authority over others, and so on. . . . Because individuals are not singly motivated but seek a concomitancy of satisfactions, however, the balance which management projects will normally reflect some combination of goals, a balance of satisfaction.[38]

Despite all this, Chamberlain ranks maximum profit as management's number one goal, although the goal may never be realized. This is true because profit can be used to secure other goals. For example, earnings (or profits) retained rather than paid out may be used for expansion, a goal separate from profit *per se*, but resulting from profit. Capturing an increasing share of either an existing or a new market by increasing the firm's proportion of total sales may be another goal, but still a goal furthered by profit.

Profit can make possible either of these alternate goals, but here again management may decide which will be emphasized, since, Chamberlain asserts, the goals may supplant rather than supplement each other. Since market share and growth are possible goals, one without the other, but neither without profit, it may be necessary to compromise with a satisfactory profit, a satisfactory market position, and satisfactory growth rather than a maximum of any one of these.[39] The definition of "satisfactory" derives from bargaining power and aspiration level.

### Summary and Conclusions

Chamberlain asserts that "it now appears that this argument [that maximal profit is the principal objective of all rational businessmen] is fairly well resolved, and its prolongation involves only the flogging of a dead horse." [40]

---

[38] Chamberlain, *op. cit.*, p. 161
[39] *Ibid.*, pp. 230-231.
[40] *Ibid.*, p. 239.

Yet there are those, like Edith Penrose, who claim to be traditionalists. But even here a compromise is apparent.[41] Although she respects profit maximization as the prime mover of business, she does not consider that maximum profit is measured as a "unique and objectively identifiable point."[42] She contends instead that businessmen in general try to make, "if they think they can, a bit more profit than they are making." On the surface this position seems quite acceptable to both factions, but in view of her contention that a particular point where marginal cost equals marginal revenue does not exist, the marginal theorist would question how long the entrepreneur could continue increasing output to make just "a bit more profit than he is making" before he passed this nonexistent point and suffered a decline in total revenue and profits.

We have reviewed several alternative theories of the firm derived from the physical sciences. The schools discussed divide on the issue of absolute control by the environment. The theory presented by Alchian, Darwin, Malthus, et al is almost nihilistic, for it assumes that because of uncertainty, not only is profit maximization impossible, but the firm's existence is jeopardized by the exigencies of the environment.

The school of Chamberlain, Knauth, and Cannon asserts that environment is controllable to a degree but that business may attempt to achieve goals preferred over profit maximization. The firm may be able to influence its environment and realize its objectives. The greater its power to influence the market and the environment, the greater is its ability to manipulate the environment to its advantage. According to this school, the satisfaction of goals depends upon power.

Could it be that the maligned theory has been too severely criticized? Could it be that it is not the theory which fails to be realistic but the applications of the theory? It is difficult to evolve a theory which is sufficiently general to be

---

41 *Ibid.*, p. 240.
42 Penrose, *op. cit.*, pp. 804-819.

useful and still sufficiently particular to be applicable. Should not businessmen and economists realize that a theory merely provides a broad, often almost unlimited, framework to direct analysis and serve as a large container within which certain assumptions are applied to the given problem and directed toward its solution?

## BIBLIOGRAPHY

Alchian, Armen A. "Uncertainty, Evolution and Economic Theory," *Journal of Political Economy*, Vol. LVIII (June, 1950), pp. 211-221.

——————; Stephen Enke; and Edith Penrose. "Biological Analogies in the Theory of the Firm: Comments and Rejoinder," *American Economic Review*, Vol. XLII (September, 1953), pp. 600-609.

Andrews, P. W. S. "A Reconsideration of the Theory of Individual Business," *Oxford Economic Papers* (New Series), Vol. I, No. 1 (January, 1949), pp. 54-89.

Arrow, Kenneth J. "Alternative Approaches to the Theory of Choice in Risk-Taking Situations," *Econometrica*, Vol. 19 (October, 1951), pp. 404-437.

Bates, Marston, and Philip S. Humphrey. *The Darwin Reader*. New York: Charles Scribner's Sons, 1956.

Boulding, Kenneth E. *A Reconstruction of Economics*. New York: John Wiley & Sons, Inc., 1950.

Cannon, Walter B. *The Wisdom of the Body*. New York: W. W. Norton & Company, Inc., 1932.

——————. "Organization for Physiological Homeostasis," *Physiological Review*, Vol. IX (1929), pp. 399-431.

——————. "Stresses and Strains of Homeostasis," *American Journal of Medical Science*, Vol. CLXXXIX (1935), pp. 1-14.

Chamberlain, Neil W. *A General Theory of Economic Process*. New York: Harper & Brothers, 1955.

Darwin, Charles. *The Origin of Species by Means of Natural Selection or the Preservation of Favored Races in the Struggle for Life.* New York: D. Appleton & Company, 1889.

Gordon, R. A. "Short-Period Price Determination in Theory and Practice," *American Economic Review* Vol. XXXVIII, No. 3 (June, 1948), pp. 265-288.

Hall, R. L., and C. J. Hitch. "Price Theory and Business Behavior," *Oxford Economic Papers*, No. 2 (May, 1939), pp. 12-45.

Knauth, O. *Business Practices, Trade Position and Competition.* New York: Columbia University Press, 1956.

Knight, Frank H. *Risk, Uncertainty, and Profit.* Boston: Houghton Mifflin Company, 1921.

Lester, Richard A. "Marginalism, Minimum Wages, and Labor Markets," *American Economic Review*, Vol. XXXVII, No. 2 (March, 1947), pp. 135-148.

Marshall, Alfred. *Principles of Economics*, Eighth Edition. London: MacMillan and Company, Ltd., 1920.

Penrose, Edith T. "Biological Analogies in the Theory of the Firm," *American Economic Review*, Vol. XLII (December, 1952), pp. 804-819.

Pfeffer, Irving. *Insurance and Economic Theory.* Homewood: Richard D. Irwin, Inc., 1956.

Scitovsky, T. "A Note on Profit Maximization and Its Implications," *Review of Economic Studies*, Vol. XI, No. 1 (1943), pp. 57-60.

Stigler, George T. *The Theory of Price.* New York: The Macmillan Company, 1952.

Veblen, Thorstein. *The Theory of Business Enterprise.* London: MacMillan and Company, Ltd., 1904.

Weiss, Paul. *Man's Freedom.* New Haven: Yale University Press, 1951.

Weiner, Norbert. *The Human Use of Human Beings: Cybernetics and Society.* Garden City: Doubleday Anchor Company, Ltd., 1950.

# Chapter 4

## ORGANIZATION THEORY AND
## BUSINESS BEHAVIOR

Charles A. Lee

---

### Introduction

Interest in theories of organization has developed tremendously in recent years. The growth and proliferation of formal organizations in modern society, the fact that organizations are the natural focal point of study for many of the social sciences, and the importance of large organizations in spheres of activity that individuals or small groups formerly dominated are all factors that have stimulated interest in the development of organization theory. Ideas concerning the formal organization have been forthcoming from such diverse groups as anthropologists, business administrators, sociologists, economists, psychologists, and political scientists.

The frame of reference and, consequently, the approach to the problems of the formal organization has been different for each of these groups. For example, the economist is concerned with the market behavior of business organizations. He has found it useful, and indeed necessary, to shroud the firm in the cloak of the entrepreneur, a perfectly rational individual attempting to maximize profits. This abstraction coupled with the assumption of competition in the markets allows the economist to study and predict the market behavior of firms without delving into the complexities of human behavior. On the other hand, the study of the behavior patterns of groups and individuals which economic theory so thoroughly obscures is the substance of the disciplines of sociology and psychology. Modern organization theory is of an eclectic nature, utilizing the applicable insights of each of these diverse disciplines to formulate a unified theory of organizational behavior.

The purpose of this chapter is to determine the contribution of the behavioral theory of organization to the explanation and prediction of the behavior of firms. The behavioral theory will be compared to the classical economic theory of the firm and the traditional theory of organization in regard to the concept of the firm, the goals of the firm, and decision making in the firm in order to determine (1) if it provides a better frame of reference for explaining the behavior of firms, and (2) if it is better as a tool for predicting the behavior of firms.

The term "organization theory" is subject to various interpretations. The businessman tends to think of organization theory as a group of principles such as span of control, specialization, functional departmentalization, unity of command, and so forth. His concepts spring from the treatment given this topic by business schools and the work of such men as Fayol, Mooney, Davis, and Urwick. The theory of organization set forth by this group of men will be referred to in this chapter as the traditional theory of organization.

Today most of the literature relevant to the development of a theory of organization is emanating from the social sciences and is usually devoted to the examination of some minute variable within the context and environment of the group. With few exceptions, this literature has tended to emphasize the dysfunctional aspects of organizations and leaves unexplained the high degree of rationality that characterizes the formal organization. The problem of a general framework for a theory of organization has usually been referred to as a problem that "somebody should do something about " Consequently, this chapter will rely primarily upon the work of those few scholars who have attempted to synthesize and organize the work of the social sciences. Their work will be referred to as the behavioral theory of organization.

Since the preceding chapters have been concerned primarily with economic explanations of the behavior of business firms, this chapter will point to the differences between the behavioral theory of organization and the classical economic theory of the firm, with a minimum of elaboration. Classical economic theory of the firm refers to the model of pure competition which has been used for many years to explain and justify business behavior.

Perhaps at this point some of the differences in the basic nature of each of these theories should be pointed out. Economic theories of the firm seek to explain only the market behavior of business organizations. Classical economic theory is normative in nature, setting forth how the business firm should act in the market system of the economy in order that maximum wealth and an optimal allocation of resources may be attained in the national economy. Traditional organization theory is also normative in nature; its principles are actually a group of *a priori* rules prescribing how the practical businessman should construct the formal structure of his organization. To a large extent these principles were distilled from historical studies of the characteristics of large organizations such as armies, churches, and states, as well as from the experience of practicing business administrators.

In contrast with the normative theories of classical economics and traditional approaches to the study of organizations, the behavioral theory of organizations is concerned with the construction and validation of empirically testable hypotheses of human behavior in complex organizations. Thus, the behavioral theorist is concerned with how organizations *do* behave, rather than how they *should* behave. Implicit in this approach is the assumption that it is possible to develop an objective science of human behavior. This fundamental assumption of the behavioral sciences has been seriously challenged by such men as Hayek,[1] Knight,[2] and Lynd.[3]

---

[1] F. A. Hayek, *The Counter-Revolution of Science: Studies on the Abuse of Reason* (Glencoe, Illinois: The Free Press, 1952).

[2] F. H. Knight, "Principles in Economics," *American Economic Review* (May, 1951).

[3] Robert S. Lynd, *Knowledge for What? The Place of Social Science in American Culture* (Princeton: Princeton University Press, 1939).

The epistemological question raised by these men is whether the scientific method is adequate for dealing with many of the complexities of human behavior. They also question the objectivity that the behavioral scientists attribute to the results obtained by the scientific method.

Aside from the somewhat philosophical questions raised by these men, the fundamental nature of the behavioral theory of organizations presents other difficulties. The requirement of rather precise definitions and concepts has presented a formidable obstacle because each of the various disciplines has developed its own vocabulary and concepts to deal with the problem. However, at the present time it appears that the behavioral scientists have been more successful in conceptualizing new hypotheses and reformulating traditional assertions in a testable form than they have been in gathering empirical evidence to test the hypotheses. The problem of validation is compounded by the fact that there is no widespread agreement among the social scientists concerning what empirical evidence is scientifically acceptable and what is not. Even when the results of a study are generally accepted, they frequently raise more questions than they answer. The most common conclusion of empirical studies of organizational behavior is that factor X makes a significant difference at the .05 level if everything else is carefully controlled. Left unanswered are the questions relating to the relative weights of the variables, the sequence of the interaction of the variables, and how to obtain the relevant information needed for prediction in a natural situation.

Some of the problems faced by the behavioral theory may be attributed to the fact that it is in a relatively early stage of development and that improved communications between the various disciplines and subsequent developments in methodology may overcome many of the difficulties. For example, the analogue computer may be used to synthesize the variables introduced by the behavioral scientist and to simulate the behavior of complex organizations in the not-too-distant future. However, at the present time, the main contribution of the behavioral theory appears to be in the rough framework it provides for examining a wide spectrum of business behavior. This framework begins with the behavioral concept of organization.

## The Behavioral Concept of Organization

Barnard defined formal organization as "a system of consciously coordinated activities or forces of two or more persons." [4] Organization, so defined, is ubiquitous. This concept of organization led to a general recognition that organization theory was the natural focus for many of the disciplines of the social sciences. For example, the sociologist views the formal organization as a fertile field for examining patterns of group relationships; the psychologist studies organizations to determine their impact upon individual behavior; and the anthropologist is concerned with the organization as a cultural institution. Thus, the development of a theory of organizations is of central concern to each of these disciplines.

The traditional theory of organization was considered inadequate by the behavioral scientists for quite a variety of reasons but primarily because of its narrow concept of organizational behavior. However, the traditionalist and the behaviorist both tend to conceive of organization as a pattern or system of relationships. Simon refers to organization as the "complex *pattern* of communications and other relations in a group of human beings." [5] Mooney defines organization as "the form of human association for the attainment of a common purpose." [6] Simon has been at the forefront in the development of the behavioral theory of organizations, while Mooney was one of the earliest of the traditional organization theorists.

The conflict between these concepts is to be found in the manner that the pattern or form is determined. The tradi-

---

[4] Chester I. Barnard, *Functions of the Executive* (Cambridge: Harvard University Press, 1938), p. 73.

[5] Herbert A. Simon, *Administrative Behavior* (New York: The Macmillan Company, 1948), p. xvi.

[6] J. D. Mooney, *The Principles of Organization* (New York: Harper & Brothers, 1947), p. 1.

tionalist views the pattern of behavior as being primarily determined by the offices and the formal relationship between offices in the organization. The problem of organization becomes one of beginning with a clean sheet of paper and carefully sketching out the ideal relationships between the parts of the organization.[7] The individual is viewed as being essentially a passive instrument, acting only in accordance with his formal role. Thus, the concept of organization postulated by the traditionalist is analogous to a well-designed machine.

Research in the behavioral sciences refutes the machine model of human organization. Beginning with the work of Elton Mayo and his colleagues, the dysfunctional aspects of human behavior in organizations have been emphasized. Organization is conceived of as encompassing not only the intended activities of the formal organization but also the activities of individuals and groups to fulfill their particular needs. They stress the modification of the pattern by the personality, knowledge, beliefs, cognition, perception of the individuals in the organization and by the interactions of these individuals. Thus, like Pandora, the behavioral concept of organization opens a box containing an almost infinite number of variables, with only hope remaining at the bottom.

In contrast to the behavioral concept of organization, the concept of the firm in economic theory presents few problems. The cloak of the entrepreneur is wrapped around the firm, and the entrepreneur and the firm are assumed to be an identity for purposes of analysis. The concept of the entrepreneur is that of a rational individual attempting to maximize his incentive function (usually profit). The activity that is examined is the market behavior of the firm, and this is determined almost entirely by the external environment (competition).

This question may now be asked: What does the concept of organization as advanced by the behavioral scientist contribute to the theory of the firm? It would appear that it

---

[7] Lyndall Urwick, *The Elements of Administration* (New York: Harper & Brothers, 1944), p. 36.

offers a more accurate and complete description of the business organization in the real world. However, this in itself is not an adequate justification, but the level of generalization used in either the economic concept of the firm or the traditional concept of organization can be defended only on the grounds that it furnishes a better basis for predicting the behavior of firms. At the present time it would be difficult to prove that any one of these concepts is superior to the others for the purpose of building a theory that would predict the behavior of firms. It should be noted that the behavioral theory does provide a frame of reference for examining a wider range of problems, and it explicitly identifies many of the important variables affecting the behavior of business organizations.

## The Goals of the Organization

All three theories are concerned with the behavior of a person or a group attempting to reach certain goals by the manipulation of given variables. In each case, behavior can be evaluated, explained, or predicted only in relation to the goal or goals of the organization.

In the economic theory of the firm, the crucial assumption was that the entrepreneur had a single goal—profit maximization. A rather naive view of the classical economic theory would contend that economists thought that man was interested only in economic goals. However, it is necessary to realize that the goal of profit maximization was only a part of a system that assumed pure competition between firms in the market. Under the rigorous assumptions of pure competition, a firm had to maximize profits in order to survive, and a firm that had competing or conflicting goals could not continue to exist if the economy was in or near equilibrium.

The general discard of the competitive model, on the grounds that it did not adequately reflect the real world, also raised the question of whether profit maximization was an adequate generalization of the goals of firms in a system of imperfect competition. Profit maximization as *the* goal of firms has been criticized in recent years by many authors on rather diverse grounds. Joel Dean summarizes many of these objections in the following manner:

> Economic theory makes a fundamental assumption that maximizing profits is the basic objective of every firm. But in recent years "profit maximization" has been extensively qualified by theorists to refer to the long run; to refer to management's rather than to the owner's income; to include non-financial income such as increased leisure for high-strung executives and more congenial relations between executive levels within the firm; and to make allowance for special considerations such as restraining competition, maintaining management control, holding off wage demands, and forestalling anti-trust suits. The concept has become so general and hazy that it seems to encompass most of man's aims in life.[8]

Organization theorists in general have refused to accept profit maximization as *the* goal of the firm. Even the traditional writers who utilized a highly rationalistic concept of the firm contended that the firm should have a multiplicity of objectives or goals. The goals espoused by these writers were moralistic in tone, emphasizing service to the various interested groups such as stockholders, customers, employees, and the general public. Profits were usually viewed as being of a residual nature, coming into existence to the extent the firm was able to fulfill the stated service objectives to these groups. It is interesting to note that their concept of the goals of the business organization is fully compatible with the economic doctrine of profit maximization over the long run because the traditional organization theorist assumes a logical ordering and complimentary relationship between the various goals. To the extent that these goals are achieved in the most efficient manner possible, the firm will maximize its profits over the long run.

The problem of appraising alternatives is simplified if a single criterion or goal is sufficient. But men have a multiplicity of goals, and the maximization of one goal frequently

---

[8] Joel Dean, *Managerial Economics* (Englewood Cliffs, N. J.: Prentice-Hall, Inc., 1951), p. 28.

conflicts with the maximization of another or even several others. Rational behavior usually requires one to determine to what extent he is willing to sacrifice the attainment of certain goals to reach other goals. The problem addressed by the behavioral theorist is the construction of a theoretical framework which will help explain how the goals of a firm are determined, how they are balanced, and how the goals and balance change over a period of time.

A behavioral theory of organizational goals has been set forth by Herbert Simon in the following manner:

> The notion of satiation plays no role in classical economic theory, while it enters rather prominently into the treatment of motivation in psychology. In most psychological theories the motive to act stems from drives, and action terminates when the drive is satisfied. Moreover, the conditions for satisfying a drive are not necessarily fixed, but may be specified by an aspiration level that itself adjusts upward or downward on the basis of experience.
>
> If we seek to explain business behavior in the terms of this theory, we must expect the firm's goals to be not maximizing profit, but attaining a certain level or rate of profit, holding a certain share of the market or a certain level of sales. Firms would try to "satisfice" rather than to maximize. . . . Models of satisficing behavior are richer than models of maximizing behavior, because they treat not only of equilibrium but of the method of reaching it as well. Psychological studies of the formation and change of aspiration levels support propositions of the following kinds. (a) When performance falls short of the level of aspiration, search behavior (particularly search for new alternatives of action) is induced. (b) At the same time, the level of aspiration begins to adjust itself downward until goals reach levels that are practically attainable. (c) If the two mechanisms just listed operate too slowly to adapt aspirations to performance, emotional behavior—apathy or aggression, for example—will replace adaptive behavior.[9]

Simon's satisficing model is built upon Chester Barnard's concept of the equilibrium of the organization.[10] Barnard

---

[9] Herbert Simon, "Decision-Making in Economics," *American Economic Review* (June, 1959), p. 263.

[10] Barnard, *op. cit.*, pp. 56-59, and Simon, *Administrative Behavior, op. cit.*, p. 111.

insisted that the customers must be considered as part of the system of organization, and that the members of the organization contribute to the organization in return for the inducements offered. The contributions of one group were seen to be the inducements offered to other groups. Equilibrium was achieved when the sum of the contributions was sufficient to satisfy all the primary groups within the organization.

A further refinement of the satisficing model may be taken from the political science concepts of bargaining between leaders. Cyert and March in their "Behavioral Theory of Organizational Objectives" proceed along these lines. They conceive of organization as a coalition of individuals, some of them organized into sub-coalitions, and present what they consider to be the three major ways in which the objectives of a coalition are determined:

> The first of these is a bargaining process by which the composition and general terms of the coalition are fixed. The second is the internal organizational process of control by which objectives are stabilized and elaborated. The third is the process of adjustment to experience, by which coalition agreements are altered in response to environmental changes.[11]

The behavioral model appears to offer a more satisfactory description of goals than the profit maximization model because it can accomodate a variety of objectives and partially explain shifts in objectives, and because it corresponds more closely to the real world. However, the vagueness of satisficing as the goal of a firm presents serious problems in building a predictive model of business organizations. The normative propositions of the traditional theory of organization provide some insight into the actual goals of the business firm, but their usefulness in constructing a predictive model is also limited by the lack of a measurable statement of goals. All three approaches are capable of giving a rather crude approximation of the goals of a firm, but each possesses fundamental flaws for purposes of prediction.

---

[11] R. M. Cyert and J. G. March, "A Behavioral Theory of Organizational Objectives," in Mason Haire, (ed.), *Modern Organizational Theory*, (New York: John Wiley & Sons, Inc., 1959), p. 79.

## Decision Making

If the assumptions of the economic theory of the firm are accepted, the *process* of decision making is relatively insignificant for purposes of explaining or predicting the behavior of firms. Given the single goal of profit maximization, the concept of the firm as a single rational entity, the environment of pure competition among firms, and the tools of marginal analysis, it is possible to predict how firms will behave without delving into the complexities of human behavior.

In recent years economists have constructed various models of the firm eliminating most of these unrealistic assumptions. Theories using utility maximization rather than profit maximization, theories using oligopoly conditions rather than pure competition, and theories incorporating expectations under conditions of uncertainty have occupied much of the recent literature of economics. At this time it is difficult to evaluate the contributions of these theories, but it should be noted that all of them still incorporate the concept of the firm as a single organism, the completely rational entrepreneur.

Decision making is treated rather vaguely in the traditional theory of organization. Most of the discussions of decision making are concerned with normative propositions prescribing the steps to be followed in choosing between alternatives. The concept would appear to be that of a single individual choosing between alternatives after receiving all of the facts and alternatives from his staff. A logically consistent set of criteria to evaluate the alternatives is normally assumed.

Behavioral theories of organization, unlike the economic or traditional theories, focus their attention on the internal process of decision making. The empirical orientation of the behavioral theories leads to a rejection of the assumptions of the economic theory of the firm, and once these hypotheses are discarded, deductive reasoning is no longer sufficient for predicting the behavior of the firm. For example, if there is pure competition between firms in an industry, we can predict with certainty that those firms surviving over the long run will have acted as if they were maximizing profits, regardless of their stated goals or actual decision making processes. With the tools of marginal analysis we can deduce what their market behavior will be, but if the assumption of competition is relaxed, deductive reasoning can no longer tell us how firms will act because a variety of alternatives may be viable in a system of imperfect markets.

The behavioral theories attempt to construct empirically testable models of human problem-solving processes from the perceptions of psychology and sociology. Accordingly, a limited rationality is hypothesized for the actors, and the organization is conceived as an instrument for increasing rationality. March and Simon present the behavioral concept of decision making in the following manner:

> The basic features of organization structure and function derive from the characteristics of human problem-solving processes and rational human choice. Because of the limits of human intellective capacities in comparison with the complexities of the problems that individuals and organizations face, rational behavior calls for simplified models that capture the main features of a problem without capturing all its complexities.
>
> The simplifications have a number of characteristic features: (1) Optimizing is replaced by satisficing—the requirement that satisfactory levels of the criterion variables be attained. (2) Alternatives of action and consequences of action are discovered sequentially through search processes. (3) Repertories of action programs are developed by organizations and individuals, and these serve as the alternatives of choice in recurrent situations. (4) Each specific action program deals with a restricted range of situations and a restricted range of consequences. (5) Each action is capable of being executed in semi-independence of others.[12]

The manner in which organization influences the decisions of its members is the subject of volumes of literature.

---

[12] James G. March and Herbert A. Simon, *Organizations* (New York: John Wiley & Sons, Inc., 1959), p. 169.

Whyte's study of roles and interactions,[13] Bakke's concept of the fusion process,[14] Simon's concepts of authority and influence,[15] and Argyris's postulates concerning the conflicts between individual and the organization provide examples of this literature.[16] The fact that decision making in an organization is a process rather than the act of a single individual has been stated in the following manner:

> It should be perfectly apparent that almost no decision made in an organization is the task of a single individual. Even though the final responsibility for taking a particular action rests with some definite person, we shall always find, in studying the manner in which the decision was reached, that its various components can be traced through the formal and informal channels of communication to many individuals who have participated in forming its premises. When all of these components have been identified, it may appear that the contribution of the individual who made the formal decision was a minor one, indeed.[17]

The emphasis upon the internal decision-making process appears to have blinded the behaviorists to the importance of the ecology of the organization in determining the firm's behavior. In both the classical theory of the firm and the traditional theory of organization extreme care was taken in sketching the relationship of the business organization to its environment. The fact that these relationships have not been defined in the behavioral theory is rather inconsistent with the fact that in the concept of the firm the behaviorist draws heavily upon the biological concepts of viability and homeostasis. That the environment influences the decision premises of the firm has been pointed out,[18] but theories attempting to explain this phenomena have been spasmodic and rather inadequate.

[13] W. F. Whyte, *Man and Organization: Three Problems in Human Relations in Industry* (Homewood, Illinois: Richard D. Irwin, Inc., 1959).
[14] E. W. Bakke, *Bonds of Organization* (New York: Harper & Bros., 1950).
[15] Simon, *Administrative Behavior, op. cit.*, pp. 123-153.
[16] Chris Argyris, "The Individual and Organization: Some Problems of Mutual Adjustment," *Administrative Science Quarterly* (June, 1957).
[17] Simon, *Administrative Behavior, op. cit.*, p. 221.
[18] Simon, "Decision-Making in Economics," *op. cit.*, p. 278.

**Summary**

Behavioral theories of organization are of an eclectic nature and result from a coalescence of the behavioral sciences. The importance of these theories in explaining the behavior of firms has been universally recognized over the past decade, but at the present time, serious problems still exist. The lack of a unifying framework in which to fit the various eclectic concepts and postulates, the large number of variables introduced, and the neglect of the ecology of the organization impair the predictive value of these theories. However, the behavioral theories do appear to be more firmly grounded in reality than either the traditional theory of organization or the economic theory of the firm.

The behavioral theory differs from the two older theories in that it is empirically oriented. The traditional theory of organization was concerned with stating how the firm should act in constructing the formal structure of the organization. The principles of this theory are actually a group of *a priori* rules developed by administrators. In the economic theory of the firm, empirical testing is not necessary if the assumption of pure competition is accepted, for profit maximization is then necessary for survival. The tools of marginal analysis permit the economist to deduce how firms will behave while maximizing profits. The fact that the real world is characterized by imperfect competition largely negates the predictive value of the economic theory.

The ultimate contribution of the behavioral theories is difficult to determine. The development of computers may eventually overcome the problem of such a large number of variables, or a higher level of abstraction may reduce the variables to a workable level. The primary contributions of these theories to date are that they are submitted in empirically testable forms, and they do provide a rough frame of reference for explaining many facets of business behavior that were obscured by the older theories.

# BIBLIOGRAPHY

Alderson, Wroe, and Reavis Cox, (eds.). *Theory in Marketing.* Homewood, Ill. Richard D. Irwin, Inc., 1950.

Argyris, Chris. "The Individual and Organization: An Empirical Test," *Administrative Science Quarterly* (September, 1959).

——————. "The Individual and Organization: Some Problems of Mutual Adjustment." *Administrative Science Quarterly* (June, 1957).

Bakke, E. Wight. *Bonds of Organization.* New York: Harper & Brothers, 1950.

——————. *Organization and the Individual.* New Haven: Yale University Labor and Management Center, 1952.

Barnard, Chester I. *Functions of the Executive.* Cambridge: Harvard University Press, 1938.

Boulding, Kenneth E. "Implications for General Economics of More Realistic Theories of the Firm," *American Economic Review* (May, 1952).

Cyert, R. M., and J. G. March. "Organization Structure and Pricing Behavior in an Oligopolistic Market," *American Economic Review* (March, 1955).

——————. "A Behavioral Theory of Organizational Objectives," in Mason Haire, (ed.). *Modern Organization Theory.* New York: John Wiley & Sons, Inc., 1959.

Dahl, R. A., and C. E. Lindblom. *Politics, Economics, and Welfare.* New York: Harper & Brothers, 1953.

Dale, Ernest. "New Perspectives in Managerial Decision-Making," *Journal of Business,* Vol. 26 (1953).

Davis, Ralph C. *The Fundamentals of Top Management.* New York: Harper & Brothers, 1952.

Dean, Joel. *Managerial Economics.* New York: Prentice-Hall, Inc., 1951.

Drucker, Peter F. *The Practice of Management.* New York: Harper & Brothers, 1954.

Edwards, Ward. "The Theory of Decision-Making," *Psychological Bulletin,* 51 (1954).

Fayol, Henri. *General and Industrial Management.* London: Sir Isaac Pitman & Sons, Ltd., 1949.

Gore, William J., and Fred S. Silander. "A Bibliographical Essay on Decision-Making," *Administrative Science Quarterly* (June, 1959).

Gulick, Luther, and Lyndall Urwick. *Papers on the Science of Administration.* New York: Columbia University Press, 1937.

Haire, Mason (ed.). *Modern Organization Theory.* New York: John Wiley & Sons, Inc., 1959.

Hayek, F. A. *The Counter-Revolution of Science: Studies on the Abuse of Reason.* Glencoe: The Free Press, 1952.

Homans, G. C. *The Human Group.* New York: Harcourt, Brace & Co., 1950.

Katona, George. "Rational Behavior and Economic Behavior," *Psychological Review* (September, 1953).

Knight, Frank H. "Principles in Economics," *American Economic Review* (May, 1951).

Lerner, Daniel, and Harold D. Lasswell (eds.). *The Policy Sciences.* Stanford, Calif.: Stanford University Press, 1951.

Litchfield, E. H. "Notes on a General Theory of Administration," *Administrative Science Quarterly* (January, 1956).

Lynd, Robert S. *Knowledge for What? The Place of Social Science in American Culture.* Princeton: Princeton University Press, 1939.

March, James G., and Herbert A. Simon. *Organizations.* New York: John Wiley & Sons, Inc., 1958.

McDonald, John. "The Theory of Strategy," *Fortune* (June, 1949).

McGuire, Joseph W. "The Concept of the Firm," *California Management Review* (Summer, 1961).

Metcalf, H. C., and Lyndall Urwick (eds.). *Dynamic Administration: Collected Works of Mary Parker Follet.* New York: Harper & Brothers, 1940.

Mooney, J. D. *The Principles of Organization.* New York: Harper & Brothers, 1947.

Papandreou, A. G. "The Concept of the Firm in the Light of the Theory of Organization," in *Selected Readings in Management,* Fremont A. Shull (ed.). Homewood, Ill.: Richard D. Irwin, Inc., 1958.

Parsons, Talcott. "Sociological Approach to a Theory of Organizations," *Administrative Science Quarterly* (March, 1956).

————, and E. A. Shils (eds.). *Toward A General Theory of Action.* Cambridge: Harvard University Press, 1951.

Selznick, Philip. "Foundations of the Theory of Organizations." *American Sociological Review* (February, 1948).

Simon, Herbert A. *Administrative Behavior,* Second Edition. New York: The Macmillan Company, 1957.

————. *Models of Man.* New York: John Wiley & Sons, Inc., 1957.

————. "Decision-Making in Economics," *American Economic Review* (June, 1959).

————, and C. P. Bonini. "The Size Distribution of Business Firms," *American Economic Review* (September, 1958).

Tannenbaum, Robert. "The Manager Concept: A Rational Synthesis," *Journal of Business* (October, 1949).

————. "Managerial Decision-Making," *The Journal of Business* (January, 1950).

Urwick, Lyndall. *The Elements of Administration.* New York: Harper & Brothers, 1944.

Wasserman, Paul, and Fred S. Silander (eds.). *Decision-Making: An Annotated Bibliography.* Ithaca: Cornell University Press, 1958.

Whyte, W. F. *Man and Organization: Three Problems in Human Relations in Industry.* Homewood: Richard D. Irwin, Inc., 1959.

Whyte, William H., Jr. *The Organization Man.* New York: Doubleday & Company, Inc., 1947.

# Chapter 5

# GRAPH THEORY AS A METHOD FOR EXPLORING BUSINESS BEHAVIOR

Leo Spier

## Introduction

In recent years, businessmen have tended to abandon many rule-of-thumb practices in favor of more scientific methods and to employ various procedures of the empirical sciences as analytical tools in the study of behavioral problems. Among such other devices as game theory, linear programing, and statistics—used to quantify and measure variables in social sciences—the mathematical theory of linear graphs has been recently introduced as a possible analytical instrument.

From an inquiry into the basic concepts of graph theory,[*] an investigation is conducted of their possible use for the analysis of business behavior.

The potential value of graph theory in the analysis of business behavior is twofold. First, it serves to illustrate the structural properties of business problems and to facilitate the understanding of complex relationships. For example, in Figure 1, the points (knots or vertices) in this graph theoretic model may represent people or work stations, and the lines (links or edges) connecting the points might conceivably illustrate the communication between the people or the flow of goods. Second, if certain conditions are met, graph theory serves as a framework for the development, analysis, and em-

---

[*] This is to acknowledge that the general concept of the fundamentals of the graph theory described above has been based upon the research study of Frank Harary and Robert Z. Norman, *Graph Theory: as a Mathematical Model in Social Science* (Ann Arbor: University of Michigan Institute for Social Research, 1953).

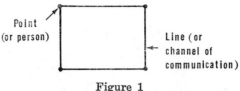

Point
(or person)

Line (or
channel of
communication)

Figure 1

pirical testing of the hypotheses of a business problem. For example, if the axioms and postulates contained in graph theory hold true in the business problem, then a theoretical framework is available to give a more rigorous, *i.e.*, systematic, explanation of this phenomenon. These theorems, however, cannot represent a dynamic state of business behavior. They apply only to its static or comparative static nature.

In addition to these two major usages, the mathematical definitions of graph theory could provide business with valuable language concepts.

*History.* The first use of graph theory may be attributed to the British mathematician J. J. Sylvester (1878). However, the major groundwork was laid by the German mathematician D. Koenig in 1936. Based on Koenig's treatise, the Americans Frank Harary (1953), Robert Z. Norman (1959), and Dorwin Cartwright (1959), and the Frenchman Claude Berge (1959) applied the mathematical theory of linear graphs more extensively to the social sciences. A bibliography of these works can be found on page 98.

## Basic Concepts of Graph Theory

*Ordinary Graph.* An ordinary graph is a linear structure utilizing geometric terms and (1) composed of points ($P_1$, $P_2$, $P_3$, ... $P_n$), also referred to as vertices or knots, and (2) connected by lines ($L_1$, $L_2$, $L_3$, ... $L_k$), also called links or edges, as illustrated by Figure 2a. The basic axioms of these points and lines as they comprise an ordinary graph have been stated as follows:[1]

---

[1] Dorwin Cartwright, "The Potential Contribution of Graph Theory to Organization Theory," *Organizational Theory*, Mason Haire, ed. (New York: John Wiley & Sons, Inc., 1959), pp. 262-266.

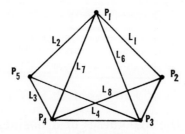

Figure 2a

1. A graph has a finite number of points.
2. Each line is a set consisting of two points.
3. Each line must join two different points. Thus a graph may not contain any loops, *i.e.*, any lines from a point to itself.
4. A graph may have at most one line joining the same pair of points.
5. No distinction is made between the "initial" and the "terminal" points of a line. If a line goes from a point $a$ to a point $b$, then the same line is said to go from point $b$ to point $a$.

The above axioms, containing points and lines as their only properties, constitute the basic mathematical rules of a linear graph structure (Figure 2a). In the application of the mathematical model of a graph to problems of business behavior, the basic mathematical definitions of (1) graph, (2) point, and (3) line may be replaced by corresponding general business terminology such as (1) organization, (2) unit, and (3) relationship (Figure 2b).

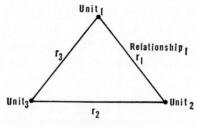

Figure 2b

From this fundamental mathematical structure, more complex concepts and relationships of linear graphs can be derived. Some of the more pertinent models and their components are defined below.

*Path and Length of Path.* A path is a line or set of lines connecting different pairs of points. The length of the path describes the number of lines required to get from any one point to another. In Figure 3, there are three paths from $P_1$ to $P_2$, ($P_1P_2$; or $P_1P_4P_2$; or $P_1P_4P_3P_2$), and their lengths are one, two, and three respectively.

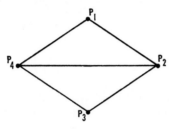

Figure 3

In business terminology, a path may be described as a set of connecting relationships or channels between different units of a business organization. The length of the path signifies the number of channels used between the units.

*Connected Graphs.* A graph is connected if there is a path joining every pair of points. This is illustrated in Figure 4 where $P_4$ and $P_5$ are not linked directly, yet are connected by a path running through a series of points ($P_4P_3P_2P_5$).

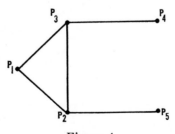

Figure 4

*Distance, Diameter, and Associated Number.* The distance between two points of a connected graph is the length of the *shortest* path connecting these points. In Figure 5, the distance between $P_1$ and $P_6$ is three. The diameter of a connected graph constitutes the maximum of the distances (or of the shortest paths) between *any* of its points. In Figure 5, the diameter is four.

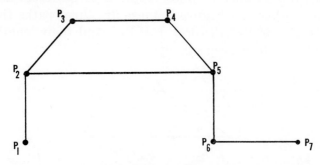

Figure 5

The associated number of a point is the maximum distance from a particular point ($P_5$) to any other point in the connected graph, in this case, two.

*Central Point and Center.* Central points designate the minimum of associated numbers in a connected graph. For example, in Figure 6, $P_2$, $P_3$, and $P_5$ represent central points. Any one or more of a set of central points in a connected graph is called the center; in Figure 6, $P_2$, $P_3$, and $P_5$ are the set of central points that constitute a tri-center in this case.

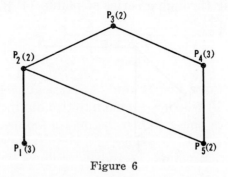

Figure 6

*Degree and Endpoint.* The number of degrees given to a point P in a graph corresponds to the number of lines touching P. Thus, in Figure 7, the degree of $P_1$ is zero, the degree of $P_2$ is two, the degree of $P_3$ is two, of $P_4$ three, and of $P_5$ one. This designates $P_1$ as an endpoint.

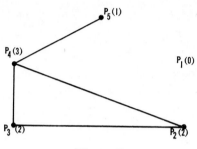

Figure 7

*Subgraph and Component.* A subgraph is *any* graph "S" within a larger graph "G" such that every point and line in "S" is contained in "G." A component is the *largest* connected subgraph within graph "G." Thus the component of a connected graph is the graph itself. In Figure 8, any combination of points or of points and lines is a subgraph; the component of Figure 8 is the figure itself.

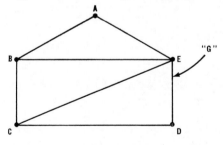

Figure 8

*Articulation Point and Bridge.* An articulation point of a graph is a point $P_1$ which is common to two distinct subgraphs and which causes the graph to become disconnected if it is removed (Figure 9a). A bridge is a single line connecting a pair of articulation points, $P_1$ and $P_2$ (Figure 9b).

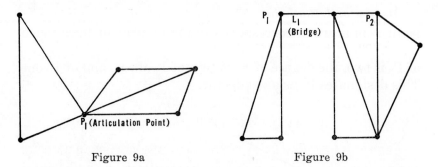

Figure 9a                    Figure 9b

*Cycle, Tree, and Root.* A cycle is a set of lines passing through three or more points ($P_1$, $P_2$, $P_3$, ..., $P_n$, $P_1$), beginning and terminating at the same point and passing through no point twice.

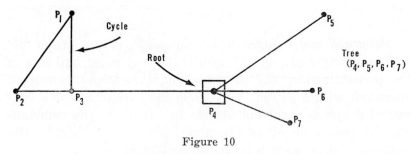

Figure 10

A tree is a connected graph or subgraph in which there is one and only one path between any pair of points, *e.g.*, $P_4$, $P_5$ (Figure 10).

A root is a distinguished point ($P_4$), *i.e.*, a point which has been circled or otherwise identified to designate its special significance (Figure 10).

*Directed and Nondirected Graphs (Digraph Theory).* A directed graph may be a cycle or tree using an arrow to specify the direction of the line connecting any pair of its points. The direction may be one-way ($P_1$, $P_2$) or two-way ($P_1$, $P_3$); however, there may be no specific direction indicated ($P_2$, $P_3$), in which case the graph is assumed to be a nondirected graph (Figure 11). The direction may indicate the strength of the graph.

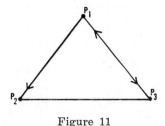

Figure 11

*Type of a Graph.* The type of a graph is merely an attempt to seek out various graphical devices indicating a subjective evaluation of relative power between any pair of its points. A root is such a device; a double line, a broken line, or various colored lines may serve the same purpose (Figure 12). The relative type of business behavior in a particular situation can thus be emphasized through the use of these graphical devices.

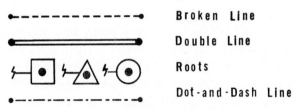

Broken Line

Double Line

Roots

Dot-and-Dash Line

Figure 12

*Matrices and Their Relation to Linear Graphs.* A matrix is the algebraic counterpart for the linear graph of a mathematical model. Although it lacks the pictorial properties of a graph, the numerical structure of a matrix facilitates the identification of complex graphic relationships. For example, in a matrix specifying the relations found in a directed graph, the sum of each row element in the matrix indicates the extent to which an element exerts an influence upon the other elements, while the sum of each column element reflects the degree to which each of the elements has been affected by the other elements.[2] These primary relations are shown in Figure 13 and are duplicated in the matrix Table 1.

---

[2] David L. Huff, "A Topological Model of Consumer Space Preferences," *Papers and Proceedings*, Regional Science Association, Vol. VI, 1960.

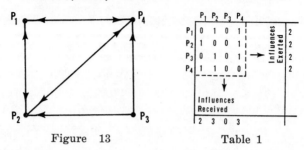

Figure   13                    Table 1

This matrix designates irreflexive relations, since all elements contained within the graph are a set of ordered pairs (a, b). For example, $P_3$ in Figure 13 obviously exerts a great deal of influence. Its exact extent, however, is far better expressed in Table 1 by the influence exerted, which is the sum of the third row (equal to two), and by the influence received, which is the sum of the third column (equal to zero).

To obtain secondary effects, for example, the matrix must be squared in the following manner. Multiply each point of a particular column by its respective point in a particular row. The sum of the products thus derived is the number of the new matrix at the intersection of the above column and row. After all the points in the new matrix have been established, the sums of their rows and columns represent the secondary effects exerted and received respectively. The squaring of a matrix with weighted elements is yet another possible application.[3]

---

[3] The weight of any matrix element exerting an influence can be varied by the emphasis placed upon it arbitrarily. The predictability of a secondary matrix with weighted factors can be preserved as follows:

1. Each element is given an arbitrary value or weight number in the primary matrix (e.g., one to five), wherever a connectivity between points exerting an influence is found from the graph pattern.

2. The matrix is then squared to arrive at secondary effects of the problems. To preserve the range of weight factors given to any element, the squared matrix is then devalued according to the cyclic group whose elements are the weight numbers (in this case, the cyclic group of order 6).

The mathematical proof of the above devaluation can be set up as follows:

Let I be the set of all positive integers (including zero).
Let S be the elements of the cyclic group of order 6, namely: 0, 1, 2, 3, 4, 5.
Then ∃ a (I,+;S,+) —homomorphism as well as a (I,×;S,×)— homomorphism between the two sets.
Additive identity in I = O; in S = O.
Multiplicative identity in I = 1; in S = 1.

*Mathematical Numbers of Points and Lines in a Graph.*  The theorem of minimal, optimal, and maximal numbers of connection required in a given number of units so as to obtain a complete organizational network is well presented by Dorwin Cartwright.[4] It ". . . provides information concerning necessary relations between the number of points and lines of a graph." [5] The links in a graph may be determined by: [6]

---

The result of a weighted matrix should show that secondary effects in the interrelation of factors, not directly discernible, can be preserved without impairing the given weight of individual elements under varying behavioral conditions. If the hypothesis proves correct, then the graph theoretic analysis can be utilized to predict individual behavior. In other words, graph theory as a methodological tool may interpret not only secondary and tertiary connectivities among variables, but also may prove to be sufficiently flexible to permit inclusion of the individual importance attributed to each variable.

*Sample*

(a)

$$m \begin{array}{cccccc} 0 & 0 & 5 & 4 & 5 & 1 \\ 3 & 0 & 1 & 5 & 4 & 2 \\ 0 & 2 & 0 & 2 & 5 & 3 \\ 1 & 5 & 0 & 0 & 2 & 0 \\ 4 & 4 & 1 & 3 & 0 & 3 \\ 3 & 5 & 0 & 3 & 3 & 0 \end{array}$$

(b)

$$m^2 \begin{array}{cccccc} 27 & 55 & 5 & 28 & 36 & 30 \\ 27 & 53 & 19 & 32 & 36 & 18 \\ 37 & 45 & 7 & 34 & 21 & 19 \\ 23 & 8 & 12 & 35 & 25 & 17 \\ 24 & 32 & 24 & 47 & 56 & 15 \\ 30 & 27 & 23 & 46 & 41 & 22 \end{array}$$

(c)

devalued by cyclic
group of order
6

$$\begin{array}{cccccc} 3 & 1 & 5 & 4 & 0 & 0 \\ 3 & 5 & 1 & 2 & 0 & 0 \\ 1 & 3 & 1 & 4 & 3 & 1 \\ 5 & 2 & 0 & 5 & 1 & 5 \\ 0 & 2 & 0 & 5 & 2 & 3 \\ 0 & 3 & 5 & 4 & 5 & 4 \end{array}$$

*Sample:*  1) range of weights given: 5
2) cyclic group order: 0  1  2  3  4  5 = 6
3) for example: 27 ÷ 6 = leaves a remainder of 3
4) cyclic group order relation:

$$\begin{array}{ccc} 0 & = & 0 \\ 1 & = & 1 \\ 2 & = & 2 \\ 3 & = & 3 \\ 4 & = & 4 \\ 5 & = & 5 \\ 6 & = & 0 \\ 7 & = & 1 \\ 8 & = & 2 \\ \dots\dots \\ 27 & = & 3 \end{array}$$

[4] Cartwright, *op. cit.*, pp. 262-266.
[5] *Ibid.*, p. 262.
[6] L = no. of lines; P = no. of points; F = no. of faces. A planar graph is a graph in which none of the lines cross. A connected planar graph is a connected graph in which none of the lines cross.

1. The number of lines in a complete graph: $L = \frac{1}{2} P (P - 1)$.
2. The number of lines in a connected planar graph: $L = P + F - 1$.
3. The number of lines in a tree: $L = P - 1$.
4. The minimal number of lines in a connected graph: $L = P - 1$.
5. The maximal number of lines in a graph: $L = \frac{1}{2} P (P - 1)$.
6. The optimal number of lines in a tree graph: $L = P - 1$.*

Figures 14a, 14b, and 14c illustrate some of these formulae.

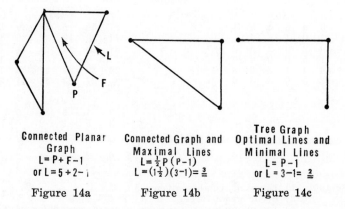

Connected Planar Graph
$L = P + F - 1$
or $L = 5 + 2 - 1$

Figure 14a

Connected Graph and Maximal Lines
$L = \frac{1}{2} P (P-1)$
$L = (1\frac{1}{2})(3-1) = \underline{3}$

Figure 14b

Tree Graph
Optimal Lines and Minimal Lines
$L = P - 1$
or $L = 3 - 1 = \underline{2}$

Figure 14c

Aside from the basic concepts in graph theory, there are higher, more complex forms depicting theorems, among them Lewin's diagrams, Hamilton lines, and Euler graphs. Due to the limited scope of this study, however, they are omitted here.

## An Application of Graph Theory Exploring the Efficiency of Bureaucracy

Efficiency, along with rationality, is probably the most disputed factor in the justification of a bureaucratic organiza-

---

* The optimum does not exist per se, but only in terms of some empirical criterion through which optimal functioning can be defined.

tion. It is also one of the areas in the behavior of bureaucracy which has not yet been explored by the mathematical theory of linear graphs. Therefore, the use of a topological model to analyze the efficiency of a bureaucracy may furnish further information about the behavior of this ubiquitous modern organization.

There is no precise definition of the term "bureaucracy." Generally, it seems to encompass an inflexible, impersonal, and centralized organization of hierarchical structure. More specifically, it is based upon the classical, ideal, or "pure" type bureaucracy as defined by Max Weber.[7] Therefore, his concept appears to be the most suitable basic model for construing a topological graph. Weber conceives this monocratic type of bureaucracy to be the "rational and *efficient* adoption of means to ends." [8] Using experience as an empirical criterion, Weber maintains that (1) regardless of the economic system (capitalistic or socialistic), (2) regardless of any changes of revolution by force or time, and (3) from a purely technical point of view, the pure bureaucracy is capable of achieving a maximum degree of efficiency. Therefore, it becomes the most rational vehicle to carry out the control over people, or "officials," in the organization. Without its precision, discipline, stability, and thus its high degree of calculability of results, a society as technical as ours could not function, much less function efficiently.

Weber suggests that the following basic concept is essential to an ideal type of construction of a bureaucracy:[9]

1. A bureaucracy must have an effective legal authority consisting of general abstract rules governing the "offices" of a corporate group.
2. The person in an "office" is an official, *i.e.*, his status of authority and his actions are of an impersonal nature.

---

[7] Max Weber, *The Theory of Social and Economic Organization*, translated by A. M. Henderson and Talcott Parsons (New York: Oxford University Press, 1947), pp. 329-340.

[8] R. A. Dahl and C. E. Lindblom, *Politics, Economics, and Welfare*, (New York: Harper & Brothers, 1953), p. 235 (Italics supplied).

[9] Robert K. Merton, *et al.*, *Reader in Bureaucracy* (Glencoe, Illinois: The Free Press, 1952), pp. 18-27.

3. Any member of the corporate group, therefore, obeys the established rules of law, not the person issuing them. Thus he owes obedience to an artificial, impersonal structure.

The operation of such a bureaucracy requires the following major rules:

1. There must be a clearly delineated sphere of functions or offices with a corresponding outline of authority and duties.
2. The offices must be (a) arranged in hierarchical order so as to achieve the technically most efficient operation, and (b) ruled by a prescribed set of procedures (always in writing and "according to Hoyle").
3. The persons (administrative staff) occupying the offices are those most qualified technically to conduct the business of the organization as defined by the procedures.
4. The administrative staff, while in the conduct of the various offices, must proceed as a robot, i.e., it is stripped of all personal feelings and of influences that are external to the organization.

The above rules are only main excerpts from a detailed description of the essential principle in a bureaucracy. However, they suffice to construct a basic topological model to explore the alleged efficiency of Weber's bureaucracy.

The graphic presentation (Figure 15) illustrates the relations of the basic concepts of Weber's ideal bureaucracy, the legal authority A, (i.e., an organization code created by the top hierarchy), consisting of general learnable rules (a), the offices (b), and the persons (c) occupying the offices. The links in this particular model represent the influences (not communications) among the vertices.[10]

The rules give the legal authority the tools by which it governs both the office and the person occupying the office. In the ideal sense, therefore, there is no direct connection

---

[10] The broken lines in this and in all models are to indicate a link of secondary nature, i.e., one dominated by the actions through other links.

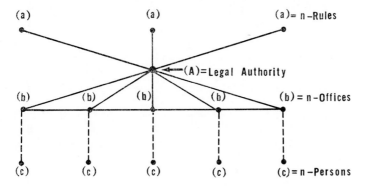

Figure 15

between the persons and offices nor is there a communication among the persons or offices, themselves. The only connection existing is through the legal authority by virtue of which (1) the person assumes a role in the office, and (2) the office is established.

From this basic topological model, it can be seen that Weber's concept of a bureaucracy actually disregards the human organism (broken line) as having any influential role in the organization.[11]

***Analysis of Weber's Bureaucratic Model.*** The more detailed graph (Figure 16a) therefore omits the human elements. However, this graph clearly indicates the functional relationship of the offices, dominated by the stimulus of the legal authority A. The appropriate rules are applied through A to the various offices ($B_1$, $B_2$, $B_3$, ..., $B_n$) of the hierarchy to obtain a present goal. Since, according to Weber, these offices (and their incumbents) are only the mechanical vehicle which carries out the rules of the stimulus, any interaction among the offices is only by way of the procedures contained in A (indicated by a broken line connecting $B_1$, $B_2$, $B_3$, ..., $B_n$).

If this topological model (Figure 16a) is a fair representation of Weber's concept of an ideal bureaucracy, it disproves

---

[11] According to Weber, the official's only function consists of providing the machine with the necessary "mechanical energy" to operate it. The human organism is merely a robot which minutely performs the tasks of the office as set forth by the rules of the organization.

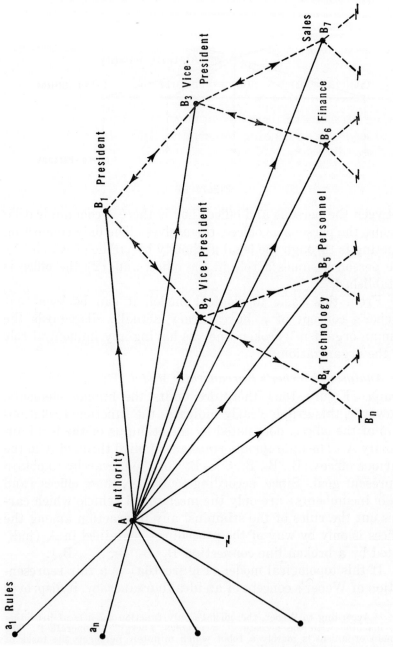

Figure 16a

his contention that it is of an efficient organization. First of all, a high number of degrees leading toward or from a unit (A) indicates overcentralization and, *ipso facto*, inefficient operation. The larger the number of tasks required from any one unit, the less attention that unit can devote to an individual problem. Thus A not only has to provide the procedures for offices $B_1$ through $B_7$, but it must be able to solve all interacting problems of procedure among all offices, to say nothing of procedures external to the organization.

Secondly, and implicit in the overcentralization, is the problem of "red tape" that is created. Any action in the organization must be cleared through A, which formulates the procedures according to the rules. Such procedure admittedly may set forth a desirable uniform procedure. It is doubtful, however, that the advantage of uniformity would outweigh the disadvantage of red tape inefficiency.

Finally, the most notable characteristic of the articulation point A is the vulnerability which it imposes upon the entire organization. By virtue of its focal position and its function as a stimulus, it would impair the entire organization, should it break down. As shown by Figure 16b, a removal of the articulation point, A, divides the graph into a series of dis-

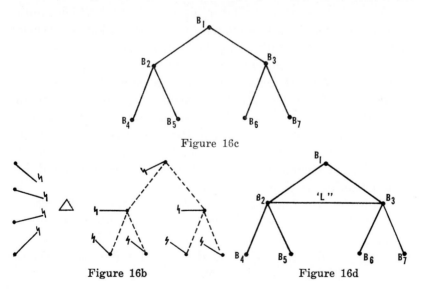

Figure 16c

Figure 16b

Figure 16d

connected subgraphs, $(a_1, a_2, \ldots a_n + B_1, B_2, \ldots B_n)$, unable to operate by themselves.

Another criticism of the efficiency of formal relationships in the hierarchy of offices B, B, ... B is the duplication of effort created through the inflexibility of such a system. Unlike a planar graph, the tree-like structure of Weber's "pure" hierarchy forces any communication to detour through a maze of channels which are often unnecessary. Figure 16c, for example, portrays the channel of communication from the finance unit $(B_6)$ to the personnel unit $(B_5)$, consisting of a diameter of four $(B_6 - B_3 - B_1 - B_2 - B_5)$. In contrast, in a modified hierarchy (Figure 16d), the diameter can be reduced to three by adding to it channel "L."

By virtue of such a focal position, of its impersonal and functional characteristic, and of its inflexibility, the entire operational apparatus of the machine model is vulnerable to a breakdown caused by unforeseen dangers. It is missing the power of free individual decisions of a democracy to maintain the organization in a state of homeostasis. Hence, the workability of Weber's bureaucratic model in actual practice appears difficult, if not impossible (Figure 16b); it portrays an ideal bureaucracy.

A further aspect of this duplication of effort which applies to any tree graph can be shown by the simplified illustration of Figure 16c. In Figure 16e, the diameter, or minimum number of channels for communication between $B_6$ and $B_5$, is four. However, the total amount of times a communication must be handled from the starting request to the final report amounts to eight (total of boxed-in numbers). By comparison, the planar graph (Figure 16f) requires an operation procedure of only two to get from $B_6$ to $B_5$. Aside from the feasibility of such a planar graph, it clearly eliminates duplication of effort in that it omits units $B_3$, $B_2$ and $B_1$.

However, the major defect of Weber's concept of bureaucracy lies in its impersonal structure. He considers the impact of human behavior upon his monocratic model irrelevant and immaterial, for the established general rules are the sole motivational force in an ideal bureaucracy.

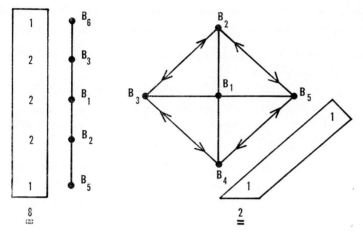

Figure 16e                    Figure 16f

This contention has since been attacked by various scholars who, while accepting Weber's basic "desirability of functional relationships between actions, offices, and organization goals . . . ," recognize the influence of dysfunctional and unintended elements upon the "ideal" bureaucracy.[12] The result is a lessening of the predictability of the behavior of the bureaucratic organization. The ensuing analysis will examine some modified models of bureaucracy set forth by J. K. Merton, P. Selznick, and A. W. Gouldner.

**Analysis of Merton's Theory of Bureaucracy.** Merton's bureaucratic model (Figure 17a) consists of three major areas or functions.[13] The first area, which is essentially a reiteration of Weber's model, is the "manifest function." It is the anticipated process of procedures in the organization. From top hierarchy $P_1$ (see Figure 17a), a demand for control $P_2$,[14] has been established by a set of rules of procedure $P_3 - P_n$. The purpose of $P_2$ is to increase the reliability of behavior $P_4$ (stimulus), so that $P_1$ can ascertain an optimum predictability $P_5$. In order to insure such reliability by means of the tech-

---

[12] Joseph McGuire, "The Concept of the Firm," *California Management Review*, Summer, 1961, p. 75.
[13] *Ibid.,* p. 18.
[14] Demand for control represents, for all purposes, the same concept as the authority in Weber's model.

niques, certain anticipated consequences ($P_6$, $P_{10}$, and $P_{13}$) ensue within relationships of the bureaucratic organization.[15]

1. "There is a reduction in the amount of personalized relationships.
2. "Internalization of the rules of the organization by the participants is increased.
3. "There is increased use of categorization as a decision-making unit."

Each of the above anticipated consequences, however, contains several unanticipated results ($P_7$, $P_8$, $P_9$), ($P_{11}$, $P_{12}$), and ($P_{14} - P_n$). It is in that second area—designated as the "latent function"—that Merton's bureaucratic model differs from that of Weber.

Merton explains these unintended results as interpretations by the human element in the organization. The value system ($P_{15}$) of a participant will not fully accept, for example, the "increased use of categorization," but will attempt to restrict the categories to a minimum ($P_{14} - P_n$). This unanticipated interpretation by the value system carries its effect to the personality behavior-perception ($P_{16}$) and hence softens the impact of the manifest function (the stimulus $P_4$) upon the personality ($P_{16}$).

Curiously enough, however, as Merton explained, the unanticipated interpretation often does not weaken the stimulus but reinforces it, as is seen by the increased rigidity of behavior ($P_{17}$), which, in its own right, increases the reliability. The element of rigidity naturally reinforces the stimulus only to the extent to which the value system's interpretation happens to coincide with the manifest functions.

Therefore, from the point of view of the top hierarchy, there are some undesirable interpretations whose rigidity weakens the stimulus. Merton describes these consequences of rigidity as (1) Group Identification $P_{18}$, (2) Defensibility of Individual Action $P_{19}$, (3) Trappings of Authority $P_{20}$, and (4) Difficulties with Clients $P_{21}$. In other words, rigidity be-

---

[15] James G. March and Herbert A. Simon, *Organizations* (New York: John Wiley & Sons, Inc., 1958), p. 28.

comes unreliable in the tendency of creating "reliable" miniature organizations with goals of their own within the main organization.

In spite of the weakened Weber model by virtue of personalized interpretation of the stimulus by the human factor, Merton maintains that the result, *i.e.*, the desired goal ($P_{22}$), is still fairly predictable in a modified bureaucracy. However, as evidenced in Figure 17a, its predictability decreased substantially in contrast to Weber's goal (see broken line to $P_n$). Since the resulting goal deviated from the manifested objectives of the top hierarchy, it caused a series of adjustments, as illustrated by the secondary effects in Figure 17b (dot-and-dash lines) and described as follows.

The impact ($P_{23}$) of the goal ($P_{22}$) modified by latent and dysfunctional interpretation arouses the stimulus ($P_4$) to improve its demand for control ($P_2$) in order to obtain a greater degree of predictability of the goal. The demand for control then attempts to adjust the behavior perception ($P_{16}$) to increase the manifest function moving the goal towards a more accurate state of predictability ($P_{24}$). However, the stringent measures enacted by the demand for control will affect the value system adversely in that the latter interprets the new rule according to its behavior perception. Such interpretation in turn may result in a protective move resulting in unintended group rigidities which tend to move the goal toward a less predictable point ($P_{25}$).

It is evident that Merton's introduction of human behavior has converted Weber's static monocracy into a dynamic concept where there remains a constant flux of predictability within the goal of the bureaucracy.

The application of Merton's model to the hypothetical case of "automation" in the XYZ Company may illustrate some of the practical usages of graph theory. Given the assumption that the top hierarchy of the company ($P_1$) decided to replace a major part of its equipment by automatic machinery, according to the rules ($P_3 - P_n$), only the information necessary to achieve the replacement is carried down from the demand for control ($P_2$) through the stimulus ($P_4$) to the behavior

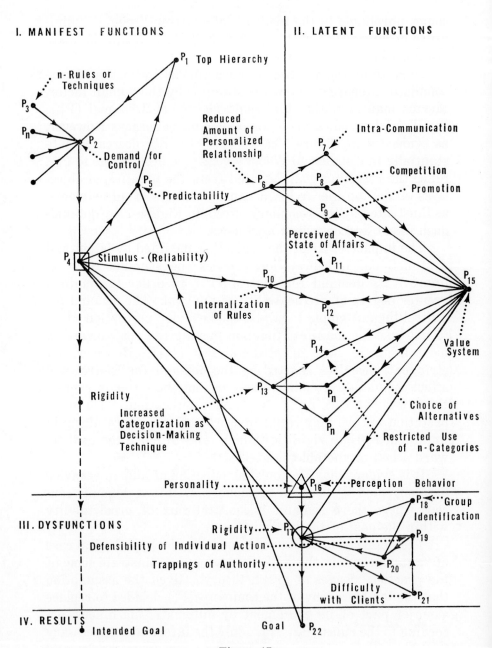

Figure 17a

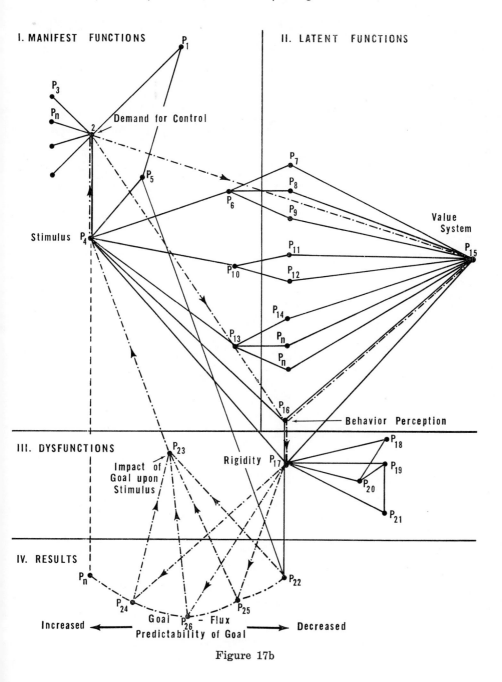

Figure 17b

| P | 1 | 2 | 3 | 4 | 5 | 6 | 7 | 8 | 9 | 10 | 11 | 12 | 13 | 14 | 15 | 16 | 17 | 18 | 19 | 20 | 21 | 22 | Row Total |
|---|---|---|---|---|---|---|---|---|---|----|----|----|----|----|----|----|----|----|----|----|----|----|-----------|
| 1 | 1 |   |   |   |   |   |   |   |   |    |    |    |    |    |    |    |    |    |    |    |    |    | 1 |
| 2 |   | 1 |   |   |   |   |   |   |   |    |    |    |    |    |    |    |    |    |    |    |    |    | 1 |
| 3 | 1 |   |   |   |   |   |   |   |   |    |    |    |    |    |    |    |    |    |    |    |    |    | 1 |
| 4 |   |   |   | 1 | 1 |   |   | 1 |   |    |    | 1  |    |    |    |    |    |    |    |    |    |    | 5 |
| 5 |   |   |   |   |   |   |   |   |   |    |    |    |    |    |    |    |    |    |    |    | 1  |    | 1 |
| 6 |   |   |   |   |   | 1 | 1 | 1 |   |    |    |    |    |    |    |    |    |    |    |    |    |    | 3 |
| 7 |   |   |   |   |   |   |   |   |   |    |    |    |    | 1  |    |    |    |    |    |    |    |    | 1 |
| 8 |   |   |   |   |   |   |   |   |   |    |    |    |    | 1  |    |    |    |    |    |    |    |    | 1 |
| 9 |   |   |   |   |   |   |   |   |   |    |    |    |    | 1  |    |    |    |    |    |    |    |    | 1 |
| 10 |   |   |   |   |   |   |   |   |   | 1 | 1  |    |    |    |    |    |    |    |    |    |    |    | 2 |
| 11 |   |   |   |   |   |   |   |   |   |    |    |    |    | 1  |    |    |    |    |    |    |    |    | 1 |
| 12 |   |   |   |   |   |   |   |   |   |    |    |    |    | 1  |    |    |    |    |    |    |    |    | 1 |
| 13 |   |   |   |   |   |   |   |   |   |    |    |    | 1  |    |    |    |    |    |    |    |    |    | 1 |
| 14 |   |   |   |   |   |   |   |   |   |    |    |    |    | 1  |    |    |    |    |    |    |    |    | 1 |
| 15 |   |   |   |   |   | 1 | 1 | 1 |   | 1 |    | 1  |    | 1  |    | 1  | 1  |    |    |    |    |    | 8 |
| 16 |   |   |   |   |   |   |   |   |   |    |    |    |    |    |    |    | 1  |    |    |    |    |    | 1 |
| 17 |   |   | 1 |   |   |   |   |   |   |    |    |    |    |    |    |    |    | 1  |    | 1  | 1  |    | 4 |
| 18 |   |   |   |   |   |   |   |   |   |    |    |    |    |    |    |    |    |    | 1  |    |    |    | 1 |
| 19 |   |   |   |   |   |   |   |   |   |    |    |    |    |    |    |    |    |    | 1  |    |    |    | 1 |
| 20 |   |   |   |   |   |   |   |   |   |    |    |    |    |    |    |    | 1  |    |    |    |    |    | 1 |
| 21 |   |   |   |   |   |   |   |   |   |    |    |    |    |    |    |    | 1  |    | 1  |    |    |    | 2 |
| 22 |   |   | 1 |   |   |   |   |   |   |    |    |    |    |    |    |    |    |    |    |    |    |    | 1 |
| Column Total | 0 | 2 | 0 | 2 | 2 | 1 | 2 | 2 | 2 | 1 | 2 | 2 | 1 | 2 | 6 | 1 | 4 | 1 | 1 | 3 | 1 | 1 | |

Row Total = Influence Exerted

Influences Received

**Primary Matrix Representation of "Game Against Nature"**

Table 2

perception ($P_{16}$). Realizing that the change in equipment will cause certain consequences ($P_6$, $P_{10}$, $P_{13}$), the top hierarchy attempts to eliminate much of the human behavior by, *e.g.*, internalizing rules or increasing categorization. This may take the form of a brief notice advising only the group directly affected by the change without detailed explanation of the advantages of the new equipment for the group.

However, the interpretation by the value system of the group ($P_{15}$) resulting from the uncertain consequences has a twofold effect. First, it may interpret the change to automation as a potential threat to job security and thus affect the personality of the workers ($P_{16}$). Secondly, it may cause group rigidity ($P_{17}$) inasmuch as the group, and possibly others indirectly affected, may want to protect themselves from the imagined loss of security.

While the impact of the human behavior not only attempts to change the stimulus ($P_{17}$ to $P_4$), it has furthermore altered the company's originally intended goal ($P_{22}$) through possible strikes or refusals to operate the new equipment.

The graph in this case aims to illustrate some of the errors which may occur in the setup of a bureaucratic model if some of the impacts of human behavior are ignored.

The matrix (Table 2) provides an example of the influences exerted (rows) and received (columns) by the various organizational units. To obtain secondary effects, for example, the matrix must be squared in the following manner. Multiply each point of a particular column by its respective point in a particular row. The sum of the products thus derived is the number of the new matrix at the intersection of the above column and row. After all the points in the new matrix have been established, the sums of their rows and columns represent the secondary effects exerted and received respectively.[16]

***Analysis of Selznick's Theory of Bureaucracy.*** Philip Selznick's model (Figure 18) essentially reinforces the features

---

[16] Since the matrix in Merton's model is one of symmetry (reciprocal digraph), the matrix cannot be squared or cubed to illustrate secondary or tertiary impacts unless each unit has a value between zero and one.

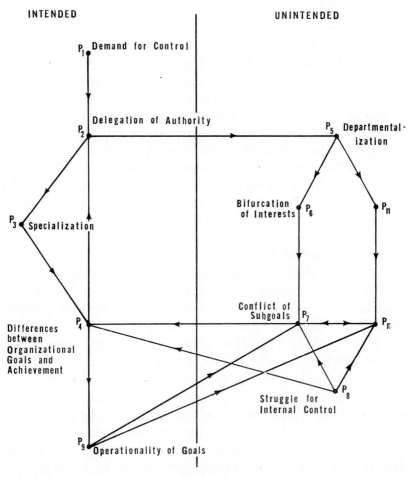

Figure 18

of Merton's bureaucracy modified by the impact of human behavior. Selznick differs merely in his approach, emphasizing individual aspirations which result in internal conflicts and thus change the intended goal. Selznick starts out with a demand for control ($P_1$) which is obtained through delegation of authority ($P_2$).[17] The delegation carries with it the following functional (intended) and dysfunctional (unintended) consequences:

_____

[17] March and Simon, *op. cit.*, pp. 40-44.

1. Functional consequences:

   a. An increased amount of specilization ($P_3$) resulting in (b).
   b. Decreased differences between organizational goals and achievements ($P_4$) which then stimulate further increase of delegation of authority.

2. Dysfunctional consequences:

   a. Departmentalization ($P_5$), *i.e.*, a collection of sub-units whose primary goal is that of their immediate groups rather than that of the entire organization which results in (b).
   b. Bifurcation (division) of interests ($P_6$) among sub-units.
   c. This bifurcation of interests often leads to increased conflicts of subgoals ($P_7$) among subunits, creating further internalization of goals ($P_4$).
   d. These conflicts often break out into struggles for internal control ($P_8$) by subunits and hence influence the internalization of the goals.
   e. At the same time, the subgoal conflicts ($P_7$) are affected by the operationality of the final intended goal ($P_9$).

From this brief excerpt and linear graph model, one can safely deduce that (1) Selznick agrees in essence with Merton's theory of bureaucracy and that (2) despite dysfunctional modification of Weber's monocracy, Selznick still regards a bureaucracy as a reliable form of organization to predict behavior.

*Analysis of Gouldner's Theory of Bureaucracy.* Gouldner's bureaucratic model (Figure 19) combines Merton's theory of impersonal rules and Selznick's theory of delegated internal powers. In the search for an effective and reliable demand for control ($P_2$), the top hierarchy ($P_1$) of the organization establishes a set of impersonal rules ($P_3$). Again, these rules create certain intended as well as unintended consequences.

The intended or manifest functions, derived from the rules, are (1) a decrease of the visible power relations ($P_4$)

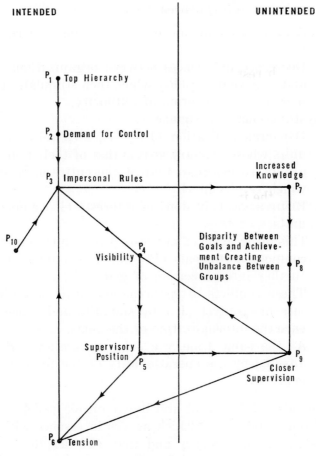

INTENDED                                    UNINTENDED

P₁ ● Top Hierarchy

P₂ ● Demand for Control

P₃ ● Impersonal Rules                        Increased
                                            Knowledge
                                                      ● P₇

P₁₀                                 Disparity Between
                                    Goals and Achieve-
              P₄                    ment Creating
         Visibility                 Unbalance Between  ● P₈
                                    Groups

    Supervisory
    Position
              P₅                                      ● P₉
                                            Closer
                                            Supervision

P₆ ● Tension

Figure 19

of the participants which leads to (2) an increase in the legitimacy of the supervisory position ($P_5$) and therefore a decrease in the tension ($P_6$) within the participant groups.

Simultaneously, however, the rules increase the participants' knowledge about minimum acceptable behavior ($P_7$) and the disparity between organizational goals and achievements ($P_8$). This, in turn, creates a disturbance among the participant groups, requiring closer supervision ($P_9$) of these groups. Once closer supervision is established, the groups receive greater visibility of the power relations ($P_4$) and therefore not only increase the tension among the subunits, but also influence the final goal (adversely or by reinforcement). It is the equilibrium, based upon impersonal rules, which has been upset by the tension created.

Gouldner therefore agrees with Merton and Selznick that a bureaucracy must take into account the impact of personal behavior which may be adverse to the intended behavior or may reinforce it. Regardless of the dysfunctional aspects, however, all three scholars seem to agree with Weber that the bureaucratic model lends itself to a relatively accurate predictability of behavior of an organization. The only difference of opinion remains in the degree of predictability achieved in this type of organization.

## Summary

With the introduction of linear graph theory as a tool for analysis in social sciences, this chapter attempts to examine the feasibility of the theory's use in exploring one facet of business behavior in organizations.

There are a great number of uses and approaches of linear graphs in the analysis of business behavior, as can be seen from the fundamental concepts of the theory. It should be stressed again, however, that the concept merely illustrates and verifies behavior; it does not explain the dynamics of behavior.

The workability and efficiency of the various theories of bureaucracy provide some illustration of the possible range in which graph theory may be employed to analyze business behavior. It may be set up to represent a hierarchical form of the bureaucracy or to illustrate the reciprocal influences exerted by functional and dysfunctional elements. These influences may then be translated into matrices for further study. The reader should keep in mind that the mathematical application in this chapter has by no means been exhausted. Many higher and more complex graph relationships might reveal further problems of the bureaucratic models as discussed above. The scope of this chapter, however, limits the discussion to an introduction of the application of the mathematical theory of linear graphs to business behavior.

## BIBLIOGRAPHY

Berge, Claude. *Theories des Graphes et ses Applications.* Paris: Dunod, 1959.

Cartwright, Dorwin. "The Potential Contribution of Graph Theory to Organization Theory," in *Organization Theory*, ed. Mason Haire. New York: John Wiley & Sons, Inc., 1959.

Dahl, R. A., and C. E. Lindblom. *Politics, Economics, and Welfare.* New York: Harper & Brothers, 1953.

Garrison, W. L. "Connectivity of the Interstate Highway System," Seattle: University of Washington Press. (Mimeographed.)

Gurvitch, Georges, and Wilbert E. Moore, *20th Century Sociology.* New York: Philosophical Library.

Harary, Frank, and R. Z. Norman. *Graph Theory as a Mathematical Model In Social Science.* Ann Arbor: University of Michigan Institute for Social Research, 1953.

Huff, David L. "A Topological Model of Consumer Space Preferences," in *Papers and Proceedings*, Regional Science Association, Vol. VI, 1960.

Koenig, Denes. *Theories der Endlichen und Unendlichen Graphen.* New York: Chelsea Publishing Co., 1950.

March, James G., and Herbert A. Simon. *Organizations.* New York: John Wiley & Sons, Inc., 1958.

McGuire, Joseph W. "The Concept of the Firm," *California Management Review*, Summer, 1961, pp. 64-88.

Merton, Robert K., *et al. Reader in Bureaucracy.* Glencoe: The Free Press, 1952.

Prihar, Z., "Topological Properties of Telecommunication Network," New York: *Proceedings of the IRE* (July, 1956), pp. 927-933.

Weber, Max. *The Theory of Social and Economic Organization*, translated by A. M. Henderson and Talcott Parsons. New York: Oxford University Press, 1947.

# Chapter 6

## UNCERTAINTY, EXPECTATIONS, AND RISK THEORIES

Bryce B. Orton

---

### Introduction

The statement has been made and is often repeated that nothing is certain except death and taxes. When uncertainty is referred to, the meaning attached to the concept in nearly all cases involves the unpredictability of, or imperfect knowledge concerning, the future. There is an important sense in which not even the qualifications of "death" and "taxes" need be made in reference to uncertainty.[1] The whole institution of insurance is built upon the uncertainty of the date of death of individuals. As for taxes, those who read about and observe legislative bodies in session must readily agree that even in this case, uncertainty as to the amount and nature of taxes hangs heavily in the background.

The business manager is constantly faced with uncertainty. In this environment of uncertainty, decisions must be made and plans formulated for the future. If the future could be known with certainty, the problems of economic decision making would fade away. In the face of certainty, the work of the business manager would become one merely of supervision. The outcome of alternative ventures would be known in advance. Under these circumstances, the only reason wrong decisions would be made would be because those responsible for decision making were not acting rationally upon the information available.

---

[1] Marshall R. Colberg, William C. Bradford, and Richard M. Alt, *Business Economics*, Revised Edition (Homewood, Illinois: Richard D. Irwin, Inc., 1957), p. 1.

In the world within which the business manager functions, that degree of certainty does not exist. The resources available for use in business organizations are not unrestricted. Limited as businesses are in the amount of capital, land, and labor available for use, business managers find themselves faced with alternative uses for which these resources might be employed. Choices must be made which will permit the business organization to achieve desired goals. In making these decisions, the business manager cannot know in advance the outcome of alternative ventures. Decisions must be made on the basis of current knowledge in anticipation of events that will occur or situations that will exist at some future time. This involves expectations, which one author has defined as "propositions with a future reference." [2] These decisions, once made, must be constantly reviewed, reshaped, and redirected as new and better data become available. The work of the business manager in decision making and planning is one of charting the business course into the uncertain future.

## Economic Theory and Uncertainty

While much criticism can be directed toward the traditional economic theory of the firm, one of the major criticisms, if not the most important, is that this theory has not provided for the uncertainty which exists in the real world. To the credit of traditional economic theory, it was the first to look into decision making in business and "presents the most diverse and developed set of ideas." [3] But as Hart stated:

> . . . in consequence of their preoccupation with "equilibrium," most theorists down to the last few years have confined themselves to the analysis of "timeless" situations— situations remaining unchanged through time—so that no explicit recognition of the problems of anticipations has been needed.[4]

---

[2] Mary Jean Bowman, "Introduction," *Expectations, Uncertainty, and Dynamic Planning* (Chicago: The University of Chicago Press, 1940), p. 3.
[3] *Ibid.*, p. 1.
[4] Albert Gailord Hart, *Anticipations, Uncertainty, and Dynamic Planning* (Chicago: The University of Chicago Press, 1940), p. 1. Copyright 1940 by the University of Chicago.

We live in a dynamic world. In decision making, all of the relevant facts are not known, and when decisions are made "under uncertainty," not every decision will turn out to have been right. Seldom, if ever, does a business executive have complete information as to what can be expected in the way of future sales, costs, and profits. Estimates must continually be made of the changes that will occur in material prices, in the cost of wages, in the changing desires of the purchasers of the goods produced, and in the changing complexion of the total economy. Such estimates are essential if the business man is going to plan for the future and carry out business operations efficiently and profitably. Dynamic uncertainty surrounds the environment of business decision; this is the environment that sets business behavior. As one writer has stated, "We can hardly hope to explain what is happening in the economic system if we do not understand how people make up their minds when they are faced by uncertainty about the future." [5]

Those who challenge the traditional economic theory of the firm on the grounds that it does not take into consideration the aspects of uncertainty have advanced a number of theories relating to business behavior. These theories themselves are subject to criticism but nevertheless are attempts to explain how the business manager proceeds in decision making "under uncertainty."

The various theories of risk, expectations, and uncertainty will be discussed under two broad classifications: (1) "those which use exclusively the language of probability distributions, and (2) those which call for some other principle, either to replace or to supplement." [6] Carter substantiates this breakdown by stating that there are only two contending theories—the one on expectation proposed by Shackle and "the belief that a businessman forms a probability distribution of the outcomes of a particular line of action, and summarizes the effect of the action by forming the mathematical

[5] C. F. Carter, "A Revised Theory of Expectation," *The Economic Journal*, LXIII (December, 1953), p. 811.
[6] Kenneth J. Arrow, "Alternative Approaches to the Theory of Choice in Risk-Taking Situations," *Econometrica*, 19 (October, 1951), p. 410.

expectation of the outcome." [7]  The theories are discussed in this chapter under the headings "Probability" and, for the want of a better title, "Other Theories of Uncertainty and Expectation."

## Probability

Only within the present century have the applications of the concept of probability to real life situations exerted a major influence in the area of decision making. This whole area of probability theory, however, dates back to 1654 when, so it is reported, a French nobleman and gambler asked the mathematician, Pascal, to help compute the proper odds in a dice game. [8]  Some mathematicians, such as Jacob Bernoulli, were of the opinion that the theory of probability was capable of providing advice "in a much wider field of human affairs" and on subjects more important than dice or card games. [9] But probability theory was destined to lie somewhat dormant until the turn of the century, when it was given a "wider" application and use in explaining business behavior. Bross points out that the reason probability theory did not emerge sooner as a decision-making tool was that it grew up in an era which acknowledged the "supremacy of reason." "Reason, and reason alone, could solve all human problems with little more than a passing reference to the real world." [10]

Theoretical mathematicians working with probability theory were able to construct elaborate models created entirely in terms of abstract symbols. In real-world situations, data had to be gathered before applications could be made. This was a tedious and wearisome task, making the application of probability theory to real-life situations of little interest to the theoreticians. Remaining withdrawn from the world, they spent their time with mathematical problems, which, while interesting, had little practical meaning. Very little effort was made to advance the use of probability theory

[7] Carter, *op. cit.*, p. 811.
[8] Irwin D. F. Bross, *Design for Decision* (New York: The Macmillan Company, 1957), p. 42.
[9] *Ibid.*, p. 43.
[10] *Ibid.*, p. 43,

in the area of explaining business behavior, pointing up the fact that "academic sterility can only be avoided by maintaining close contact with the real world—unpleasant as the contact may be at times." [11]

*Probability, Uncertainty, and Risk.* Many different concepts of the meaning of the probability relation exist, each stemming from one of the various theories of knowledge.[12] None of these concepts may currently claim universal approval. Pfeffer has noted questions that remain unresolved.

> Is the probability relation a matter of subjective belief, or is it a clearly defined objective phenomenon independent of the mind of the inquirer? Is it purely a feature of syntax, or is it a characteristic of the real universe? Is the notion of probability relevant in the case of the single unique event, or is it applicable only to series of events? Must probability be expressible as a cardinal number? Is the idea of *a priori* probability meaningful? [13]

The final answers to these problems will undoubtedly be provided only with future research and study.

Among those who describe uncertainty by means of probability, several groups may be distinguished. Arrow, in his discussion, lists three:

> (1) those who treat the probability distributions of the consequences of alternative actions as subjectively given to the individual and who do not attempt further analysis; (2) those who derive all probability judgments from a limited number of *a priori* probabilities; (3) those who attempt to relate the degree-of-belief and frequency theories to each other through the law of large numbers.[14]

Others, such as Georgescu-Roegen, speak of two: the "Laplacian or Classical School" and the "Frequency School." [15] This, in general, includes the classifications made by Arrow.

---

[11] *Ibid.*, p. 43.

[12] Irving Pfeffer, *Insurance and Economic Theory* (Homewood, Illinois: Richard D. Irwin, Inc., 1956), p. 167.

[13] *Ibid.*, pp. 167-168.

[14] Arrow, *op. cit.*, p. 410.

[15] Nicholas Georgescu-Roegen, "The Nature of Expectations and Uncertainty," *Expectations, Uncertainty, and Business Behavior*, Mary Jean Bowman, (ed.) (New York: Social Science Research Council, 1958), pp. 12-13.

*The Classical View.* The classical view is "that a degree of probability is a measure of the strength of conviction with which a particular belief is held." [16] Those holding this view see probability as a purely subjective conception of the weight to be attributed to any hypothesis. Irving Fisher's theory is typical of those who accept this position. For Fisher, "chance exists only so far as ignorance exists; varies with different persons according to their comparative ignorance of the matter under consideration and is in fact a measure of ignorance." [17] At another time he wrote, "Risk is synonymous with uncertainty—lack of knowledge." [18] In Fisher's view, probability is simply an expression of ignorance; "risk varies inversely with knowledge." [19]

Fisher has illustrated this viewpoint with the example of a coin in a man's hand. "If a man holds a coin in his hand and, without letting it be seen, asks his neighbor what the 'real' chance is that heads are up," he will reply, "one half." [20] To the man who holds the coin and who has looked upon it there is no uncertainty. He knows that the coin lies in a given position; for him the probability is not "one half," but is certain. Ignorance of all the facts made the man's neighbor assert a probability value equidistant between zero and unity. The application of this concept does not depend on whether the subject about which probability statements are made is a single unique event or a number of events. Statistics may provide us with some information, but it has no more value than information from any other source of knowledge.

Numerous other writers have accepted this subjective view; included among them are Marshall, Hicks, Friedman, Savage, and Lange. The latter writer's intention seems to be, however, "not so much a philosophical position as a view that the relevant phenomena can be explained by theories

---

[16] Pfeffer, *op. cit.*, p. 168.
[17] Irving Fisher, *The Nature of Capital and Income* (New York: The Macmillan Company, 1906), p. 268.
[18] Irving Fisher, *The Theory of Interest* (New York: The Macmillan Company, 1930), p. 221.
[19] *Ibid.*
[20] Fisher, *The Nature of Capital and Income, loc. cit.*

using only probability language, such theories being preferred on grounds of simplicity." [21]

*The A Piori View.* Another group has worked on the theory of, or at least derived all probability judgments from, a limited number of *a priori* probabilities. In the games of chance, for instance, an *a priori* (*i.e.* prior to experience) judgment is usually made as to certain probabilities. When business affairs are dealt with, however, there is no natural way of making these judgments. For the subjectivists, the appeal is to past observations. Judgment becomes a matter of inference of probabilities from empirical evidence.

Much of this thought is built around Bayes' rule which was the first systematic study of the inference of probabilities from empirical evidence.[22] The work of Bayes was published after his death by some of his friends and has had a most controversial history.[23] Bayes' theorem shows that the *a priori* probabilities which are set up on the basis of past information are affected by the *a posteriori* (*i.e.*, through experience) probabilities. The *a priori* probabilities, in any particular context, are the *a posteriori* probabilities of the preceding time period. This becomes a "continuous circle" and was one of the major criticisms leveled at the classical view.

In order to overcome this criticism, the classicists developed and introduced the "principle of nonsufficient reason." This was first formulated by Jacob Bernoulli in the Seventeenth Century. The principle asserts that "if there is no *known* reason for predicating of our subject on one rather than another of several alternatives, then relative to such knowledge, the assertions of each of these alternatives have *equal* probability. Thus, *equal* probabilities must be assigned to each of several arguments, if there is an absence of positive ground for assigning unequal ones." [24]

Keynes preferred to call it the "principle of indifference" and found it "clumsy and unsatisfactory." In his work,

---

[21] Arrow, *op. cit.*, p. 411.
[22] *Ibid.*, p. 412.
[23] Bross, *op. cit.*, pp. 81-83.
[24] John Maynard Keynes, *A Treatise on Probability* (London: Macmillan & Company, Ltd., 1921), p. 42.

Keynes has demonstrated the paradoxical conclusion to which this principle leads. For example, assume that we have a book of which we know nothing about the color. If we should assign equal weights to the proposition that the book is blue and that it is not blue, we would obtain a value of one half that it is blue. Keynes makes modifications in the principle, making it even more difficult to apply.[25]

In addition to the criticism already given, two more have been made against the subjective view. Some argue that this concept of probability is far too limited in its application. From the standpoint of its mathematical formulation, it requires that all events be classified into sets of equipossible alternatives. This is a condition that is not met in the inductive areas of research where the probability concept is most useful.

The second criticism is that there is some question as to whether probability measures an actual belief or measures the strength of conviction which ought to be associated with belief. If the first position is taken, it then presents the problem of showing how these beliefs can be subjected to arithmetic. This problem has its analogue in the issue of interpersonal and intertemporal comparisons of utility in economics.[26] The "strength of conviction" view is the one held by Keynes and is discussed later.

*The Frequency School.* There are a number of variants of the relative frequency interpretations of probability. The most common attempts to relate the degree-of-belief and frequency theory to each other by means of the law of large numbers.[27]

The law of large numbers, in more popular but less exacting language than that used in mathematics, means that as the number of trials increases, the proportion of results approaches the underlying probability. For example, if we

---

[25] *Ibid.*, pp. 42-64.
[26] Arrow, *op. cit.*, pp. 420-426.
[27] As variants of the frequency school, some regard frequency as pertaining to propositions about events; others hold it is the frequency of events themselves that is involved; and others define probability as the limit of frequencies of events.

were to draw a single card from a well-shuffled deck, it may
be any one of 52, but, since one fourth of the cards are clubs,
the probability of drawing a club is one fourth. This does not
mean that if only four cards are drawn, one, and only one,
will be a club. It can be shown that there is a strong probability *against* this exact result. Furthermore, it does not
mean that if 40 are drawn, exactly 10 will be clubs. It does
mean that as the number of trials is increased, the ratio of
drawings of clubs to the total drawings tends to become one
fourth, though the actual departure may be great.

In its applications, the law of large numbers is not
subject to exact proof, except under purely mechanical and
artificial conditions similar to those used in defining probability. The concept is useful, however, under modern statistical theory in providing rational rules of inductive behavior.
The law of large numbers is a statistical concept designed to
reveal the probability of the occurrence of specified characteristics in random samples of various sizes drawn from their
respective universes of data. The law is derived from mathematical theorems and is valid for experience only to the
extent that the postulates derived by induction are identical
with those employed in the mathematical construct.

## Other Theories of Uncertainty and Expectation

*Keynesian View.* Keynes' theory, although he was an advocate of a degree-of-belief theory, differs from the probability
views already presented. Keynes held the view that probability is an "ultimate, undefinable, primitive" relationship
between propositions by virtue of which, if we know the first,
we can attach to the latter some degree of rational belief.[28]
For Keynes, no proposition may be regarded as probable
except in relation to other propositions.

In explaining his views, Keynes sets up a formula such
as $A/H = K$. He then argues that it is rational to entertain
a degree of belief of K in the validity of a conclusion A based
on all of our relevant knowledge of H. As we obtain additional

---

[28] Pfeffer, *op. cit.*, p. 171.

and perhaps better information, the probability values assignable to our hypothesis changes. Since all information affects the value of K, and since the relative importance and accuracy of our evidence varies widely, we can only occasionally assign numerical values to our probabilities. For Keynes, a rule can be given a numerical measurement only "when the conclusion is one of a number of equiprobable, exclusive, and exhaustive alternatives, but not otherwise." [29]

Comment needs to be made relative to Keynes' concept of rational belief. For Keynes, knowledge is defined in terms of "certain rational belief," i.e., "when the outcome of an event is known, a rational person will be certain of his belief in the result." [30] In the case of an unknown (uncertain) outcome, a rational person will hold the degree of belief that is warranted by the knowledge or evidence he has. "Symmetry between our degree-of-belief and the conviction warranted by the objective facts which determine our knowledge is the test of rationality." [31]

Keynes contends that this concept of probability provides a more general and complete theory than that offered by the statistical interpretation of the frequency school. For Keynes and others accepting this point of view, more rational grounds exist than statistical frequencies for preferring one belief over another.

**Frank H. Knight—Risk and Uncertainty.** Frank H. Knight, through his work in the early 1920's in the area of profit theory, helped to bring probability and economics together.[32] In addition, his work drew the first real distinction between risk and uncertainty. Knight gave this distinction considerable emphasis. He states:

> (risk) . . . really covers two things which . . . in their casual relations to the phenomena of economic organization, are categorically different . . . the essential fact is that "risk" means in some cases a quantity susceptible of measurement,

---

[29] Keynes, *op. cit.*, p. 112.
[30] Pfeffer, *op. cit.*, p. 172.
[31] Pfeffer, *op. cit.*, p. 171.
[32] Bowman, *op. cit.*, p. 1.

while at other times it is something distinctly not of this character . . . a *measurable* uncertainty, or "risk" proper . . . is so far different from an *unmeasurable* one that it is not in effect an uncertainty at all.[33]

For Knight, risk is measurable uncertainty.[34] Risk is measurable when anticipations may be guided by statistical probability.[35] Uncertainty is restricted to cases of the nonquantitative types.[36] Unmeasurable uncertainty does not signify complete lack of knowledge but lack of quantitative data or basis for "classifying instances." [37]

How does this affect the business man? If the entrepreneur had complete knowledge of all relevant economic circumstances and no uncertainties of the nature and behavior of the future events, under perfect competition there would be no profit. In this case, each factor would be paid its marginal value product. According to Knight:

> . . . The reason for the inaccuracy of distribution and the occurrence of profit is essentially the inaccurate forecasting of demand by producers, and to a lesser degree the impossibility of predicting the physical result of a productive operation and so controlling it with precision. . . . It is fairly apparent that if business men could foresee future conditions exactly, and if the relations between them were those of competition only, cost and price would always be equal, there would be no pure profits. . . . Not all "risks" necessarily give rise to profit, or loss. Many kinds can be insured against, which eliminates them as factors of uncertainty . . . the uncertainties which persist as causes of profit are those which are uninsurable because there is no objective measure of the probability of gain or loss.[38]

For those types of risks that are measurable, Knight seems to derive statistical probabilities from experience with

---

[33] Frank H. Knight, *Risk, Uncertainty, and Profit* (Boston: Houghton Mifflin Company, 1921), pp. 19-20.

[34] *Ibid.*

[35] *Ibid.*, p. 255.

[36] *Ibid.*, p. 21.

[37] *Ibid.*, p. 255.

[38] Frank H. Knight, *The Economic Organization* (New York: Augustus M. Kelley, Inc., 1951), pp. 119-120.

the aid of the *a priori* in the manner of Bayes' theorem.[39] The "unmeasurable" risks are sharply distinguished by Knight from both *a priori* and statistical probabilities. These are true uncertainties which arise when there is no valid basis for classification "and are usually applied to situations which are in some sense unique." [40] Under these circumstances, according to Knight, what is done is to form an estimate of the situation and to make a judgment as to the reliability of it. These, it would appear, must be made on an intuitive basis.

He does not present a formal method of describing uncertainties or estimates. He states that the economic organization deals with uncertainty by reducing it or by specializing the function of meeting it. This reduction is done by consolidation of many cases, analogous to the law of large numbers. Insurance is the chief device for consolidation, but is not the only method available for dealing with risk.[41]

One of the objections that has been directed toward Knight and his ideas is that there is not a dichotomy between "risk" and "uncertainty." Between these two extremes which he describes, there is a continuum of graduations varying with the amount of information that is available and with the factors involved. It appears, however, that Knight was fully aware of this fact but that perhaps he purposefully exaggerated the distinctness of the two categories in order to emphasize the role of "uncertainty" or the unique.

*G. L. S. Shackle—Expectational Theory.* In 1949, G. L. S. Shackle, with his book *Expectation in Economics,* led a revival of interest in the problem of expectations as it relates to economics.[42] This was done by offering a new set of conceptual tools for coping with the problem of entrepreneurial decision making.

Shackle and Knight share a common viewpoint on a number of points. Both hold that "where the frequency of occur-

---

[39] Arrow, *op. cit.,* p. 417.
[40] *Ibid.*
[41] Knight, *Risk, Uncertainty, and Profit, op. cit.,* Chapter 8.
[42] G. L. S. Shackle, *Expectation in Economics* (Cambridge: Cambridge University Press, 1949).

rence is sufficient, the case is one amenable to the methods of mathematical expectations as a measurable, objective, statistical risk." [43]   Shackle accepts the Knight point of view described earlier, that these cases do not constitute a problem because they can be eliminated by insurance or other means. When it comes to new and unique situations, Shackle believes that one cannot satisfactorily employ the statistical theory. New and unique situations require that decisions be made under circumstances where it is impossible to obtain statistical data for dealing with them. In these cases, businessmen are confronted with situations which do not repeat themselves. Resorting to the law of large numbers would be out of the question. The nature of the problem makes the relative-frequency approach of probability of no use, and a different approach must therefore be used.

The analysis of choice in new and unique situations becomes, for Shackle, the basic problem in the theory of expectations.[44] Shackle isolates the problems for treatment by means of the use of a set of psychological postulates which he has developed and manipulates mathematically. No empirical evidence is offered in support of the postulates; they rest entirely upon the author's "intuition and logic." [45]

The mathematical model that Shackle constructs contributes to the numerous alternative hypotheses about the outcome of some particular event or activity values representing the "enjoyment" or "distress" attached to the anticipation of each event's outcome.[46] Associated with each value is a subjective probability or degree of belief in the "likelihood" of its occurrence. The degree of conviction with which each hypothesis is held is measured in terms of the "surprise" that would be felt if the particular outcome failed to materialize. These variables are labeled the "potential surprise." Thus, for each event, there is a series of possible outcomes, each with its associated degree of "potential surprise."

---

[43] Pfeffer, op. cit., p. 102.
[44] Ibid.
[45] Shackle, op. cit., p. 49.
[46] C. F. Carter, "Expectation in Economics," The Economic Journal, LX (March, 1950), p. 93.

One author has demonstrated the application of this with
the example of Adam, a primeval entrepreneur, trying to
make up his mind whether to buy an orchard.[47] The value of
the orchard to him is determined by the size of next year's
crop. As the weather outside Eden is uncertain, this may
amount to 2, 3, 4, 5, 6 or more tons of apples. As Adam
contemplates the prospective purchase, he asks himself a
series of questions:

> Shall I get only 1 ton of apples?—Quite impossible.
> Shall I get 2 tons?—Surprised if it is so low.
> Shall I get 3, 4, 5 tons?—All perfectly possible.
> Shall I get 6 tons?—Surprised if it is so high.
> Shall I get 7 tons?—Very surprising, but just possible.
> Shall I get 8 tons?—Quite impossible.

The answers to these questions determine Adam's decision.

Adam's choice is whether to buy or not to buy the orchard.
For Shackle, the decision will be based upon the course of
action which Adam might take which will offer "the most
enjoyment by anticipation of its outcome." [48] In order for
Adam to make up his mind, he must assess the various possible outcomes that might occur if he purchased the orchard.
These comparisons will be made from Adam's present "viewpoint" looking at a future "image-date" and imagining what
the future will bring. These possible outcomes are assigned
some weight or degree of belief, and it is these weighted
hypothetical outcomes which he compares. The way that
Adam measures this degree of belief is by the "degree of
surprise" which he would feel if the expected event failed
to occur.

How are choices made in new and unique situations?
Shackle says that we consider in the imagination the most
compelling favorable and unfavorable hypotheses about the
results. These he calls the "standard focus gain" and
"standard focus loss," which are the values associated with
the degree of potential surprise. Once these focus outcomes

---

[47] *Ibid.*, p. 93.
[48] Shackle, *op. cit.*, p. 10.

have been determined, the next step is to construct a "gambler indifference map" which will summarize comprehensively everything about the attitude of uncertainty of one particular person, in his circumstances of a particular moment, that is relevant for determining his actions." [49] Once this is done, the rule for decision is made clear.

> Among the courses of action that are open to the individual he must choose that which will bring him to the "best" indifference curve—*i.e.*, that whose focus-gain or given focus-loss is highest. If there are two or more choices offering equal attractions, he must toss a coin to make the final choice.[50]

***Other Theories of Uncertainty.*** There are numerous other theories of behavior and decision making that are connected with the question of uncertainty and risk. Building on Shackle's work, C. F. Carter has suggested a revised theory in which he states that "the problem of making up one's mind in face of uncertainty is a problem of simplification." [51]

The question of uncertainty and risk arises in the work of Alchian, who claims that where the economic system includes uncertainty, "profit maximization" is meaningless as a guide to specific action.[52] We find also the question of uncertainty as a factor to be considered in the liquidity theories, the theory of games, the organizational, sociological and psychological theories of firm behavior. While in these business behavior theories uncertainty is not given a prime role to play, it has been recognized as an important force in the area of decision making.

## Summary

None of the theories discussed here has gone unchallenged. The whole area of risk, uncertainty, and expectation, as it

---

[49] Shackle, *op. cit.*, pp. 29-30. See: G. L. S. Shackle, "Expectation and Liquidity," *Expectations, Uncertainty, and Business Behavior*, Mary Jean Bowman, (ed.) (New York: Social Science Research Council, 1958), pp. 30-44.

[50] Carter, "Expectation in Economics," *op. cit.*, p. 94.

[51] Carter, "A Revised Theory of Expectations," *op. cit.*

[52] A. A. Alchian, "Uncertainty, Evolution, and Economic Theory," *Journal of Political Economy*, 58 (June, 1950), p. 211.

relates to business behavior needs and is receiving additional research and study.

There seems to be, however, a somewhat general feeling held currently that the business manager in his decision-making activities is faced with two types of outcomes: risk, and uncertainty. The dichotomy that is perhaps held in widest favor is the original distinction made by Frank Knight. From the business standpoint, risk is usually defined as being the quantitative measure of an outcome, whatever it might be, in such a manner that the probability of the outcome can be predicted. Risk is measurable when anticipations may be guided by statistical probability. The risk concept has two major characteristics, first that it can be measured, and second, that it may be used to predict the likelihood of some eventuality or contingency.

What is the significance of risk as it applies to decision making and determining business behavior? Business executives are placed in a position in which they must make the decisions and lay the plans that will chart the business course into the uncertain future. Since risk can be measured and used as a predictive tool, the expected outcomes can be incorporated in advance into the business plans. This is done, for example, by taking out insurance or by merely considering it a regular cost of doing business.

Uncertainty on the other hand presents a different challenge. Like risk, uncertainty is forward-looking in nature. Uncertainty, however, is not measurable; "the observations are not repeated often enough to establish a probability figure based on repeated, homogeneous trial, as in the case of risk." [53] Uncertainty does not imply complete lack of knowledge but lack of *complete* knowledge. Business executives making decisions under these circumstances must do so by forming "expectations" as to the future that cannot be verified in a quantitative manner. "It follows from this that uncertainty is not insurable, and cannot be integrated within the firm's cost structure as can risk." [54]

---

[53] Milton H. Spencer and Louis Siegelman, *Managerial Economics* (Homewood, Illinois: Richard D. Irwin, Inc., 1959), p. 8.
[54] *Ibid.*

**Conclusion**

In any activity where knowledge of the future is imperfect, decisions are made in the present based on expectations of the future, and, therefore, prediction forms the connecting link between the known facts of today and the uncertain events of the future. Businessmen work in an environment where the future is uncertain and the knowledge available for decision making is incomplete. This fact stands in bold relief and as a challenge to the traditional economic theory of the firm as an explanation of business behavior.

## BIBLIOGRAPHY

Alchian, A. A. "Uncertainty, Evolution, and Economic Theory," *Journal of Political Economy*, 58 (June, 1950), pp. 211-221.

American Economic Association. *Readings in the Theory of Income Distributions*. Philadelphia: The Blakiston Company, 1949.

Arrow, Kenneth J. "Alternative Approaches to the Theory of Choice in Risk-Taking Situations," *Econometrica*, 19 (October, 1951), pp. 404-437.

Bowman, Mary Jean (ed.). *Expectations, Uncertainty, and Business Behavior*. New York: Social Science Research Council, 1958.

Bross, Irwin D. F. *Design for Decision*. New York: The Macmillan Company, 1957.

Carter, C. F. "Expectation in Economics," *The Economic Journal*, LX (March, 1950), pp. 92-105.

————. "A Revised Theory of Expectation," *The Economic Journal*, LXIII (December, 1953), pp. 811-820.

Colberg, Marshall R., William C. Bradford, and Richard M. Alt. *Business Economics*, Revised Edition. Homewood: Richard D. Irwin, Inc., 1957.

Dow, J. C. R. "The Inaccuracy of Expectations," *Economica*, (May, 1941), pp. 162-175.

Fisher, Irving. *The Nature of Capital and Income*. New York: The Macmillan Company, 1906.

——————. *The Theory of Interest.* New York: The Macmillan Company, 1930.

Georgescu-Roegen, Nicholas. "The Nature of Expectations and Uncertainty," in *Expectations, Uncertainty, and Business Behavior,* ed. Mary Jean Bowman. New York: Social Science Research Council, 1958.

Harris, C. Lowell. *Selected Readings in Economics.* Englewood Cliffs: Prentice-Hall, Inc., 1958.

Hart, Albert Gailord. *Anticipations, Uncertainty, and Dynamic Planning.* Chicago: University of Chicago Press, 1940.

Keynes, John Maynard. *A Treatise on Probability.* London: Macmillan & Company, Ltd., 1921.

Knight, Frank H. *Risk, Uncertainty and Profit.* Boston: Houghton Mifflin Company, 1921.

——————. *The Economic Organization.* New York: Augustus M. Kelley, Inc., 1951.

Margolis, Julius. "The Analysis of the Firm: Rationalism, Conventionalism, and Behaviorism," *The Journal of Business,* University of Chicago Press, July, 1958.

Marschak, Jacob. "Rational Behavior, Uncertain Prospects, and Measurable Utility," *Econometrica,* 18 (April, 1950), pp. 111-141.

Mowbray, Albert H., and Ralph H. Blanchard. *Insurance, Its Theory and Practice.* New York: McGraw-Hill Book Company, Inc., 1955.

Pfeffer, Irving. *Insurance and Economic Theory.* Homewood: Richard D. Irwin, Inc., 1956.

Schlaifer, Robert. *Probability and Statistics for Business Decisions.* New York: McGraw-Hill Book Company, Inc., 1959.

Shackle, G. L. S. *Expectation in Economics.* Cambridge, England: Cambridge University Press, 1949.

Spencer, Milton H., and Louis Siegelman. *Managerial Economics.* Homewood: Richard D. Irwin, Inc., 1959.

Tintner, Gerhard. "The Theory of Choice under Subjective Risk and Uncertainty," *Econometrica,* 9 (July, 1941), pp. 298-304.

Weston, J. F. "A Generalized Uncertainty Theory of Profit," *The American Economic Review,* XL (March, 1950), pp. 40-60.

# Chapter 7

# MATHEMATICAL PROGRAMMING

Richard J. Trainor

## Introduction

Economists for the past fifty years have been aware of many of the techniques of linear economics. However, until quite recently, these techniques have been disregarded basically because economists had considered the linear aspects of the program as trivial and an oversimplification of the explanation of business behavior. Instead, for many years, economists have turned to marginal analysis to explain why firms behave as they do. However, it has been demonstrated by Richard Lester and others that marginal analysis often does not provide a satisfactory method for explaining what businessmen will do in a given situation. It therefore becomes the problem in this chapter to outline two mathematical approaches and to see if these will provide a more satisfactory explanation of behavior of the firm.

## Linear Programming

One of the most common mathematical techniques used to explain business behavior is linear programming. Linear programming has been variously described, but possibly the most correct definition is "the analysis of problems in which a linear function of a number of variables is to be maximized (or minimized) when those variables are subject to a number of restraints in the form of linear inequalities."[1] Linear

---

[1] Robert Dorfman, Paul A. Samuelson, and Robert M. Solow, *Linear Programming and Economic Analysis* (New York: McGraw-Hill Book Company, Inc., 1958), p. 8.

117

programming was developed in 1947 by George B. Dantzig, some three years after the publication of Von Neumann and Morgenstern's *Theory of Games and Economic Behavior.* The technique was first used for planning the diversified activities of the Air Force. The main applications have since been in problems of resource allocation. Linear programming has been particularly successful in scheduling of salesmen, geographical distribution of warehouses, and inventory control.

*An Application of Linear Programming.* Before discussing the application of linear programming to theory of the firm, it is desirable to review briefly the technique in one of its more familiar roles—maximizing of profits in an atmosphere of linear restraints. For this purpose it is desirable to choose a problem that has only two processes, since this allows the technique to be displayed in graphic form. Obviously, application of linear programming usually involves several processes and is therefore solved algebraically, not graphically.

Let us assume a hypothetical problem of a construction firm in the business of building carports and garages. This company has two limited resources: labor and the ability to finance its construction efforts. In addition, there are market limitations with the profit structure that has been assumed. The company can build carports and/or garages in any combination so long as the 100% capacity of either resources or market is not exceeded. The capacities are shown in Table 1 and plotted in Figure 1.

Table 1

Yearly Capacity of a Firm Constructing Carports and Garages

|  |  | UNITS PER YEAR | |
|  |  | CARPORTS | GARAGES |
|---|---|---|---|
| Market Limits | Carport Market | 500 | — |
|  | Garage Market | — | 260 |
| Resource Limits | Labor | 600 | 420 |
|  | Financing | 800 | 300 |

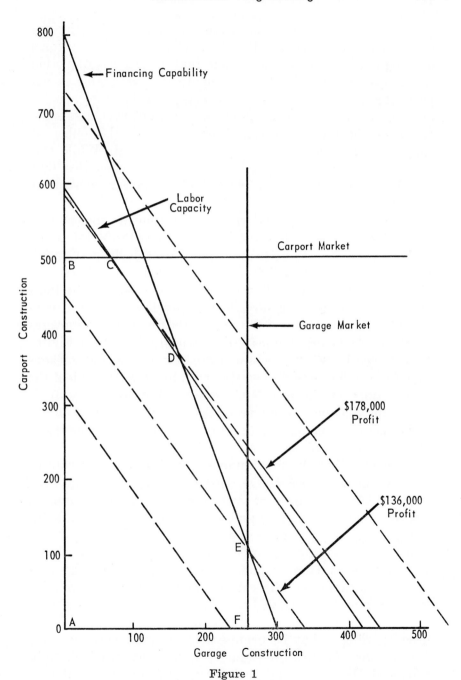

Figure 1

**Carport and Garage Construction Possibilities, Constant Profits Per Unit**

Figure 1 shows that feasible construction possibilities are enclosed in the hexagon ABCDEF. (Restraints in the form of inequalities are written such that negative production which would otherwise be mathematically acceptable is not permitted.) In this example, it can be seen that the capacity of each resource and market imposes a limit, over a selected range of construction possibilities, on the total number of carports and garages that could be constructed. While this is not a requirement of a linear program, capacities that do not impose a constraint can be disregarded in subsequent computations.

The problem is to find the combination of carport and garage construction that will yield the greatest total profit without exceeding the resource limits previously postulated. It is assumed, arbitrarily, that each carport completed will yield a net profit of $300 and each garage, $400. The total profit per year is, therefore, $300 times the number of carports constructed plus $400 times the number of garages constructed. Isoprofit lines are shown graphically in Figure 1 as dashed lines. Any combination of carports and garages that fall on the same dashed line will, by definition, yield the same profit. The largest feasible profit, $178,000 per year, is the profit that will result from the combination at point C. Construction at point D with a profit of $175,400 is nearly as profitable as at point C.

The fact that the maximum profit occurs at a vertex of the hexagon is not accidental. Instead, it illustrates that even with a large number of variables, linear programming problems have a definite number of possible solutions. Solution to a linear program is a problem of searching (by iteration) for the optimum vertex of the $n$ dimensional shape. It can be seen from Figure 1 that only two of the four possible constraints (the carport market and the available labor) are at 100% capacity in the achievement of maximum profits; this illustrates a fundamental theorem of linear programming. That is, profits will be maximized by using just as many facilities to capacity as there are products to be produced. In a more general form, "maximum output may always be obtained by using a number of processes which does not exceed the number of factors in limited supply, if this number is greater than zero." [2]

This result is surprising and is a basis for explaining some aspects of business behavior—if the statement can be believed. Suppose, for example, a company has successfully diversified and is deriving a good rate of profit by making thirty different products with ten factors. Linear programming tells us that if the factors are fixed, the product line should be dropped to ten. Now, this may be mathematically palatable but it is probably economic nonsense. If the products are compatible and help create a relatively constant overall production program, then it may be perfectly logical to produce a large number of products with a limited number of fixed factors. The limitations of linear programming as expressed by this theorem are twofold: first, it ignores the demand side of the economic problem; second, connected to the first limitation, is the fact that linear programming is basically static, not dynamic. Linear programming ignores the possible cyclical demands for various products because the answer it gives is good for only one point in time. But let it be added that linear programming apparently gives a definite non-time oriented answer—that is, drop twenty products from production and concentrate on the other ten. The question is, which ten products? Linear programming techniques will tell us to produce the ten currently most profitable. However, this answer is not necessarily the correct answer viewed from a long-term profit situation. It doesn't account at all for the fact that demand for some of these products may diminish in the near future. The theorem will not even allow the introduction of a new product line unless it is profitable from the outset. It is possible to set up a series of linear programs time-sequenced to handle variations in product demand. However, it is not clear when one has finished whether he has really utilized linear pro-

[2] Robert Dorfman, "Mathematical, or 'Linear,' Programming: a Non-mathematical Exposition," *The American Economic Review*, XLIII (December, 1953), p. 812.

gramming or rather has actually performed a marginal analysis by a most devious route.

*Simplifications Required in Linear Programming.* It is clear that we did not need a technique such as linear programming to solve the problem of optimum carport-garage construction. However, the problem does illustrate some of the characteristics of more difficult models. We should first examine some of the simplifying assumptions necessary to the solution of this type of linear program. The model assumes that each unit can be sold at a constant profit. However, this assumption implies that if revenue is constant, costs must be constant; or if costs vary, net revenue must vary proportionately. Since net revenue is very unlikely to rise with higher production, we are back to an assumption of constant cost and constant revenue up to capacity limits, whereupon costs then rise to infinity. The assumption of a constant revenue is basically one of perfect competition and is probably justifiable with moderate capacity limits of a plant.

It is particularly useful to recognize that the isoprofit lines in a linear program are linear and parallel. That is, if $x$ production yields $y$ profits, a production of $2x$ yields profits of $2y$. While this assumption will bother marginal analysts no end, the following quotation is an indication of the importance attached to linearity by those who advocate the use of linear programs in the analysis of business behavior. "In our formulation we shall assume that deviations from proportionality are unimportant and shall neglect them." [3]

If, in a linear program, we start by making a profit, moving to higher curves will always increase profits. (If both carport and garage construction is unprofitable from the outset, moving to higher profit curves results in larger negative profits, *i.e.* losses). Because of the lack of diminishing returns to scale, production could be profitably expanded infinitely. Of course, the situation is kept under control by the constraints imposed, in this case by resource

---

[3] Dorfman, Samuelson, and Solow, *op. cit.*, p. 132.

and market limits. However, from a theoretical viewpoint, these constraints were quite arbitrarily selected. Another example could be used to show that it is as profitable to build five million cars per week as it is to build twenty thousand. In short, unlike marginal analysis, the demand side of the picture is ignored completely. Dorfman attributes the neglect of the demand side of economic problems to the fact that the initial appearance of linear programming was in scientific management rather than in economics.[4] However, excuses notwithstanding, the neglect of demand is considered by the writer to be one of the most serious shortcomings of linear programming.

Dorfman makes specific reference to characteristics of linear programming that he considers to be particularly important. These are linearity, divisibility, additivity, and finiteness.[5] The effect of linearity will be discussed in greater detail later. Divisibility is the assumption that all the products of an enterprise can be profitably produced independently of one another. For example, it was assumed that either carports or garages could be produced within the resource and market limitations. This assumption is quite limiting in that many industries have interrelated products. It would be possible, based on prices, floor space, labor, etc., to prove with the assumption of divisibility that a contractor should build twice as many garages as he does houses. The assumption of divisibility disregards the fact that only one garage is usually required per house. The assumption of additivity requires that the result of production with nonidentical processes will be additive. It is, of course, easy to find situations in which the assumption of additivity is violated. The assumption of finiteness refers to the manner in which resources can be combined without changing the basic process. This assumption is perhaps the most limiting of the four mentioned because there are a large number of processes which allow infinite variation in the amounts of various

[4] Robert Dorfman, *Application of Linear Programming to the Theory of the Firm* (Berkeley: University of California Press, 1951), p. 5.
[5] *Ibid.*, p. 80.

factors used. For example, in agriculture and in the chemical industry, the range of productive processes is virtually infinite.

*Effect of Linearity.* An interesting conflict concerning the effect of linearity for the analysis of business behavior appears in various publications. Dorfman, for example, in his writings tends to belittle the effect of linearity. Although he does not adequately explain his reasons, Dorfman says the contrast between mathematical programming and marginal analysis with respect to linearity is "more verbal than substantive." [6] To substantiate this claim, he gives a number of examples of industry processes in which he claims factor prices and productivity do not change in response to changes in scale. Dorfman does, of course, admit that complete linearity is not often present, but he believes that in most cases minor variation in scale change reportedly can be ignored for purposes of theoretical analysis. Dorfman summarizes by justifying the linearity assumption because it serves two purposes: it permits the definition of processes by means of their constant input-output ratios, and it simplifies computation.

By the above, it seems clear that Dorfman, right or wrong, has satisfied himself that the assumption of linearity is not particularly restrictive for a very broad class of economic problems—that is, until the book *Linear Programming and Economic Analysis* by Dorfman, Samuelson and Solow, is examined. In this book the authors say that although they have assumed marginal utilities were constant, this assumption is "galling to any economist worthy of the name." [7] They continue by admitting that diminishing marginal utilities have been most important to economic theory. Finally, they conclude on the note that the use of mathematical programming techniques without assuming linearity is indeed quite difficult. The reader may be justified by this time in feeling a little bewildered concerning the effect of the assumption

---

[6] Dorfman, "Mathematical, or 'Linear,' Programming: a Non-mathematical Exposition," *op. cit.*, p. 808.

[7] Dorfman, Samuelson, and Solow, *op. cit.*, p. 186.

of linearity. However, even admitting Dorfman is correct (when he writes as a sole author), linearity appears to this writer to be an oversimplification for purposes of theoretical analysis.

*Comparison With Marginal Analysis.* Another point of conflict concerns the use of linear programming and marginal analysis. The apparent conflict of ideas again appears in the writings of Dorfman.

> Mathematical programming has been developed as a tool for economic and business planning and not primarily for the descriptive, and therefore predictive, purposes which gave rise to the marginal analysis. Nevertheless, it does have predictive implications. Insofar as firms operate under the conditions assumed in mathematical programming, it would be unreasonable to assume that they acted as if they operated under the conditions assumed by the marginal analysis.[8]

In contrast, in *Linear Programming and Economic Analysis* the following quote appears:

> In cases where a firm has an infinite number of processes available to it, the traditional marginal analysis of smooth curves is likely to be more appropriate than the methods of linear programming. It would be misleading to contrast the linear programming model with marginal analysis in general. Linear programming *is* marginal analysis, appropriately tailored to the case of a finite number of activities. "Traditional" marginal analysis is tailored to the case of a differentiable production function.[9]

The above remarks have been sufficiently qualified by the authors to leave doubt as to any real difference of opinion among the writers. However, the quotations are submitted to indicate the vagueness concerning the differences between marginal analysis and linear programming. Such vagueness is characteristic of many writings on the subject.

*Reasons for Using Linear Programming.* Justification for the use of linear programming for theoretical analysis usually

---

[8] Dorfman, "Mathematical, or 'Linear,' Programming: a Non-mathematical Exposition," *op. cit.*, p. 823.

[9] Dorfman, Samuelson, and Solow, *op. cit.*, p. 133.

involves discussions of the inadequacy of marginal analysis
and the basic simplicity of thought behind the linear program.
The following quotation provides a typical example.

> The essential simplification achieved in mathematical pro-
> gramming is the replacement of the notion of the production
> function by the notion of the process. The process is a highly
> observable unit of activity and the empirical constants which
> characterize it can be estimated without elaborate analysis.
> Furthermore, in many industries the structure of production
> corresponds to operating a succession of processes, as we have
> conceived them. In brief, mathematical programming is mod-
> eled after the actual structure of production in the hope it
> thereby will involve only observable constants and directly con-
> trollable variables.[10]

One of the main advantages cited for the linear programming method of analysis is its ability to handle constraints or side conditions in the form of inequalities.
Conversely, a marginal analysis technique cannot adequately
treat inequalities. Advocates of linear programming claim
the firm may often be limited by some factor (commonly
facilities) from approaching the point of production where
marginal cost equals marginal revenue. In such cases, marginal analysis is reported (by W. J. Baumol) to be useless as
an analytic tool.[11] Actually the need to discard marginal
analysis at this point is not obvious. Since the curves in
marginal analysis are typically smooth with regular changes
in slope, the most profitable production level in a marginal
analysis will usually be at the MC=MR point minus the
distance to the furthest constraint. However, this formula
is difficult to apply and does not always yield a correct result.
Therefore, because of the complication involved in the analysis, it is recognized that the inability of marginal analysis
to treat inequalities is a point in favor of linear programming.

The use of linear programming is also justified by the
specific objection that marginal analysis simply is not ap-

---

[10] Dorfman, "Mathematical, or 'Linear,' Programming: a Nonmathematical Exposition," *op. cit.*, p. 819.
[11] William J. Baumol, "Activity Analysis in One Lesson," *The American Economic Review*, XLVIII (December, 1958), p. 840.

plicable under certain conditions. Dorfman is particularly adamant on this subject and insists that marginal analysis is useful in agriculture, but in nonagricultural industries it is often inappropriate. "The use of marginal analysis depends on being able to differentiate the production revenue and cost factors independently with respect to each input and output." [12] In agriculture and selected other industries, marginal analysis is applicable since it is possible to vary labor, seed, fertilizer, etc., over a wide range without changing the operating techniques. In industrial processes, due to the high interrelation of the factors, it is usually not possible to vary the factors independently. For example, the selection of a particular machine often predetermines the amount of electricity consumed and the amount of labor associated with the process. In the situations described, linear programming, designed for selection among discrete alternates, is reportedly much more applicable than marginal analysis. This form of justification is basically negative and tends to presuppose that marginal analysis and linear programming are the only techniques available. While today this may be valid, the introduction of new theoretical tools will require advocates of linear programming to be more specific in outlining the advantages of its use.

*Nonlinear Programming.* From the foregoing discussion, it has been evident that one of the problems with the application of linear programming is the assumption of linearity. It seems appropriate to examine the use of nonlinear programming. To be specific, an examination of the carport-garage problem will be helpful in determining the usefulness of nonlinearity. Suppose, for example, the demand curve for carports slopes downward while the demand for garages remains constant. We can describe this situation with two equations:

---

[12] Dorfman, *Application of Linear Programming to the Theory of the Firm, op. cit.*, p. 10.

$$Z_1 = 300 - \frac{X_1}{2} \qquad \text{(Equation 1)}$$

$$Z_2 = 400 \qquad \text{(Equation 2)}$$

where $Z_1$ = net revenue per carport

$Z_2$ = net revenue per garage

$X_1$ = volume of carport sales

From Equation 1, it can be seen that with 100 carports sold, the net revenue per carport is $300 - \frac{100}{2} = 250$. The profit per carport drops to zero at 600 units. Combining the two equations results in isoprofit parabolas instead of the straight isoprofit lines common to linear programs.

It can be seen (Figure 2) that the highest isoprofit parabola touches the accessible region at point P, which is not at a corner. Depending on the assumption of profit, point P could have been anywhere on the boundary of BCDEF. It is apparent that in a problem with a complex nonlinear program, the search for point P becomes very difficult. If, in addition, the demand curve for garages is allowed to vary, the problem becomes even more complicated. In this case, the isoprofit lines become nests of ellipses, and the maximum profit is at point Q. Depending on the profit assumptions, point Q could lie anywhere within the accessible region. It is therefore not likely even to fall on the boundary, much less at a vertex. The reader can easily imagine the difficulty of searching for point Q in a difficult program with the use of iterative techniques.

Nonlinear programming, through the relaxation of the linearity assumption, allows us to realistically evaluate the effect of demand on production. In fact, in this sense, nonlinear programming is similar to marginal analysis, the chief difference being the use of resource restraints. Because of the addition of resource restraints, nonlinear programming may someday be more useful than marginal analysis. This day has not arrived, however, since no one yet has found a way to solve nonlinear programs having any degree of difficulty. This difficulty does not necessarily preclude the theorist

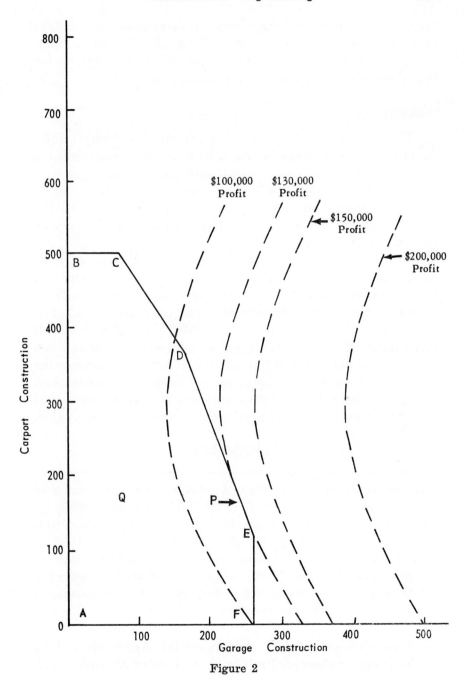

Figure 2

Carport and Garage Construction, Variable Profit for Carports

from using nonlinear programming to examine the salient characteristics of a good program. Used in this manner, non-linear programming may provide the necessary link between linear programming and marginal analysis.

## Summary

The discussion of linear programming indicates, in a general way, that the technique is difficult to use and requires a number of simplifying assumptions that are not especially palatable to economists. Most of these simplifying assumptions are associated with linearity or the ignoring of the demand side of economics. It also becomes painfully clear that when the program attempts to avoid the simplifying assumptions, it either becomes unsolvable or approaches a complicated form of marginal analysis. Linear programming has, of course, made an important contribution in the solving of complex operational problems. Its contribution to solution of inventory problems and distribution problems is well recognized. However, the reader should recognize that when he starts to use linear programming to analyze business behavior, he is not developing a theory; he has just chosen one. He has chosen a theory (constant return to scale, etc.) that is cumbersome to use and is of questionable theoretical value.

## BIBLIOGRAPHY

Baumol, William J. "Activity Analysis in One Lesson," *The American Economic Review*, XLVIII (December, 1958).

Chorafas, D. N. *Operations Research for Industrial Management*. New York: Reinhold Publishing Corp., 1958.

Crawford, Robert W. "Operations Research and Its Role in Business Decisions," *Planning for Efficient Production*, Manufacturing Series No. 206, New York: American Management Association, 1953.

Dantzig, G. B.; D. R. Fulkerson; and S. M. Johnson. "On a Linear-Programming, Combinatorial Approach to the Traveling-Salesman Problem," *Operations Research*, Vol.

VII, No. 1, Baltimore: Operations Research Society of America, 1959.

Dorfman, Robert. *Application of Linear Programming to the Theory of the Firm.* Berkeley: University of California Press, 1951.

——————. "Mathematical, or 'Linear,' Programming: a Nonmathematical Exposition," *The American Economic Review,* XLIII (December, 1953).

——————, Paul A. Samuelson, and Robert M. Solow. *Linear Programming and Economic Analysis.* New York: McGraw-Hill Book Company, Inc., 1958.

Dreyfus, Stuart E. "Computational Aspects of Dynamic Programming." *Operations Research,* Vol. V, No. 3, Baltimore: Operations Research Society of America, 1957.

Fetter, Robert B. "Management Science: The Quantitative Analysis of Management Problems," *The Manager's Key,* Vol. XXXI, Indiana University, May, 1957.

Klahr, Carl N. "Multiple Objectives in Mathematical Programming," *Operations Research,* Vol. VI, No. 6, Baltimore: Operations Research Society of America, 1958.

Klein, Burton, and William Meckling. "Application of Operations Research to Development Decisions," *Operations Research,* Vol. VI, No. 3, Baltimore: Operations Research Society of America, 1958.

McCloskey, Joseph F., and Florence N. Trefethen. *Operations Research for Management.* Baltimore: The Johns Hopkins Press, 1954.

Rohde, F. Virginia. "Bibliography on Linear Programming," *Operations Research,* Vol. V, No. 1, Baltimore: Operations Research Society of America, 1957.

# Chapter 8

# GAME THEORY AND THE BEHAVIOR OF THE FIRM

William F. Boore

---

## Introduction

The serious student of business and the economist want to know how the individual (firm), pursuing his (its) best interest, should act in a given market situation. "Sound economic theory must therefore indicate how the firm or the individual should behave under all conceivable conditions." [1]

In *The Theory of Games and Economic Behavior*, the classic work of Von Neumann and Morgenstern,[2] the authors begin by considering the conditions under which economic decisions are made. Taking the simplest kind of economy, one which might be typified by the situation of Robinson Crusoe marooned on an uninhabited island, they point out that Crusoe's problem is a simple maximum problem in which the external conditions are given. Under these conditions, Crusoe is concerned only with behaving in such a way as to maximize the goods he can obtain from nature. In pure monopoly, the absence of any competitor creates essentially the same situation.

At the other extreme, if an individual had many competitors, the advantage which they could gain by combining against him would be small. Under these same conditions, his ability to affect external conditions through his own

---

[1] Oskar Morgenstern, "Oligopoly, Monopolistic Competition, and the Theory of Games," *American Economic Review*, XXXVIII (May, 1948), p. 11.

[2] John Von Neumann and Oskar Morgenstern, *The Theory of Games and Economic Behavior* (Princeton, N. J.: University Press, 1944).

actions is negligible. In certain fundamental respects, each individual (firm) is in the position of Robinson Crusoe, confronted with a maximization problem in a situation which he must accept as given, since he is incapable of making any significant alteration in it by his actions. Under these conditions, classic economic theory asserts that the firm (individual) achieves its optimum when its marginal costs equal its marginal revenue, and it should produce until these two are equal.

Typically, in attacking its problems, classical theory has assigned a fundamental role to the device of parametrisation. Using this device, quantities which are in fact variables of the system are taken as given for certain economic actors, who respond accordingly; these responses in turn affect the values of the parameters taken as given. The legitimacy of the parametrisation device is postulated in competitive situations, *i.e.*, those where the individual has no reason to consider his influence on the market in planning his actions. However, the classical theory has recognized certain cases in which this parametrisation process is clearly inappropriate; the best known example of this is the duopoly problem. In this instance, "solutions" have depended upon the assignment of some reaction function to one of the duopolists which linked his actions to those of his rival. Such a procedure is essentially arbitrary and can produce no more than many particular solutions, each appropriate to the special circumstances assumed in the generation of the reaction function itself.[3]

The condition of duopoly is not essential. Similar difficulties arise whenever the outcome depends not simply on the actions of one individual but on those of others as well. In such circumstances, the individual is faced with trying to maximize a function containing some variables he does not control. As McKinsey puts it, ". . . each member has control of some, but not all, of the factors which determine how the commodity is to be distributed. The behavior of each,

---

[3] Carl Kaysen, "A Revolution in Economic Theory?" *The Review of Economic Studies*, XIV, 1 (1946-47), p. 186.

then, if it is to be rational, must take into account the expected behavior of the other." [4]  This is no longer a simple maximum problem, and classical economics has had difficulty in anticipating or explaining the events which occur under such circumstances.

It was through considerations of this sort that mathematician John Von Neumann was led to believe that economics could more profitably be viewed under the analogy to games of strategy than under the simpler analogy to the analytic problem of finding maxima and minima. In their book *The Theory of Games and Economic Behavior*,[5] John Von Neumann and Oskar Morgenstern propose an entirely new foundation for economic theory.

## The Theory of Games

In Von Neumann's view, the theory of games is, in essence, a science of strategy. As such, game theory was designed to narrow the gamble to a point where it would be irrational to act otherwise than by a known, optimum policy. It was developed through study and analysis of situations in which the reactions of competitors must be taken into account. It is therefore essentially a theory of strategy which deals with certain situations of conflict that exist in various activities of men, regardless of whether the particular arena is a playing table, a specific industry or market, or political in nature. Whatever the particular competitive situation may be, it is described through the precise formulation of individual objectives, through precise descriptions of the "strength" of each player, the state of "information" existing in the game, the method of play,[6] and payoff functions for a set of at least two alternatives.

A "game" as the word is construed in game theory is rigorously defined and very restricted in structure. As a result, one of the principal difficulties in applying game theory

---

[4] J. C. C. McKinsey, *Introduction to the Theory of Games* (New York: McGraw-Hill Book Company, Inc., 1952), p. 3.
[5] Von Neumann and Morgenstern, *op. cit.*
[6] Martin Shubik, "The Role of Game Theory in Economics," *Kyklos*, VI (Fasc. 1, 1953), p. 28.

has been the necessary reduction of real situations to game structure. Rules, players, moves, strategies, payoffs, information, imputation, dominance, coalitions, and some concepts of competition or cooperation are all associated with the games of game theory. As Shubik points out, these words and ideas have immediate intuitive meaning when they are associated with one's conception of conflict in economic life. However, everyday usage of these terms is often not precise, and it is important that the student of the theory become thoroughly acquainted with the formalized concepts of their meaning when associated with a game.[7]

A thorough acquaintance with game theory obviously cannot be developed in the confines of this chapter. However, a limited exploration of game-theory concepts seems a necessary prerequisite to discussion of their potential contribution to the understanding of business behavior.

The number and variety of games of strategy is enormous. Their classification can be based on the number of players, the nature of payments, the number of moves, the amount of information in the game, or combinations of these. The ensuing sketch of game theory is entirely devoted to a consideration of a two-person, zero-sum game. Those who desire a thorough treatment of the formal aspects of game theory will find an examination of the book by McKinsey and the book by Luce and Raiffa, both of which are cited in the bibliography, well worth the effort.

The designation "two-person" means that there are two interested parties involved. Either or both of the parties may be an individual person, a legal person, or a group of people with identical interests insofar as the game is concerned. Thus, bridge is a two-person game, each "person" being a pair of allied players. "Zero-sum" means that the interests of the players are diametrically opposed. What one gains, the other loses.

In the play of the game, a "pure strategy" is defined as a complete plan. It is complete in the sense that it prescribes

---

[7] Martin Shubik, *Strategy and Market Structure* (New York: John Wiley & Sons, Inc., 1959), p. 4.

a specific choice for the player at every conceivable opportunity and for all possible situations, *i.e.*, a plan that cannot be upset by anything the opponent may choose to do. The specification of such a strategy as a sequence of decisions in the actual play of the game is extremely difficult. In fact, the version of a game designed for actual play is exceedingly complicated and is referred to as the "extensive form."

A game may have many pure strategies. A major contribution of Von Neumann and Morgenstern was the proof that each game having a finite number of pure strategies has a "normalized form" that reveals the essential strategic structure of the game. In the normalized form of the game, each player makes a single decision consisting of the selection of one from among his possible pure strategies. Once the players have made this choice, it is possible to trace out what would occur were the extensive form used. Thus, a pair of pure strategies in the normalized form of a two-person game completely determines the outcome of a play of the game in its extensive form except for chance effects.[8]

It is conventional to represent a game in its normalized form as a matrix in which the rows correspond to the pure strategies of one player and the columns the pure strategies of the other. An entry in the matrix indicates the expected outcome, or payoff, when the players have selected the corresponding pair of pure strategies. When the original analysis of a problem has been structured such that all strategies with their attendant payoffs to each player are contained in a matrix, all relevant information is present and a game theory analysis can begin.

| Player #1 Strategies | Player #2 Strategies | | |
|:---:|:---:|:---:|:---:|
| | A | B | C |
| X | 4 | 3 | 2 |
| Y | 7 | 9 | 5 |

---

[8] The role of chance is noted for the sake of descriptive accuracy but represents a sophistication that will not be pursued further in this simplified exposition.

The above example of a payoff matrix for the normalized form of a game has a simple structure.[9] It could be assumed to represent a duopoly, each firm having alternate strategies at its disposal. Each player (firm) has one pure strategy that he should choose in each play of the game. Game theory approaches the question of what is the best procedure for the players through a well-defined philosophy. The assumption is that each player argues as follows:

> For every choice that I can make, I must fear that my opponent makes that choice which makes my gain (or average gain, if there is a chance move) the smallest possible under the circumstances. Hence, if I make that choice which makes this smallest gain as large as possible, then I am as safe as I can ever reasonably expect to be.[10]

Edwards expresses this philosophic approach to the theory in these terms:

> ... the crux of the theory of games is the principle of choosing the strategy which minimizes the maximum expected financial loss; and the theory defines a solution of the game as a set of imputations which satisfies this principle for all players.[11]

Thus, the core of the strategy problem is for each player to select a strategy in order to guarantee himself a certain minimum return regardless of the opponent's action. Employing this concept, Player #1 finds "Y" as his optimum strategy; this insures his expected payoff as at least 5. Player #2 identifies "C" as his optimum strategy since this insures that his expected loss will be no greater than 5. The element "5" illustrates what is defined as a "saddlepoint," i.e., an element of a matrix that is maximal in its column and minimal in its row. When the payoff matrix has a saddlepoint,

---

[9] It should be noted that such a game actually has two payoff matrices, one for each player. In this instance, because it is a zero-sum game, entries in one matrix are simply the negatives of the entries in the other, hence one matrix suffices. By convention, positive entries represent the payoff for the player on the left side of the matrix.

[10] S. Vajda, *The Theory of Games and Linear Programming* (New York: John Wiley & Sons, Inc., 1956), p. 6.

[11] Ward Edwards, "The Theory of Decision Making," *Psychological Bulletin*, 51 (July, 1954), p. 408.

each player of the game will have an optimal pure strategy. Also, it should be noted that the "value" of the game is that of the saddlepoint element, in this case, 5.

The following payoff matrix presents a slightly more complicated situation:

| Player #1 Strategies | Player #2 Strategies | |
|:---:|:---:|:---:|
| | A | B |
| X | 5 | 3 |
| Y | 2 | 7 |

This matrix has no saddlepoint. The most that Player #1 can insure as his expected gain is 3. The smallest loss Player #2 can insure for himself is 5.[12] The discrepancy between 3 and 5 indicates that neither player has a single pure strategy that is optimal. Actually, each player can determine an optimal mixed strategy. For Player #1 this gives "X" a probability of 5/7 and "Y" a probability of 2/7. In the course of mixing his strategies in this ratio, Player #1 should use a randomizing device to eliminate any detectable regularity in his sequence of choices. This mixed strategy gives Player #1 an expected return of 4.14, which is independent of the choice of strategies made by Player #2. This expected return is the value of the game, since by mixing strategies in the manner indicated, Player #1 can insure that his expected payoff is at least 4.14, while Player #2 can act to insure that it is no greater. Said another way, the conjunction of the optimal mixed strategies of the two players is a saddlepoint with a value of 4.14.[13]

---

[12] The reader should verify these statements with his own reasoning.

[13] An important theorem in Von Neumann and Morgenstern's classic work states that each two-person, zero-sum game whose normalized form has a matrix with a finite number of pure strategies has a value. In this specific case, Player #1 would analyze the given matrix as shown by:

$$\frac{5}{7} \times 5 + \frac{2}{7} \times 2 = \frac{5}{7} \times 3 + \frac{2}{7} \times 7 = 4.14$$

The reader is reminded that this examination of game theory has been perhaps excessively simplified; for example, many games are so complicated and involved that it is impractical (or impossible) to actually write out even the normalized form. Game theory does not try to model all the complexities in any situation. The matrix of a game is simply a model of a conflict situation, and as such, it is an abstraction from reality. Nevertheless, a game-theoretical analysis of the abstract model will reveal aspects which otherwise might not be detected, and these properties may have some significance in connection with the analysis and understanding of the actual situation. Obviously, the degree of validity will depend on the adequacy of the abstraction. From this point forward, the game-theoretical analysis involves operations on the matrix and is primarily a technical problem requiring ingenuity and proficiency in mathematics rather than a conceptual one.

In the words of Lindsay:

> In mathematical analysis, the word "model" is used to mean a mathematical description of an activity which expresses the relationships among the various elements with sufficient accuracy that it can be used to predict the actual outcome under any expected set of circumstances. . . . The obvious advantage of a model is that it, instead of the organization it simulates, can be manipulated in a variety of ways until the best solution is found. . . . The great disadvantage is that no model can completely duplicate reality; therefore, both the construction of the model, and the translation of the results to the actual problem, must be done with both sophistication and humility. The function of model building and analysis is not to replace intuition and judgment, but rather to support them with tools for handling complexity and uncertainty with which the human intuition cannot cope unaided.[14]

Salveson makes essentially the same points in his discussion on mathematical techniques for decision making. He says, "The 'game' of game theory, like any economic model,

---

[14] Franklin A. Lindsay, *New Techniques for Management Decision Making* (New York: McGraw-Hill Book Company, Inc., 1958), pp. 13-14.

is an abstraction of real-life circumstances." [15] Wagner gives
a simple characterization of a game as follows:

> Given the variables subject to each player's control, all
> possible eventualities in a conflict situation must be ascertain-
> able. Nature may influence the game by operating chance
> devices at various stages. If Nature's probability distributions
> are known to the players, she assumes a dummy role; the
> potential outcomes are then specified in terms of the proba-
> bilities associated with each possible event. Otherwise, Nature
> is a bona fide player. Each opponent must choose from all the
> actions open to him, taking into account that his adversaries
> are doing the same thing.[16]

Thus the "game," like any mathematical economic model,
is an abstraction of the essence of real-life economic situations. With this admittedly rudimentary discussion of game
theory as a base, it is now appropriate to examine those applications of game theory which relate to the theory of the firm.

## Applications to Business Behavior

Game theory provides a new set of concepts and relationships in terms of which firm behavior can be discussed. These
technical terms such as move, strategy, payoff, etc., have been
given careful definition. In fact, Shubik considers this sharp-
ening of concepts and terminology and the extra insights
given into the nature of competition to be the principal contribution of game theory in its present state of development.[17]
Hurwicz supports this same point of view. He feels that,
". . . Even where the theory of games does not provide satisfactory answers, it has contributed to a more lucid, rigorous, and natural formulation of many problems." [18] A further
development, which he attributes at least partly to the influence of game theory, is the trend toward axiomatic formu-

---

[15] M. E. Salveson, "An Analysis of Decisions," *Management Science*, 4
(April, 1958), p. 216.
[16] Harvey M. Wagner, "Advances in Game Theory," *American Economic Review*, XLVIII (June, 1958), p. 369.
[17] Shubik, "The Role of Game Theory in Economics," *op. cit.*, p. 28.
[18] Leonid Hurwicz, "What Has Happened to the Theory of Games?"
*American Economic Review*, XLIII (May, 1953), p. 405.

lation in economic theory. This trend has been accompanied by an increase in rigor and greater transparency in the relationships between assumptions made and conclusions reached. Lindsay contributes to the same general line of thought in his statement: "Game theory does, however, provide important insights into situations of conflict, insights which will be of considerable value in approximating optimum solutions by means less rigorous than formal game theory." [19]

In the early development of game theory, the two-person, constant-sum games were of particular interest. In these games, a player's strategy is characterized by the different payoffs he would obtain depending on the strategy chosen by his opponent. (If chance factors are present, expected or long-run average gains should be substituted in order to maintain precision.) As Hurwicz points out, "The solution proposed by Von Neumann and Morganstern makes each player choose that strategy for which the minimal gain is at least as high as, and possibly higher than, the minimal gain guaranteed by any alternative strategy. Thus, the player is maximizing the minimum payoff, or playing the 'maximin.'" [20] (His opponent, reading the matrix in the opposite but more conventional way, is minimizing his maximal loss or "minimaxing.") The proof of this theorem, *i.e.*, that there is a single stable or rational course of action that represents the best strategy or saddlepoint in nonstrictly determined, zerosum games, indicates that, at least for this narrow set of games, a behavior is prescribed by theory.

The literature contains a number of discussions of alternative formulations of optimal behavior under uncertainty which are broader than the minimax principle. Hurwicz commented as follows:

> Among many examples of alternatives to the maximin (minimax) principle, one may mention the principle (formulated by L. J. Savage) of minimizing the regret (or the disutility), the maximax principle of maximizing the maximal (rather than the minimal as in maximin) expected gain (sug-

---

[19] Lindsay, *op. cit.*, p. 53.
[20] Hurwicz, *op. cit.*, p. 399.

gested by F. Modigliani), and the principle of maximizing some
weighted average of the maximal and minimal expected gains
(suggested by the present writer). . . .[21]

Even this limited listing of alternative behavior patterns
suggests that there is no single formulation of optimal behavior under uncertainty which has no weaknesses or which
finds general acceptance. These behavioral alternatives suggest a design for a logical way to anticipate behavior. It
seems reasonable to suppose that analysis would reveal
whether an individual (or firm) was following, either implicitly or explicitly, some particular uncertainty behavior
principle. If some one of these principles explained the behavior pattern of a given individual (firm) under uncertainty, such knowledge should prove useful in prediction.

To return to the minimax concept, it is here that game
theory makes an important connection with, and contribution
to, statistical decision theory. In his article, Hurwicz also
observed that the nature of individual behavior in situations
involving nonprobabilistic uncertainty is a problem which
will yield to certain tools of the theory of two-person games.
In fact, an important class of statistical problems has been
reformulated into the framework of a zero-sum game against
Nature; the latter defined as a nonmalevolent opponent.
Given this formulation, it is natural for the statistician to
use minimax as the solution to these problems.[22]

Most of the work of Von Neumann and Morgenstern
applied to cooperative games, that is, games constructed out
of situations where every player is completely informed about
the payoff values of the game to himself and every other
player. The solution which they derived for the general case
of this type of game is the minimax strategy which was illustrated in the earlier example using the special case of the
two-person, zero-sum game. As they derived it, the minimax
strategy has two important properties: (1) rationality of
the player's behavior in terms of their following an uncertainty principle, and (2) the equilibrium property, since

---

[21] *Ibid.*, p. 399.
[22] *Ibid.*, p. 400.

neither player has any incentive to change his strategy. This coincidence of rationality (minimax) and equilibrium (saddlepoint) is a special feature of the constant-sum, two-person game.

Another major contribution to the understanding of business behavior came directly from Von Neumann and Morgenstern's application of the theory to a three-man game. The important new feature introduced by this step was the possibility that two of the players would band together and form a coalition against the third. The formation and dissolution of coalitions, the problems of side payments, and many other facets of monopolistic competition have been developed and treated as a result of this extension of the theory. The three-player and more-than-three-player games offer a means for manipulating the symbolic structure of monopolistic competition. A thorough and up-to-date review of current game theory capability for explaining and/or predicting behavior in this area is contained in Shubik's recent book.[23]

In the case of nonconstant-sum games, Von Neumann and Morgenstern suggest that all competitors will act jointly so as to maximize their joint gain from the environment and then will work out a scheme for division of the proceeds among themselves. In real life this rarely seems to occur, the weakness in the analysis being the assumption that all players are completely informed about the environment.[24]

Nash made a separate attack upon a simpler class of game situation. His work on the equilibrium point in noncooperative games, i.e., games free of communication among the players, illustrates another concept which game theory has added to the analysis of business behavior. Nash suggests a pattern of behavior which results in the establishment of equilibria; in fact, his solution is defined in terms of the equilibrium property. While the Nash model also has certain inadequacies, his model and solution concepts appear

[23] Shubik, *Strategy and Market Structure, op. cit.*
[24] Martin Shubik, "Studies and Theories of Decision Making," *Administrative Science Quarterly*, III (December, 1958), pp. 295-296.

to be useful in the area of the allocative properties of the market mechanism.[25] Flood has run some experimental games to test the predictive value of Nash's theory. These games have produced outcomes that correlated well with predicted results.[26]

The preceding discussion has made it apparent that as soon as the game is variable-sum or when it involves more than two persons, one or the other of the two important features of the minimax strategy must be sacrificed. For all games of three or more players, and for nonconstant-sum games with two players, there are many theories of optimal behavior. Each of these theories amounts to a description of the rational decision behavior of each involved individual under the particular conditions modeled.

## Limitations on Game Theory

It appears that the major obstacle to the application of game theory to a wide variety of practical situations is the enormous complexity of the mathematical computations involved.

Consider the notion of strategies, both pure and mixed, since these notions are very useful for the mathematical development of game theory. It must be recognized that even for simple parlor games the number of strategies is too large ever to have been completely given. Chess, for example, has been played and analyzed for years, yet only a small fraction of partial strategies has ever been discussed and listed.[27]

Morgenstern discussed the case of two competing auto manufacturers each of whom may have a large number of product-market strategies involving the choice of body design, the addition of new accessories, the best time to announce new models and price changes, etc. He points out that it has been estimated that the calculations for a game in which one

---

[25] Hurwicz, *op. cit.*, pp. 401-403.
[26] Shubik, "Studies and Theories of Decision Making," *op. cit.*, p. 296.
[27] R. Duncan Luce and Howard Raiffa, *Games and Decisions: Introduction and Critical Survey* (New York: John Wiley & Sons, Inc., 1957), p. 159.

manufacturer had 100 possible strategies and his competitor had 200 possible strategies (not an uncommon situation) would take about a year on an electronic computer.[28] This example suggests that in all but the simplest cases, the calculations become astronomical.

Alternatively, one can consider the problem introduced by increasing the number of participants in a game to a more realistic number than 2 or 3. The difficulty in handling situations involving more than 3 persons is formidable, even with powerful mathematical methodologies. Here we will consider the complications which participants introduce only in terms of their possible coalitions. (The reader is left to speculate concerning their effect on the number of strategies.) A necessary condition exists in that the basic aim is to deduce all the solutions of a game; that is, to determine from the conditions of the game what coalitions will be formed, what the payoffs will be, and how the game will be played if it is played rationally. Stone shows that the number of distinct games which can be derived from 3 participants is 5, while the total number of games when there are 10 participants is 115,975.[29]

In addition to the computational difficulties which have been mentioned and the extremely high degree of abstraction which the theory involves, the other major problems seem to be that there are no objective mathematical ways to formulate "rational" behavior or to measure the value of a given outcome to a particular player.

McKinsey states that it is convenient ". . . to speak as though all games were played for money; thus, we shall usually speak of the payments as sums of money." [30] Though he acknowledges that something other than money might be involved, he closes this part of his discussion with, "But we do not want to enter these knotty problems about value, which

---

[28] Oskar Morgenstern, "The Theory of Games," *Scientific American*, 180 (May, 1949), p. 24.

[29] Richard Stone, "The Theory of Games," *The Economic Journal*, LVIII, 230 (June, 1948), pp. 194-196.

[30] McKinsey, *op. cit.*, p. 5.

lies in the province of economics or philosophy rather than in that of mathematics." [31]

The material from McKinsey illustrates two important problems of game theory. First, and most obvious, is that of utility. Von Neumann and Morgenstern in the appendix of the revised edition of their classic prove that their axioms of utility make utility a number up to a linear transformation, *i.e.*, without fixing a zero or a unit of utility. However, their axioms regarding utility have failed to satisfy all the workers in the field. Shubik mentions that in the last few years a considerable amount of literature has sprung up on the economic, psychometric, and axiomatic problems of utility measurement. [32] Luce and Raiffa present a detailed survey of the major problems encountered in the treatment of utility. [33] Suffice it to say that the adequate handling of utility is a fundamental difficulty in the path of expanding the applicability of game theory.

The second problem is discussed at some length in an article by Bodenhorn. [34] In the article, he points out that there are two potential dangers in using mathematics in economics: (a) making assumptions which are convenient mathematically but poor economically, and (b) concluding that mathematics is a substitute for good economics. In a subsequent illustration, he shows that *implicit* assumptions concerning important economic considerations may not be made *explicit* and that in some cases these assumptions can turn out to be very restrictive. This provides the opportunity for the unsophisticated mathematical user to leap to the conclusion that no assumption is needed if none is stated. [35]

In the conclusion of his article he adds,

> However, it is one thing to state mathematical assumptions clearly and another thing to state economic assumptions clearly. There are no well-defined procedures for exhausting all the economic implications of any set of mathematical as-

---

[31] *Ibid.*, p. 6.
[32] Shubik, *Strategy and Market Structure, op. cit.*, p. 341.
[33] Luce and Raiffa, *op. cit.*, Ch. I.
[34] Diran Bodenhorn, "The Problem of Economic Assumptions in Mathematical Economics," *Journal of Political Economy*, LXIV, 1 (February, 1956), p. 25. Copyright 1946 by the University of Chicago.
[35] *Ibid.*, pp. 30-31.

sumptions or conclusions, nor are there any well-defined procedures for determining whether any statement concerning the
economic implications of a mathematical model is true. Thus,
there is nothing inherent in the mathematical technique itself
which required a mathematical economist to state his economic
assumptions and conclusions either clearly or correctly.[36]

One final specific "for instance" will perhaps suffice. As
the discussion in the section "The Theory of Games" indicated, game theory is built upon the basis of precise definitions of a game, the structure of information available, and
the final payoffs. The theory has also been structured to be
consistent with the common assumption in economic theory
that rationality is a condition of an optimum. It is this latter
aspect of game theory that caused Simon to observe that the
concept of economic man (an individual who has a complete
and consistent system of preferences that allows him always
to choose among alternatives open to him; who is always
completely aware of what all these alternatives are; and who
has no limit to the complexity of calculations which he can
perform in order to determine which alternatives are best)
when extended to competitive game situations reaches a state
of refinement that may have considerable narrative interest,
but has little discernible relation to the actual or possible
behavior of human beings.[37]

There are, of course, other problems which are obstacles
to the application of game theory to a wide variety of practical situations. The nature of some of these other complications were suggested in the book *The New World of Math* [38]
by the following illustrations: (1) those games in which the
players are not strictly competing with one another. An
example is a labor-management negotiation; both sides lose
unless they reach an agreement; (2) collusion, *e.g.*, an agreement among two buyers not to bid against each other, is
another complicating factor; (3) payments made outside the

---

[36] *Ibid.*, p. 32.
[37] H. A. Simon, *Administrative Behavior*, Second Edition (New York:
Macmillan Co., 1951), p. xxiii.
[38] G. W. Boehm and editors of "Fortune," *The New World of Math*
(New York: Dial Press, 1959), pp. 58-59.

game, as when a large company holds a distributor in line by subsidizing him.

The specific problems used as illustrations in this chapter were chosen partly because of their own inherent interest and importance. However, their real significance lies in the fact that each is representative of a large number of specific problems lying within the general problem areas from which they were chosen. What they serve to illustrate is that game theory is confronted with technical problems, conceptual problems, and problems which arise from the necessity for merging technical and conceptual material within the framework of the theory.

## Summary and Evaluation

For years, an intuitive connection between games of strategy and economic and social behavior has found wide expression in the language and writing of business, *e.g.*, a market strategy. Modern mathematical methodology applied to the examination of social and economic behavior has made it evident that many of the forms of economic and social behavior are, in fact, analogous to games of strategy.

Williams states his assessment of game theory in these terms:

> While there are specific applications today, despite the current limitations of the theory, perhaps its greatest contribution so far has been an intangible one: the general orientation given to people who are faced with overcomplex problems. Even though these problems are not strictly solvable—certainly at the moment and probably for the indefinite future—it helps to have a framework in which to work on them. The concept of a strategy, the distinctions among players, the role of chance events, the notion of matrix representations of the payoffs, the concepts of pure and mixed strategies, and so on, give valuable orientation to persons who must think about complicated conflict situations.[39]

[39] J. D. Williams, *The Compleat Strategyst* (New York: McGraw-Hill Book Company, Inc., 1954), p. 217.

Review of the literature has suggested that, though the concepts of game theory are broad enough to cover all conditions, it is in the area that lies between the extremes of monopoly and perfect competition that it has made its most significant conceptual contributions to the understanding of firm behavior.

In taking a somewhat more optimistic approach, Luce and Raiffa suggest that, though they are aware of the relatively limited contributions of game theory to date, they see no reason to suppose that the theory could not ultimately make significant and vital contributions to applied problems.[40]

It appears that game theory may be useful for representing a situation or for testing policy or enterprise decisions through an extension into the area of operational gaming. One of the certain aids of the theory is that it aids the decision maker (or analyst) by forcing him to formalize through a model what he knows and what he doesn't know about the decision situation. Thus, one can suppose that it leads to an improved ability to predict behavior because one can, in turn, be more sure that management is aware of the interplay and magnitude of the forces involved—of the "ball park" in which they are playing. However, at present it appears that the computation of any real game requires more time and expense than can be justified for almost any applicable decisions.

Aside from the conceptual contributions of the theory, its few practical applications appear to be concentrated in the areas where game theory ties in with linear programming, statistical decision making, and operational gaming, respectively. It is obvious that much work remains to be done if game theory is to live up to its early promise. The mathematicians must advance their technical capability, the economists must apply effort to their conceptual problems, and the attention of both must be given to those problems generated out of the marriage of their respective product in game theory.

---

[40] Luce and Raiffa, *op. cit.*, pp. 10-11.

# BIBLIOGRAPHY

Bodenhorn, Diran. "The Problem of Economic Assumptions in Mathematical Economics," *Journal of Political Economy*, LXIV, 1 (February, 1956), pp. 25-32.

Boehm, G. W., and editors of "Fortune." *The New World of Math.* New York: Dial Press, 1959.

Edwards, Ward. "The Theory of Decision Making," *Psychological Bulletin*, 51 (July, 1954), pp. 380-417.

Hurwicz, Leonid. "What Has Happened to the Theory of Games?" *American Economic Review*, XLIII (May, 1953), pp. 398-405.

Kaysen, Carl. "A Revolution in Economic Theory?" *The Review of Economic Studies*, XIV, 1 (1946-47), pp. 1-15.

Lindsay, Franklin A. *New Techniques for Management Decision Making.* New York: McGraw-Hill Book Company, Inc., 1958.

Luce, R. Duncan, and Howard Raiffa. *Games and Decisions: Introduction and Critical Survey.* New York: John Wiley & Sons, Inc., 1957.

McKinsey, J. C. C. *Introduction to the Theory of Games.* New York: McGraw-Hill Book Company, Inc., 1952.

Morgenstern, Oskar. "Oligopoly, Monopolistic Competition, and the Theory of Games," *American Economic Review*, XXXVIII (May, 1948), pp. 10-18.

—————. "The Theory of Games," *Scientific American*, 180 (May, 1949), pp. 22-25.

Salveson, M. E. "An Analysis of Decisions," *Management Science*, 4 (April, 1958), pp. 203-217.

Shubik, Martin. "The Role of Game Theory in Economics." *Kyklos*, VI (Fasc. 1, 1953), pp. 21-34.

—————. *Strategy and Market Structure.* New York: John Wiley & Sons, Inc., 1959.

—————. "Studies and Theories of Decision Making," *Administrative Science Quarterly*, III (December, 1958), pp. 295-296.

Simon, Herbert A. *Administrative Behavior*, Second Edition. New York: The Macmillan Company, 1951.

Stone, Richard. "The Theory of Games," *The Economic Journal,* LVIII, 230 (June, 1948), pp. 185-201.

Vajda, S. *The Theory of Games and Linear Programming.* New York: John Wiley & Sons, Inc., 1956.

Von Neumann, John, and Oskar Morgenstern. *The Theory of Games and Economic Behavior.* Princeton: Princeton University Press, 1944.

Wagner, Harvey M. "Advances in Game Theory," *American Economic Review,* XLVIII (June, 1958), pp. 368-387.

Williams, J. D. *The Compleat Strategyst.* New York: McGraw-Hill Book Company, Inc., 1954.

# Chapter 9

## PERCEPTION, MOTIVATION, AND BUSINESS BEHAVIOR

Alvar O. Elbing, Jr.

As has been indicated in previous chapters, traditional explanations of firm behavior have tended to be based on the premise that the primary if not the single motivation of the businessman is profit maximization. Implicit in this premise is the assumption that to achieve this goal, the profit maximizing individual rationally chooses the best of all possible courses of action based on his omniscient analysis of all the available alternatives. Investigations in the social and behavioral sciences, however, have opened a number of roads of inquiry into human behavior which bring this assumption into question and which offer considerable insight into the issues which must be faced in building a generally applicable theory of firm behavior.

It is the purpose of this chapter to examine certain of the current concepts in theories of perception and motivation which offer insight into the processes of human behavior and which, therefore, must be considered in the building of any theory of firm behavior. There will be no attempt to develop a general theory of firm behavior based on these concepts nor to answer all of the many unanswered questions about firm behavior. Rather, it will be the purpose here to identify appropriate questions raised by current concepts of perception and motivation which must be faced in any eventual construction of a general theory of firm behavior.

Traditional economic theory has considered the firm to be an abstract unit separate from the individuals who are a part of it. Actions of the firm have been explained in terms of rational goals of a business enterprise, *e.g.*, maximization of profit; these goals were then assumed to be those of the individuals who made up the firm. Can we, however, consider an organization apart from the individuals who form that organization? E. Wight Bakke of Yale University suggests that we cannot. He states:

> When we observe an "organization" we are observing people organized, and when we observe "organizational activity" we are observing the behavior of people acting as agents of the organizations. When, therefore, we refer to an organization and its activities, we are referring to agents of the organization and their behavior. The substance of an organization is human behavior; the structure of an organization is defined simply as human behavior which is systematized and stabilized.[1]

If we accept Bakke's assumption, then, that firm behavior is the composite of the behavior of individuals who make up the firm, it is appropriate that we examine the current concepts of individual perception and motivation as essential considerations in any theory of firm behavior.

## Perception

What are some of the currently advanced key concepts of human perception that must be applied to behavior in a firm? The assumption that human beings simply perceive precisely "what is there" is no longer considered a safe assumption. It is no longer generally accepted that there is a necessary, obvious, and inevitable correlation between objective factors in the environment and human perception of them. According to Mason Haire,

> If we make a separation between the physical world outside of us, on the one hand, and the psychological environment, or the world that we see, on the other, we come to see that the order and organization is not in the physical stimulus but in the observer. . . .[2]

---

[1] E. Wight Bakke, *Organization and the Individual* (New Haven: Yale Labor and Management Center, 1952), p. 7.
[2] Mason Haire, *Psychology in Management* (New York: McGraw-Hill Book Company, Inc., 1956), p. 40.

Psychologists, today, in advancing the theory that there is no fixed correlation between data in the environment and perceived data, describe perception as a process. Any data perceived might be described appropriately as "processed data." The processing of data through perception operates in certain general ways. First we know that persons tend to selectively perceive data in ways that enable them to cope most readily with it. On the visual level of perception, for example, we tend to take in primarily that visual data which enables us to judge distance quickly for the immediate purpose of reaching an object or taking a step down a stair or otherwise carrying out an immediate practical purpose. Thus, we do not register all sense data on an equal basis; we tend to focus on those factors in the environment which enable us to make a ready adjustment. The individual, in fact, never perceives an entire situation, nor does he construct what he does see in the same way on different occasions.

Further, our perceptions tend to have fixity. If a certain perceptual framework for coping with a repeated problem has worked before, that perception tends to become fixed. We then tend to think of the perceptual judgments as existing in the reality "out there," rather than recognizing that we are merely using a portion of what is out there to pick up certain clues which will enable us to maintain stable behavior. If we accept these two concepts—that perceptions do not necessarily have direct correlation with "reality" and that perceptions, whether corresponding to reality or not, have fixity—we must call into question a basic assumption of traditional economic theory: that the businessman is able to perceive and take into account all factors objectively in making a business decision.

*The Organization of Perception.* Another concept of perception is that individuals tend to perceive data as organized wholes. This perceiving of data as organized wholes is one of the ways we "process" data. We do not register data as an audiometer might record units of sound; rather we tend to organize what we perceive automatically. Numerous illustrations of this human tendency have been provided through psychological experiments. As just one example, the following group of dots in parentheses (::) normally is perceived as forming a square, *i.e.*, as forming an organized whole. This organizing tendency obviously could affect firm behavior in numerous ways. A businessman in hiring employees may fail to "see" certain aspects of individuals under consideration because he may perceive each as an "organized whole" personality type. As Haire states, "In putting together items of information, we tend to make organized wholes which may distort the meaning of some of the parts which are included. This is particularly true when the items are aspects of a personality." [3]

It should be pointed out that this tendency to perceive things as organized wholes involves certain very important processes that affect the data perceived: (1) In perceiving things as organized wholes, we tend to leave out certain factors which spoil the neatness of our organization. For example, a businessman may be unable to notice certain data which indicate his product is becoming obsolete because such an observation would spoil the neatly organized picture he has of his firm. (2) In perceiving data in terms of organized whole, we tend to add to the data to make our "organized wholes" more reasonable. For example, a sales manager in preparing a market analysis that gives some sort of organized picture, may unconsciously add to the data, overemphasizing certain factors to make for a more organized report. (3) In perceiving data in terms of organized wholes, we tend to structure the data, *i.e.*, to perceive it in some kind of intelligible pattern. An executive may see an authoritarian personnel manager as highly effective because he has always perceived authoritarian behavior as part of the role-pattern of any managerial position. Or, an executive may assume that his competitors will move in a certain direction on the assumption, or projection, that they will act as he would act if in their situation, a situation which he may see as an

---

[3] Haire, *op. cit.*, p. 161.

organized whole different from that "whole" which his competitor sees. It is apparent, then, that an individual constantly distorts data in a number of ways to fit in with the organizing tendency of his perception.

Another concept of perception is that an individual tends to perceive data in terms of his already existing picture of reality. Each person has his own unique frame of reference through which he perceives data, based on his own particular past experiences, biases, sets, attitudes, goals, etc. Herbert Simon expresses a variation of this "picture of reality" concept when he states that people are constantly engaged in mentally building organized "models" of the world. He states that people never see the real world as it "is," but continually perceive that "model" of the world which they themselves have built.[4] They are engaged in a continuous process of perceiving miscellaneous data in terms of their model, again leaving out that which cannot fit within the framework of the model, adding to in order to make the model complete, and structuring to keep the pattern of the model safe from disturbances. The concept that there is a certain set of objective data which all executives or managers would perceive in the same way and from which any two of them would make the same decision with regard to maximizing profit would not stand up under current analysis with regard to perception theory.

*Perception as Factual and Rational.* Even the supposed "factuality" of certain data may be a relative matter. Research in the social sciences has suggested that we tend to perceive only that data as "factual" which society generally agrees upon as being "factual." It has been pointed out that the only way an individual can adjust to other human beings is by checking his own impressions and observations against others' opinions. Only when his perceptions are adjusted to correspond sufficiently with the perceptions of others can he relate to others and communicate with them at all. Thus,

---

[4] Herbert A. Simon, *Models of Man: Social and Rational* (New York: John Wiley & Sons, Inc., 1957), p. 199.

perceptions of everyone in a society or social group tend to conform to one another. Persons actually tend to perceive only those things which fit in with an agreed-upon picture of things. As a result of this conformance to socially accepted actuality, it may be difficult for a manager not only to raise as a problem something which he feels his superiors will not see as a problem, but it may be difficult for him even to perceive such a problem in the first place.

The two opposing processes—that of building our own unique perceptual framework from our own individual experiences, and that of trimming and supplementing our perceptual framework to conform with others' perceptions (others' opinions being part of our individual experience)—go on continuously. However, it should be clear that neither of these perceptual processes results necessarily in objective perception of data. When a part of a person's unique perceptual processes conforms to society, this does not mean it conforms to "reality."

Another factor affecting human perception in our culture is that persons want to perceive data as having a rational basis and want to give rational explanations for data. This concept suggests the possibility that the entire theory of firm behavior proposed by traditional economists may have been created in an effort to perceive firm behavior as having an objective rational basis. Once such a rational theory is created, most people would be more willing to hold onto that rationality than to begin investigation again in a realm of nonrational flux.

Despite the fact that we may view the perceived data as rational, emotion and many other nonrational factors may strongly affect perception.[5] Karen Horney stresses particularly the distorting effect of anxiety upon perception. Horney has pointed out that states of anxiety or perceived threat cause the perceiving individual to narrow significantly his perceptual framework.[6] An anxious person, a person who

---

[5] See Warren J. Wittreich, "Visual Perception and Personality," *Scientific American* (April, 1959), pp. 56-60.

[6] Karen Horney, *The Neurotic Personality of Our Time* (New York: W. W. Norton & Company, Inc., 1937), Chapter 3.

perceives himself under threat, actually does not observe as much as he does when not threatened. Individuals in a firm who are operating more or less continually under threat will have correspondingly limited perceptual behavior. Surely this is a factor of importance in any theory which attempts to account for the behavior of firms when dealing with crucial problems under threatening conditions.

*Persistence of Perceptual Framework.* The great attachment man has for his perceptual framework can scarcely be overemphasized. He is highly reluctant to give up any of his perceptions, his organized wholes, his models which seem to work. If a frame of reference for perception allows the individual to operate without too much stress and without blocking him with too many problems, he will cling vigorously to that perceptual frame. One of man's strongest desires is for the security of an ordered environment. According to Haire, man "is reluctant to give up any organizations that seem to work, because of the danger that is involved in being lost in a disorganized environment." [7] Man does not wish to upset areas of order except when forced to do so, even though such order may be only illusional. Since a man's own self concept is involved in that perceptual frame, giving up his perceptual frame may mean giving up his sense of his own identity and meaningfulness. Thus, in many businesses, we observe that outmoded techniques continue to be retained longer than the concept of "maximization of profit" and other traditional concepts of firm behavior would suggest.

## Motivation

In the search for a theory of firm behavior, it is also important to be aware of certain assumptions about human "motivation." It no longer appears possible to assume that executives and managers are simply embodiments of the motivation for profit maximization and that their behavior can be explained merely in terms of this single motive. In

---

[7] Haire, *op. cit.*, p. 41.

order to attempt to understand the behavior of businessmen, we must take into account other concepts of motivation.

It should be noted at the outset, however, that concepts of motivation cannot be separated from related concepts of perception. The separation of these two aspects of behavior for the purposes of this chapter should be considered as a method which, although useful in analysis, is somewhat unrealistic in that behavior is seamless.

*Definition of "Motive."* The idea of a "motive" is so common in lay conversation and thinking that it might be well to outline briefly the concept of motivation as it is used here. Motivation may be meaningfully discussed from two angles. First, it may be discussed in terms of its internal aspect, its reference to a state of inner dissatisfaction, a state of needs, wants, or desires, a state in which bodily energy is mobilized, a state of a drive which the organism is impelled to relieve. Secondly, motivation may be discussed from its outer aspect, as a sequence of behavior selectively directed in terms of a goal. Goal, then, refers to the outer directional aspect of behavior in a given situation. Thus, we may define motivation as characterized both by a state of drive and by the direction of behavior toward some goal selected in preference to other possible goals. Since all thories do not give equal emphasis to these two aspects of motivation, let us begin by considering the two approaches separately.

*"Inner Motivation": Emphasis on the Individual.* One widely accepted concept is that all persons are motivated by certain needs. Various lists of such needs have been advanced by a number of investigators and though we find differences among the lists, they are generally similar. Perhaps most investigators would agree upon this basic list of needs: Physiological needs (need for air, food, water, etc.), social needs (need to belong to a group and to have social relations with others), and ego or individual needs (need for approval, acceptance, mastery, etc.). There are certainly many longer lists which include such items as need for security, need for wider experience, need for a sense of meaningfulness, etc.

Theodore Brammeld, however, considers a list of even three needs too long, since it implies that man is somehow composed of separate compartments. Brammeld points out that there is no sense of ego separate from the socially perceived ego; and therefore the self is a social self. Further, the physical components of the organism cannot be separated from the mental or psychological components. Brammeld therefore suggests that man has but one basic drive or motivating force: "social self-realization." [8]

The assumption that businessmen are motivated for maximization of profit is very different from the assumption that men have certain basic needs or drives seeking fulfillment. Maximization of profit certainly may serve in some ways several of these physiological, social, and ego needs, but it is evident that other channels as well present themselves as means for serving these drives in the atmosphere of the business organization. Some of the opportunities for serving man's needs may be in actual conflict with the firm's maximization of profit.

*"Outer Motivation": Emphasis on the Situation.* On the other end of the continuum there are those theorists who see motivation as having its roots primarily in the situation or in environment. Karl Mannheim, a representative of this view, states that "both motives and actions very often originate not from within but from the situation in which individuals find themselves." [9] Allport suggests that "situational variability has led many social scientists to the conviction that any search for a consistent personality with specifiable motives and traits is doomed to failure." [10] He goes on to quote William James to the effect that each situation has different motives: "A man has as many selves as there are distinct groups about whose opinion he cares." [11] When con-

---

[8] Theodore Brammeld, *Toward a Reconstructed Philosophy of Education* (New York: The Dryden Press, 1956), p. 119.

[9] Karl Mannheim, *Man and Society in an Age of Reconstruction* (New York: Harcourt, Brace & Co., 1940), p. 249.

[10] Gordon W. Allport, "What Units Shall We Employ?" in *Assessment of Human Motives*, ed. Gardner Lindzey (New York: Holt, Rinehart and Winston, Inc., 1958), p. 243.

[11] *Ibid.*, p. 244.

sidering the motives of businessmen, one must be aware of the influence of the business situation. At the same time, it is a dangerous generalization to assume that any two situations are ever the same or that any two individual businessmen will perceive any situation in exactly the same way or even that one businessman will perceive the same situation the same way on two different occasions. Further, it may be readily seen that the business environment may provide many motives for the individual in addition to that of profit maximization. The businessman may be motivated by titles, large offices, or personal friendships as well as by his personal or family security. Such motives may have no direct connection with the goals of the firm.

*Role Theory in Relation to Motivation.* This emphasis on the situation borders on the concept of "role theory," which assumes that individuals take on certain motives as they assume different roles. A "role" is defined by Sargent as "a pattern or type of social behavior which seems situationally appropriate to the individual in terms of the demands and expectations of those in his group." [12] Role theory suggests that as the individual's position in the group changes, his motivations may also change. Mannheim, for example, posits that businessmen change their motives as they assume different roles on the way up the business ladder. ". . . There is normally a graduated scale of motives by which men from different social classes are driven to work. . . . Whenever a man rises to a higher class . . . he switches over from one set of motives to another." [13] It should be noted, however, that not all writers on role theory place this much emphasis on role as a motivating factor. The sociologist Nelson Foote, for example, states that "Roles as such do not provide their own motives." [14] Mason Haire suggests that the "social definition" of a role is not specific enough to completely govern the be-

---

[12] S. Stansfeld Sargent, *Social Psychology—An Integrative Interpretation* (New York: The Ronald Press Company, 1950), p. 279.

[13] Mannheim, *op. cit.*, p. 316.

[14] Nelson N. Foote, "Identification as the Basis for a Theory of Motivation," *American Sociological Review*, Vol. XVI, No. 1 (February, 1951), p. 14.

havior of an individual.[15] According to Herbert Simon: "Any particular concrete behavior is a resultant of a large number of premises, only some of which are prescribed by the role."[16] Although role theory does not appear to give a total explanation to individual motivation in a particular setting, it does suggest one additional source of motivation. If we can become aware of how individuals perceive their role at a particular time, we may be able to gain insight into behavior at that time.

*The Middle of the Continuum.* A number of writers stress the importance of understanding both the "inner" individual and the "outer" situation in order to understand the motivation of the individual. George Kelly, while stating that a knowledge of the situation is essential to understanding psychological motives involved,[17] indicates the reciprocal relationship between the two. Allport is another who gives both factors weight: "The perceiver himself may . . . be the principal source of variance; the situation in which the object-person acts may be the second source of variance; and the fixed traits and motives of the object-person may be only a minor factor."[18]

*Complexity and Multiplicity of Motivations.* Traditional economists suggest a single business motivation, that of profit maximization. Recent psychological and sociological research, however, seems to indicate the interrelatedness of motives. Maslow, as a result of his investigations, concludes: "Most behavior is multimotivated. Within the sphere of motivational determinants, any behavior tends to be determined by several or all the basic needs simultaneously rather than by any one of them."[19] According to Allport, "It seems clear that the units we seek in personality and in motivation are

---

[15] Haire, *op. cit.*, p. 184.

[16] Herbert A. Simon, "Decision Making in Economics," *American Economic Review* (June, 1959), p. 274.

[17] George A. Kelly, "Man's Construction of His Alternatives," in *Assessment of Human Motives*, ed. Gardner Lindzey (New York: Holt, Rinehart and Winston, Inc., 1958), p. 63.

[18] Allport, *op. cit.*, p. 243.

[19] A. H. Maslow, *Motivation and Personality* (New York: Harper & Brothers, 1954), p. 102.

relatively complex structures, not molecular." [20] An attempt to explain business behavior based on a single overriding motive appears unrealistic in view of current research. A businessman's personal goals probably are not the same as those of the "organization" and, in fact, as Festinger points out, the satisfaction of either the goals of the business or of the individual may prohibit the satisfaction of the other's goals.[21] However, Festinger also suggests that in a situation in which the goals of the individual conflict with the goals of the firm, "there will be some tendency for the person to attempt to change one of them so that they do fit together, thus reducing or eliminating the dissonance." [22] Yet it may be the organizational goals he attempts to change in favor of his own.

*Aspiration Level.* One aspect of motivation which has received some attention recently and which proponents feel offers considerable insight into understanding and predicting human behavior is the concept of "level of aspiration." J. D. Frank, an early writer on this concept, defines "level of aspiration" as "the level of future performance in a familiar task which an individual, knowing his level of past performance in that task, explicitly undertakes to reach." [23] Kurt Lewin found from his experiments that "success and failure influence deeply the emotional status of the person, his goals, and his social relations. . . . After success, a person generally sets himself a higher goal. After failure, his level of aspiration generally goes down." [24] Lewin states, "The stronger the success the greater will be the percentage of raising the level of aspiration, and the stronger the failure the greater the percent of lowering the level of aspiration." [25]

---

[20] Allport, *op. cit.*, p. 242.

[21] Leon Festinger, "The Motivating Effect of Cognitive Dissonance," in *Assessment of Human Motives*, ed. Gardner Lindzey (New York: Holt, Rinehart and Winston, Inc., 1958), pp. 65-86.

[22] *Ibid.*, p. 70.

[23] J. D. Frank, "Individual Differences in Certain Aspects of the Level of Aspiration," *American Journal of Psychology*, Vol. XLV (1935), p. 119.

[24] Kurt Lewin, "Psychology of Success and Failure," *Occupations*, Vol. XIV, No. 9 (June, 1936), p. 926.

[25] Kurt Lewin, Tamara Dembo, Leon Festinger, and Pauline Sears, "Level of Aspiration," in *Personality and the Behavior Disorders*, ed. J. McV. Hunt (2 vols.) (New York: The Ronald Press Company, 1944), p. 338.

Simon stresses the correspondence of the two from his findings, stating, "In the long run the level of aspiration and attainable maximum will be very close together." [26] Such findings suggest that if we know the level of aspiration of a particular businessman we could begin to predict his behavior in certain situations. For example, if the owner of a construction firm had aspirations of a future large job, such an individual might retain his employees in relation to such aspirations rather than let workers go when work is slack. In such a case, prediction of behavior in terms of aspiration levels might be considerably different from a prediction in terms of maximization of profit.

The concept of "aspiration level," however, is not without criticism. John Gardner suggests that there may be a "region" of aspiration or a "direction" of aspiration but that a "level" does not appear to be a realistic term. He views the concept of a "level of aspiration" as an attempt to quantify something which is qualitative. He also suggests that there may be two or more aspiration levels operating in an individual at a particular time.[27] Katona questions the concept of individual "levels of aspirations" in that "aspirations are influenced by the performance of the members of the group to which one belongs. . . ." [28] Here again we are confronted with those internal-external factors of motivation discussed earlier. Nevertheless, the concept of "level of aspiration" with regard to motivation is a concept which must be faced by the businessmen and economists in attempting to develop a general theory of firm behavior.

In summary, it may be said that modern psychological concepts of motivation do not support the traditional economic theory that firm behavior may be explained by the single motivation of maximization of profit. Human motivation is not single but complex and even conflicting. Further,

---

[26] Simon, *op. cit.*, p. 272.
[27] John W. Gardner, "The Use of the Term *Level of Aspiration*," *Understanding Human Motivation*, ed. C. L. Stacey and M. F. Martino (Cleveland: Howard Allen, Inc., 1958), pp. 229-234.
[28] George Katona, "Rational Behavior and Economic Behavior," *Psychological Review* (July, 1953), p. 316.

human motives based on a number of needs or drives may well be satisfied through the firm in ways other than through maximization of profit.

## Comments and Conclusions

This chapter has presented some general concepts in the theories of perception and motivation. Although the two subjects were separated for the purposes of analysis, they are inherently interrelated, and their contributions toward an understanding of firm behavior are of the same nature. There are, however, certain limitations to the usefulness of the concepts of perception and motivation.

*Problems in Ascertaining Motivations and Perceptions.* Probably the most serious limitations of these theories involve the difficulty of ascertaining perceptions and motivations. Two methods for determining perceptions and motivations are (1) to have the individual state what his motivations are and how he sees or perceives the world, or (2) to observe overt actions and draw assumptions from these actions.

A problem in the first method is that we are faced with the task of interpreting the individual's statement about his motivations. Even though he desired to communicate his perceptions and motivations accurately, we find that his word symbols for his subjective experiences may be difficult to interpret with assurance. The problem is further complicated because of the fact that an individual's verbal behavior is not necessarily indicative of his attitudes. Behavior which is visible to others may be edited so that it appears acceptable to others. A number of writers have asked businessmen what their motives are, yet the results may be no more valuable than the original concept of profit maximization.[29]

The second alternative for ascertaining perceptions and motivations—that of observing behavior—adds the problem of the projection of the motivations and perceptions of the observer on to the observed and the fact that the observa-

---

[29] C. A. Hickman and M. H. Kuhn, *Individuals, Groups and Economic Behavior* (New York: The Dryden Press, 1956), Chapter 2.

tions are recorded in the vocabulary of the observer rather than that of the observed. As noted above, the observer may influence the data with his own specific individualized meaning.

*Other Criticisms of Motivation and Perception Theory.* Certain aspects of motivation theory have been criticized on several grounds other than the difficulty of ascertainment. Maslow has stated that "too many of the findings that have been made in animals have been proven to be true only for animals and not for human beings. There is no reason whatsoever why we should start with animals in order to study human motivation." [30] This criticism seems to suggest that much of the investigation about theories of motivation has been "zoo-morphic." Maslow also points out that many of the findings in motivation theory have come from the study of seriously disturbed people and that these generalizations may not hold true for individuals who appear to be able to cope with society, *e.g.*, businessmen. Further, motivation theory has been criticized as being static, *i.e.*, based on a premise of static properties in individuals. Finally, as has been suggested previously, motivation theory has been criticized as being highly prone to the dangers of projection. It has been suggested that possibly we can tell more about the person who attributes certain motives to another than we can about the person to whom the motive was attributed. Methods of investigating motivations must involve specific means of offsetting the dangers presented above.

Despite certain specific criticisms of motivation theory, however, it seems to be well established that human motivation is so complex that no single explanation of motivation, such as that of profit maximization, can be applied to all businessmen or to all business behavior. It may be difficult to accommodate ourselves to this conclusion, however, because it makes the building of a tight business model very difficult.

*Conclusion.* The problem of building a theory of firm behavior *today* can readily be seen to be a highly complex

---

[30] Maslow, *op. cit.*, pp. 103-104.

one. It is possible that in a previous era, motivation of the individual in the firm could have been conceived in more singular terms than it is today. Indeed, Schumpeter points out that during the late nineteenth century, a primary emphasis of the businessman appeared to be the acquisition of a large home, a large family, and a large estate to leave to his descendants.[31] Thus, perhaps it is possible that during the late nineteenth century the motivations of businessmen could be explained in more single terms, *i.e.*, by the motive of profit maximization, than they may be today. However, the problem of constructing a theory of firm behavior, in view of recent investigations into individual perception and behavior, can no longer be resolved by the simple positing of a single and rational profit motive.

Nevertheless, while the explanation of business motivation in terms of a single primary motivation of profit maximization appears to be an unwarranted oversimplification of business behavior, we cannot altogether reject the profit motive as an important factor in business behavior. As Katona stated: "There can be no doubt that in present-day American business thinking the function and role of profits is substantial." [32] What must be thrown open to question and further investigation is the extent to which actions of businessmen can be explained by the profit motive as well as by the many other motives that propel human behavior.

In this chapter, presentation has been made of current investigations into motivation and perception which must be considered in constructing a new theory of firm behavior. It may be seen that perception and motivation theories do not in themselves provide a ready-made general theory of firm behavior applicable to all situations. It may be, in fact, that such an all-encompassing theory is not feasible. Katona suggests that "the proximate aim of scientific research is a body of empirically validatable generalizations and not a theory

---

[31] Joseph A. Schumpeter, *Capitalism, Socialism and Democracy*, Third Edition (New York: Harper & Brothers, 1950), pp. 156-163.

[32] George Katona, *Psychological Analysis of Economic Behavior* (New York: McGraw-Hill Book Company, Inc., 1951), p. 194.

that is validated under any and all circumstances." [33] Yet, in the search for a variety of such generalizations capable of explaining behavior under given circumstances, motivation and perception theory will offer considerable insight into firm behavior.

## BIBLIOGRAPHY

Allport, Gordon W. "What Units Shall We Employ?" in *Assessment of Human Motives*, ed. Gardner Lindzey. New York: Holt, Rinehart and Winston, Inc., 1958.

Argyris, Chris. "The Individual and Organization: Some Problems of Mutual Adjustment," *Administrative Science Quarterly* (June, 1957), pp. 1-24.

Bakke, E. Wight. *Organization and the Individual.* New Haven: Yale Labor and Management Center, 1952.

Brammeld, Theodore. *Toward a Reconstructed Philosophy of Education.* New York: The Dryden Press, Inc., 1956.

Dearborn, DeWitt C., and Herbert A. Simon. "Selective Perception: A Note on the Departmental Identification of Executives," *Sociometry* (June, 1958), pp. 140-144.

Festinger, Leon. "The Motivating Effect of Cognitive Dissonance," in *Assessment of Human Motives*, ed. Gardner Lindzey. New York: Holt, Rinehart and Winston, Inc., 1958.

Foote, Nelson N. "Identification as the Basis for a Theory of Motivation," *American Sociological Review*, XVI, 1 (February, 1951), pp. 14-21.

Frank, J. D. "Individual Differences in Certain Aspects of the Level of Aspiration," *American Journal of Psychology*, XLV (1935), pp. 119-128.

Frank, Lawrence K. "Psychology and Social Order," in *The Human Meaning of the Social Sciences*, ed. Daniel Lerner. New York: Meridian Books, Inc., 1959.

---

[33] Katona, "Rational Behavior and Economic Behavior," *op. cit.*, p. 317.

Gardner, John W. "The Use of the Term *Level of Aspiration*," in *Understanding Human Motivation*, ed. C. L. Stacey and M. F. Martino. Cleveland: Howard Allen, Inc., 1958.

George, Frank, and J. H. Handlon. "A Language for Perceptual Analysis," *Psychological Review* (January, 1957), pp. 14-25.

Griffin, Clare E. *Enterprise in a Free Society*. Homewood: Richard D. Irwin, Inc., 1949.

Haire, Mason. *Psychology in Management*. New York: McGraw-Hill Book Company, Inc., 1956.

Hickman, C. A., and M. H. Kuhn. *Individuals, Groups and Economic Behavior*. New York: The Dryden Press, Inc., 1956.

Horney, Karen. *The Neurotic Personality of Our Time*. New York: W. W. Norton & Company, Inc., 1937.

Jones, Marshall E. (ed.). *Nebraska Symposium on Motivation*, 1958. Lincoln: University of Nebraska Press, 1958.

Katona, George. *Psychological Analyis of Economic Behavior*. New York: McGraw-Hill Book Company, Inc., 1951.

—————. "Psychological Analysis of Business Decisions and Expectations," *American Economic Review* (March, 1946), pp. 44-62.

—————. "Rational Behavior and Economic Behavior," *Psychological Review* (September, 1953), pp. 307-320.

Kelly, George A. "Man's Construction of His Alternatives," in *Assessment of Human Motives*, ed. Gardner Lindzey. New York: Holt, Rinehart and Winston, Inc., 1958.

Lewin, Kurt. "Psychology of Success and Failure," *Occupations*, XIV, 9 (June, 1936), pp. 926-930.

—————, Tamara Dembo, Leon Festinger, and Pauline Sears. "Level of Aspiration," in *Personality and the Behavior Disorders*, ed. J. McV. Hunt. 2 vols. New York: The Ronald Press Company, 1944.

Lindzey, Gardner (ed.). *Assessment of Human Motives*. New York: Holt, Rinehart and Winston, Inc., 1958.

Mannheim, Karl. *Man and Society in an Age of Reconstruction*. New York: Harcourt, Brace & Co., 1940.

Maslow, A. H. "A Dynamic Theory of Human Motivation," *Psychological Review*, L (1943), pp. 370-396.

——————. *Motivation and Personality*. New York: Harper & Brothers, 1954.

Mills, C. Wright. "Situated Actions and Vocabularies of Motive," *American Sociological Review* (December, 1940), pp. 904-913.

Newcomb, Theodore. *Social Psychology*. New York: The Dryden Press, Inc., 1950.

Sargent, S. Stansfeld. *Social Psychology—An Integrative Interpretation*. New York: The Ronald Press Company, 1950.

Schumpeter, Joseph A. *Capitalism, Socialism and Democracy*, Third Edition. New York: Harper & Brothers, 1950.

Sherif, Muzafer, and Carolyn Sherif. *An Outline of Social Psychology*, Revised Edition. New York: Harper & Brothers, 1956.

Siegel, Sidney. "Level of Aspiration and Decision Making," *Psychological Review* (July, 1957), pp. 253-262.

Simon, Herbert A. "Decision Making in Economics," *American Economic Review* (June, 1959), p. 274.

——————. *Models of Man: Social and Rational*. New York: John Wiley & Sons, Inc., 1957.

Wittreich, Warren J. "Visual Perception and Personality," *Scientific American* (April, 1959), pp. 56-60.

Zaleznik, A., C. R. Christensen, and F. J. Roethlisberger. *The Motivation, Productivity and Satisfaction of Workers*. Division of Research, Harvard University, Graduate School of Business Administration. Boston: Harvard University Press, 1958.

Chapter **10**

# FIELD THEORY AND BUSINESS BEHAVIOR

Mark J. Gibson

## Introduction

Since an iconoclast shattered the traditional economic golden egg, conceived as the *raison d'être* of business, a deluge of alchemists has experimented in gilding baser objects as replacements. By such actions, they had hoped to eliminate the frustration incurred by the goose on the demise of her potential progeny. The success of these efforts is somewhat dubious, for it appears thus far the alchemists have only succeeded in acquiring frustration themselves while the goose continues to produce.

The numerous schools established, *ceteris paribus*, to encase this lusterous deposit in various settings for admiration and adulation by all, have been guilty of the habits of another of the fowl species, the "floo floo" bird.[1] This bird had the peculiar habit of flying backward, observing the glory of its past while it backed into the future.

> For the chief obstacle to progress is not ignorance but knowledge; and just such knowledge as medieval physicians had of medicine. They were stuffed with information. They knew all there is to know about the habits of the unicorn and dragon. They knew the importance of the horoscope and they learned the peculiarities of the salamander. They had piles of books dealing with all aspects of medicine. But medical progress dates, in fact, from the moment when the physician stopped looking at the books and tried looking at the patient.[2]

---

[1] Frederick Gutheim, *Frank Lloyd Wright On Architecture*, The Universal Library (New York: Grosset & Dunlap, Inc., 1941), p. 243.

[2] C. Northcote Parkinson, "Science in Politics," *Saturday Review*, Vol. 43 (February 27, 1960), p. 37.

The psychologist George A. Kelly might attribute such a fallacy of Western man, *i.e.*, an implication of business existing for profit, as placing the onus of choice among alternatives, on the object itself. He claims that Western man has impaled all objects "on the horns of the dilemmas he chose to fashion out of his language." [3] Western man has succeeded in confusing himself with an ambiguity (and possibly often expressed equivocation) among cognition, conation, and emotion when viewing an object which has an intrinsic value; but such an object, when placed as the sole criterion for predication, becomes real or unreal, rational or irrational, as constructed by the viewer. It is in this context that business behavior, explanation for or prediction of, has been submersed.

A theory of business behavior must be generally applicable. It must seek to explain; it must seek to predict such behavior. Replacements of motives for business behavior either singular or multiple should not direct the study of business *per se*. Some students of business behavior always view the "Emperor in new clothes," but the scholar must continually observe the "Emperor."

There are certain terms in addition to motivation that are inherent in a study of business behavior. A list of such terms might include, among others: goals, roles, equilibrium, decision, uncertainty, risk, alternatives, and expectations. A few terms may be definitive, some are dichotomous, but most are ambiguous. Much of the confusion in any particular application of terminology arises from precedent. This occurs from structured viewing in a restricted time perspective. A disciple of Freud could attribute any "decision" to the omnipresent past. A disciple of Marx could attribute the "equilibrium" as being resolved only in the future. It is in the resolution of this dilemma that field theory becomes significant; wherein a view from the bridge between past and future is implicit.

---

[3] George A. Kelly, "Man's Construction of His Alternatives," *Assessment of Human Motives*, ed. Gardner Lindzey (New York: Holt, Rinehart and Winston, Inc., 1960), Ch. 2.

## Field Theory

In field theory, behavior depends neither on the past nor on the future but on the present, in its individually structured dynamic totality. This "present" in field theory does have a certain time perspective. It includes the psychological past as well as the psychological future in a study of the relationships between phenotypical facts and constructs and the relationships between constructs.[4]

Kurt Lewin, a Gestalt psychologist, became interested in social psychology and developed the concepts of field theory in order to study the dynamic totality of behavior. Gestalt psychologists had studied the inferred properties of personality as manifested in behavior and asked: "What do the facts mean?" To Lewin, the question "What are the facts?" was more important. He believed that behavior must be related not only to inner needs but also to a much more complex inference of variables—the total present situation as organized or structured by the organism—in order to determine what traits will be manifested and how.[5] Other psychologists had attempted to define the interrelationship of the individual and his environment, but attempts in conceptualization were abortive. The barrier to their methods was in the too literal use of the symbolization of the physical sciences and the attempt at application without a reconstruction of terms.

Lewin was convinced that it was possible to undertake experiments in the social sciences, which have as much right to be called scientific as those of physics and chemistry. To him, social space appeared as real as physical space. He stated that it should be studied by the students of geometry and mathematics to develop laws of the processes in social space which would have theoretical and practical importance.

In developing a method for the conceptualization of social space, Lewin contrasted Aristotelian with Galilean modes of thought in the physical sciences. The criteria of lawfulness

---

[4] Robert W. Leeper, *Lewin's Topological and Vector Psychology: A Digest and a Critique,* University of Oregon Monographs, Studies in Psychology, No. 1 (Eugene, Oregon: University of Oregon Press, 1943), p. 27.
[5] *Ibid.,* p. 28.

of an event was, in Aristotelian concepts, dependent upon its regularity or frequency; in Galilean concepts of lawfulness, regularity of occurrence was not necessary. Lewin stated that the real difference lies in the kind and direction of the physical vectors in Aristotelian dynamics, which are completely determined by the nature of the object concerned; while the procedure of Galileo included a thorough investigation of the situational forces.[6] The problem in developing a theory for experimentation in, and observation of, unique as well as frequent events in social space must then be capable of being defined and measured.

The solution of the problems inherent in defining and measuring social space can be equally applicable to a solution of problems in the development of a theory for the explanation of business behavior. How can the present field in which the firm operates be constructed to show the relationship between environmental factors and the firm's goal constructs and the relationship between constructs? Environmental forces *per se* are nothing more than empirically derived averages used in Gestalt concepts to derive motivation.

Lewin criticized "what" is treated statistically, and asserted that the "phenotypical" or surface data had been studied rather than "genotypical" or inferred abstract factors that really might possess some strict relationships.[7] To erect the necessary bridge between the concrete and the abstract, between social action and social theory, between the unique and the frequent, Lewin used three concepts: topological (as adapted by hodology), dynamic psychology, and field forces. These concepts are embodied in the system of thought described as field theory.

The use of topological principles enables the student of spacial relationships to work without regard to quantitative measurement. Topology deals with mathematical relationships definable in terms of finitely structured parts and wholes but does not consider ordinary concepts of direction

---

[6] Kurt Lewin, *A Dynamic Theory of Personality* (New York: McGraw-Hill Book Company, Inc., 1935), pp. 22-29.
[7] Leeper, *op. cit.*, p. 32.

and distance. Each item of "connectedness" or "nonconnect-edness" can be used to describe a region in the "framework of events possible in a life space." [8] The "life space" of a firm could be the dynamic totality of its construed psychological and environmental factors within the time perspective of the present.

The parts and wholes of topology, in order to have direction, are described in terms of "hodological space" (borrowed by Lewin from the Greek *hodos* for way or path—hence, hodology, the science of paths).[9] Hodology enables a description of movement, whether physical or psychological, towards a specified goal through nongeographic or non-Euclidean space. "Steps" that lead to a goal in a causal or sequential sense can approach or attain the goal "by moving away from it geographically, by approaching it geographically, or sometimes by not moving at all through ordinary space." [10]

The second class of concepts is anchored in the dynamic psychology of the individual, which could, for our purposes in studying business behavior, be the firm. It could be feasible to use either the rationalistic concept wherein the firm is a unified acting entity or the behavioristic concept in which the firm is the interaction of several.

The concepts that Lewin used to depict the dynamic totality of the present were divided between the "life space" and the "foreign hull of the life space" of the individual.

The "life space" is the totality of factors which determine behavior at a certain moment. It represents the perception of environment (or motor perceptual region) and numerous inner-personal needs as constructed by the individual. The motor perceptual region may react on the individual through his personal constructs of its facts or through actual facts. The inner-personal regions are those systems of needs and hypothesized paths which lead to their attainment. These inner-personal regions may be or may not be in a state

---

[8] *Ibid.*, p. 217.
[9] *Ibid.*, p. 37.
[10] Joseph Clawson, "Lewin's Vector Psychology and the Analysis of Motives in Marketing," in *Theory in Marketing*, ed. Reavis Cox and Wroe Alderson (Homewood: Richard D. Irwin, Inc., 1950), p. 45.

of tension: tension being determined by the balance of positive or negative valences assigned to needs or cell-paths. The change in the tension system depends upon the time interval and the fluidity as manifested in the valences. The possibility of stable equilibrium in the valences does not indicate any cessation of tension; on the contrary, it may produce the most extreme tension. A decision must be reached, and neither the negative nor the positive structured valences dominate. In the case of stable equilibrium, action must be taken; yet the alternatives are not present as dynamic wholes but only as equal parts; this produces a state of conflict. Conflict may occur, also, when the differences between existing forces are in opposite or partially opposite directions. The tensions within the inner-personal regions may spread from one region to another and be satisfied or intensified dependent upon the communication between "connected" and "nonconnected" regions. This change of tension through communication may be evidenced in the satiation or co-satiation of one "need" having greater force than another on the inner-personal regions, but its attainment may shift the existing valences of other regions in the life space of the individual.

The "foreign hull of the life space" may be described as "outside the pale of perception" of the individual. Though considerable confusion exists in Lewin's uses and the interpretations of Lewin as to whether the motor perceptual region is not, in itself, a part of the "foreign hull," it is generally used as a cognitively unstructured region of the environment. It may then actually induce physiological or psychological change through the manifestation of facts alien to the individual. The boundaries of this "foreign hull" as constructed by the individual may be perceptions of the real or the unreal which act as barriers in the tension system existing at the present. Further experience by the individual may extend these boundaries and lead to more rational decision among alternatives as the barriers are decreased.[11]

In hypothesizing that the firm could be studied by Lewin's system regardless of rationalistic or behavioristic concepts, it

---

[11] Leeper, *op. cit.*, pp. 51-76.

may be sufficient to say that the behavior of an individual or an unresolved group is determined in its dynamic totality of the present as perceived by the group's perception of the real or the unreal. Both concepts involve change through spirals of perception and re-evaluation. What is real at the moment is the membership in the firm by all individuals. If criteria for membership is merely the acceptance of a salary or wage, a group exists that can be studied for purposes of its motives. Members of larger social structures—whether individual or group, micro-economic unit or macro-economic unit—make their decision and act through a synthesis of the authority inherent in the relationships between and inter-relationships among the organization.[12]

The concept of "field forces" is used by Lewin whenever he wishes to indicate the interaction of the tension systems of the individual and the pressures emanating from sur-rounding fields. Force fields as constructed by Lewin for a systematic approach to indicate the behavior of an individual in his dynamic totality of the present, are marked by three things: strength, direction, and point of application.

The strength of a force field is the determination of the stability or differences existing in the valences of the regions in the life space which are inducements to observable be-havior. The existence of a tension system sufficient to cause locomotion, actual or anticipated, is the weight of the force.

The direction of the force is the anticipated or actual hodological locomotion within the regions of the inner-personal of the "life space." These are represented by vec-tors of various lengths to indicate the weight of the force. Direction may also be indicated without symbols as $d_{A, B}$ or "direction in region A from region A to B."

The point of application of the force is indicated by the vector pointed against the person or region with which the force is involved.

The concept of locomotion which indicates movement through time may be included in the direction but also is

---

[12] Daniel Lerner and H. D. Lasswell, *The Policy Sciences* (Stanford: Stanford University Press, 1951), p. 67.

often referred to when only psychological motion is involved or when direction is anticipated on a path.

The three concepts of Lewin (topological, dynamic, and force fields) may then be incorporated into what is known as a topological diagram. For example, such a diagram might be constructed to illustrate the possible reactions when a firm's share of the market is threatened by a competitor's introduction of a new patented product.[13]

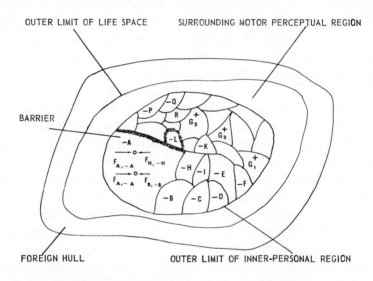

A.  Fear of losing share of market
B.  Advertising-sales engineering
C.  Location of the firm
D.  Better retail outlets
E.  Adoption of product by consumer
F.  Income $\geqq$ Costs
$G_1$  Maintain share of market
$G_2$  Survival
$G_3$  Profit

H.  Innovation
I.  Advertising
K.  Income > Costs
L.  Patent infringement
P.  Costs > Income
Q.  Efficiency in production and distribution
R.  Income = Costs

Management of the firm regularly checks sales figures and competitors' positions in the market. At present a competitor has developed a new patented product which, from

---

13 Clawson, *op. cit.*, pp. 46-48.

indications of sales figures, is cutting into the firm's share of the market. The need is —A, which is now a tension system with a negative valence (to restore the market position). The longer arrow points to the right out of region —A and indicates that there is a strong impulse or vector acting on management to escape from that region. Management considers traditional possibilities. But it is deterred from entering region —L (infringement of patent rights) by the legal risks; thus it is a closed pathway at present. The first of the open pathways is $AHIEFG_1$, but this involves more effort and expense and is less desirable, as indicated by the relative length of the vector force $F_H$, $_{-H}$ (innovation). The second open pathway is $ABCDEFG_1$, which management selects as requiring less effort. This pathway, as indicated by the length of the vector $F_B$, $_{-B}$ is exerting a greater force. The lengths of vectors $F_A$, $_{-A}$ and $F_B$, $_{-B}$ indicate that equilibrium can be more quickly resolved. Management then sets out on its first step by moving into region —B. This is the first observable objective behavior that results from what can, in reality, be a complex field of subjective possibilities. Management may continue along that path or be interrupted at point —P, where the costs of producing and marketing the product exceed income, and thus achieve equilibrium more rapidly for stockholder approval or inter-departmental financial responsibility by following pathway $PQRG_2$ (survival). This stable equilibrium will not necessarily reduce the tension. After reasserting the firm's cost-income ratio, management may return to the path $AHIEFG_1$. In developing a new product rather than engineering sales through advertising, management finds at region E that acceptance by consumers is such that direction is shifted to region —K and thence to goal $G_3$ (profit). If direction is continued to $G_1$, profit may or may not be obtained since the goal is merely to maintain the share of the market.

We might then ask: What determines the valence of motives? The need or motive is an energy-releasing process which tends to produce an organization of the life space which will lead to a process of satisfaction of a positive motive or an escape from a negative.[14] Motives are determined, according to Lewin, by achievement, aspiration, and ideal levels. The achievement level is the status quo, *i.e.*, that amount of profit, prestige, or share of the market which is at present satisfying the entrepreneur or firm. The ideal level is the largest amount of something which the firm would like to have for all purposes (perhaps a monopolistic position). The aspiration level is that amount which the individual expects after expending energy. This may be doing, producing, or buying an additional something. The choice of a quantitative valuation for the aspiration level is subject to revision with experience, involving relative valences of variations in the same activity. The factor of realism (realistic appraisal) in choice of an aspiration level is defined by the individual as to his perception and constructs of the facts and may be revised and become more realistic with experience. Lewin states that the strength of the seeking of success, the avoidance of failure, and the cognitive factor of a probability judgment depend on many aspects of the life space of the individual at that time, the way he sees his past experience and the scales of reference which are characterized for his culture and his personality.[15]

What is reality and unreality? Lewin states that the differentiation of levels of reality is less for the psychological past and the psychological future than for the psychological present. Unreality may be expressed as either positive—hopes and wishes, or negative—dreads and fears. In the case of negative unreality, the individual has constructed barrier regions within the life space, perhaps because of his limited understanding of his environment. Within the time perspective of the long run, the individual or firm may have more realistic expectations as his experience in satisficing grows.

Perception of reality may change, in the topological diagram of the motives of the entrepreneur, if a move to manufacture in countries not abiding by the international patent

---

[14] Leeper, *op. cit.*, p. 212.
[15] Kurt Lewin, *et al.*, "Level of Aspiration," in *Personality and the Behavior Disorders*, ed. J. McV. Hunt (New York: The Ronald Press Company, 1944), p. 316.

agreements was contemplated and the negative force which established the barrier between the entrepreneur and the existing design of the product diminished, so that eventually he may perceive as real that which was unreal according to law at a previous time space.

Causal factors and their effects are separated by some span of time, but both are included within a closed system.[16] This time perspective of the real and the unreal, as related to topological diagrams and the choice of alternative pathways, was one of the more important concepts developed by Lewin in later work. Experimentation in diagramming four-dimensional topological diagrams provides a more rational approach to the perception of realistic goals. The diagrams provide conceptualization of the unique situation which is generally not perceived within the present time structure. Topological diagrams present alternatives to reach a firm's goal; other diagrams deal with one barrier to a goal. Thus, the student of business behavior may have a visual reminder of the connections which may be possible in the choice among several alternatives. The firm in analyzing its own alternatives in terms of topological diagrams may thus more quickly perceive what steps are necessary to reach a certain goal and if that goal in itself is permissible within the socio-legal structure of the environment in which it operates.

## Field Theory and Business Behavior

A field theory of personality which sees behavior and personality as functions of a total field of which they are subparts is the form of theory which today seems best suited for the conceptual representation of personality. Such a theory is slowly emerging from the work of many investigators. On the psychological side, this theory will take account of both mask and substance aspects of personality, fully recognizing that much that looks like specificity of behavior, and is specificity if viewed from the standpoint of action *qua* action, is actually an expression of generality and consistency, if the setting of the behavior and its meaning for the total personality is considered. On the logical and mathematical side this

---

[16] Leeper, *op. cit.*, pp. 67-69.

theory will recognize that the traits of factors of personality range from the most specific to the most general and that the difference between specificity and generality is formal rather than material, relative rather than fixed.[17]

Field theory, in essence, may be described as encompassing the fields of psychoanalysis, cultural anthropology, and social psychology. Much criticism that has been aimed at the work of Lewin implies that his theory involves more art than science. This may be true. The analysis of the dynamic totality of the individual as he perceives it at the present moment makes the situation relative. If that situation is relative, it cannot be scientific prediction or it would, in its course, become historical determinism. Historical determinism would, in its conception of progress, eliminate man as an individual—to become merely the means for the machine of evolution that culminates in justice and equity for all. The justice by its own determinism, reaches the ultimate in nihilism—history is rational; man, a forcefully applied means—gives to man complete justice only by his total subjugation; to history a definitive end.[18] The analytical methods of the present situation as defined by Lewin give possibilities for probability prediction within a loop of present time perspective and, as such, may be scientific. But utilization of his methods for the prediction of the unlimited future based on scientific rationality would only become determinism—thus, application to the future necessarily becomes an art as created by the individual or the firm.[19]

In answer to the child's questioning what water is,[20] a field theorist might take refuge in an Oriental dictum by

---

[17] Donald W. MacKinnon, "The Structure of Personality," in *Personality and the Behavior Disorders*, ed. J. McV. Hunt (New York: The Ronald Press Company, 1944), p. 43.

[18] Albert Camus, *The Rebel* (New York: Vintage Books, Inc., 1956), p. 197.

[19] It is this author's opinion that much of the criticism of Lewin was based on the very flexibility which Lewin provides with his method; refusing to give method as dogma and, by such act, destroy its intent. Lewin never wrote a text; confining his writing to innumerable articles and monographs. As such, it leaves his methods as being *scientific* for analysis and experiment but *art* in attempting to predict.

[20] Joseph W. McGuire, "The Concept of the Firm," *California Management Review*, Summer, 1961, p. 28.

saying that water is the hardest thing in the world and the softest. He would then have provided an analysis of diametrically opposed alternatives of equal weight and direction (without being at a stable equilibrium), oriented the subject within the culturally perceived environment of the child, and yet not construed the object with predication. The whole process of learning through scientific observation and experiment might then be established.

When stating that the motive of business behavior is profit maximization or any other singular motive, the field theorist could perhaps conclude that such a compulsive drive was a sign of immaturity, being indulged by a permissive society or a dominant implication of a behavior disorder requiring psychiatric attention, or that the learning process was totally impossible within the structured thinking of its dynamic totality.

The infant industry as first protected by such laws as tariff legislation could be feasibly explained by the permissive society concept. When an industry grows, if it matures, it does not persist in the maximization of profits because its perception of the environment has increased, and it cannot trespass the social and legal barriers without running the risk of being charged with violation of the cultural tradition—the socio-legal *modus vivendi* for business behavior—and merely satisfices. As the firm grows, it acquires experience. With experience, it perceives more of the reality of the actual environment. This perception might preclude ego-fulfillment action and be realized in responsible action through participation in that environment, solely to enhance that environment. Economists (such as Galbraith) have suggested this possibility.

The perception of the environment in which it operates provides the firm or businessman with the possibilities of rational judgment for optimal planning through choice among those alternatives possible to decrease the risk, insure the survival, and provide realistic profits as means of attaining its goals and existence. With perception, it participates and becomes something more than the equivalent of a legal human aberration. But by what means does the scholar of business behavior or the firm in self-actualization proceed?

The meaning and effect of group decision depend upon the nature of the process itself and upon the position of the group within its environment. Lewin, in experimenting with social steering, suggests that forces of action act as channels which are decisively different in constellation before and after passing or not passing a gate region.[21] The question then is, who controls the gate and what is his psychology? He suggests that this method defines more precisely how certain "objective" sociological problems of locomotion of goods and persons may intersect with certain "subjective" psychological and cultural problems, and points to sociologically characterized places where attitudes and decision have great effect. A product may have little or no value, but should an advertising agency (acting as gatekeeper) attribute qualities to that product and their campaign be effective, the sales of the product may soar.

To analyze alternatives existing within the group, a series of steps of "planning, fact finding, decision, fact finding, modification of decision, and execution" are isolated. Frequently, the steps are circular and often work in spiral fashion. Fact finding itself should evaluate the action by indicating whether what has been achieved is above or below expectation, and, through planning each successive step as modified, may give the planners a chance to learn. If objective standards of achievement do not exist, those responsible for planning on a realistic basis of fact finding cannot learn or evaluate. A correct perception of the result of action is essential before discussion of any next step.[22]

In experimenting with groups, Lewin ascertained that the culture determines under what conditions aggression will be manifested. For the individual concerned toward the goal, it determines how easily a situation might indicate a cognitive structure where aggression may be possible as a path

---

[21] Kurt Lewin, "Group Decision and Social Change," in *Readings in Social Psychology,* ed. Theodore M. Newcomb, Eugene L. Hartley, and others (New York: Henry Holt & Co., Inc., 1947), pp. 330-336.
[22] *Ibid.*

for his action. This was demonstrated in experimentally established groups of totalitarian, democratic and *laissez-faire* components, rigidly observed by movies, stenographic records, impressionistic write-ups by group leaders, minute-by-minute group structure analyses, and quantitative running accounts of the social interaction.[23] If aggression occurs within the environment of the firm or within the firm itself and it is possible to isolate the elements responsible, how may a permanent change be effected to provide a more favorable environment?

It is possible to change the strength of the opposing forces without changing the level of social conduct. In this case, tension increases. Two methods of changing the level of conduct are possible: add forces in the desired direction, which will result in increased tension; diminish the forces opposing the change, which will effect a relatively low level of tension. The latter method is preferable. If a firm is contemplating a reduction of employees, two methods of reducing tension may be possible. First, ignore the reaction within the firm and concentrate on favorable public relations. Second, ignore the overt public relations and concentrate on the advantages such a reduction might have for those within the firm. The change itself, to be permanent, must unfreeze—move—refreeze at a new level the perceptions of the group. This is most effectively done by democratic processes with effective leadership.[24] By participation in its environment, the firm may, to achieve its own goals, discover the forces of those goals mitigated by the increased alternatives of action but will be able to plan more realistically.

## Conclusion

Field theory, if applied to business behavior, could not be borrowed *in toto* from Lewin. In attempting to explain the behavior of an individual or a group, Lewin and other psy-

---

[23] Kurt Lewin, Ronald Lippett, and Ralph K. White, "Patterns of Aggressive Behavior in Experimentally Created 'Social Climates,'" *Journal of Social Psychology*, Vol. 10 (May, 1939), p. 271.

[24] Kurt Lewin, "Group Decision and Social Change," *op. cit.*

chologists had a wealth of material which indicated normal cultural standards of acceptance even if, at times, the entire nation was abnormal. They had case histories of adjustment and behavior for reference. They had standards of learning which separated the exceptional from the normal. They had several fields (*e.g.*, social psychology, cultural anthropology, psychoanalysis) already established, if not perfected, to combine into that analysis of the individual behavior in his dynamic totality at the present. Such is not the case if field theory were to be applied to business behavior.

In the field of business, isolated case studies of the decision process at critical moments in a firm do exist, but little has been accomplished. (It may be that these case studies have no factors existing in sufficient quantity to merit analysis.) Some business firms are now being studied over a period of years in their entirety; this might eventually reveal how the firm reacts to its socio-legal environment. Yet even these admirably conceived studies may be insufficient for a total view towards a theory of business behavior.

It appears that the analysis of business behavior is at the stage in psychoanalysis where Freud first began to study the personality of the individual and could use only those subjects for analysis who had actually deviated from the normal and had been subjected to some sort of punishment (whether self-imposed or socio-legal punishment) for that deviation. If field theory is to be applied to the study of business behavior, we may have to begin with those firms which failed and those firms which are prosecuted under the legal structure before we can begin to indicate motives that could be considered as normal. We might then construct a maze of all socio-legal barriers (topological diagrams) to which a business might be subject in its routine existence, and from its selection of paths and successive states of lack of tension, construct or determine motives for those actions as inferred from studies of case histories. Which goals are attained? Which motives are changed? What does the business perceive from its life space in a certain environment, and how does it adjust? When is the firm in a state of lack of tension? The scientific observer and experimenter must construct a maze before observation of the behavior of the rat in that maze. Thus, field theory could offer some valid possibilities for observing business behavior.

## BIBLIOGRAPHY

Bavelas, Alex, and Kurt Lewin. "Training in Democratic Leadership," *Journal of Abnormal and Social Psychology*, 37 (January, 1942).

Camus, Albert. *The Rebel*. New York: Vintage Books, Inc., 1956.

Clawson, Joseph. "Lewin's Vector Psychology and the Analysis of Motives in Marketing," in *Theory in Marketing*, ed. Reavis Cox and Wroe Alderson. Homewood: Richard D. Irwin, Inc., 1950.

Cox, Reavis, and Wroe Alderson (eds.). *Theory in Marketing*. Homewood: Richard D. Irwin, Inc., 1950.

Gutheim, Frederick. *Frank Lloyd Wright on Architecture*. New York: Grossett & Dunlap, Inc., 1941.

Kelly, George A. "Man's Construction of His Alternatives," in *Assessment of Human Motives*, ed. Gardner Lindzey. New York: Holt, Rinehart and Winston, Inc., 1960.

Leeper, R. W. *Lewin's Topological and Vector Psychology: A Digest and a Critique*. University of Oregon Monographs, Studies in Psychology, No. 1. Eugene: University of Oregon Press, 1943.

Lerner, Daniel, and H. D. Lasswell. *The Policy Sciences*. Stanford, California: Stanford University Press, 1951.

Lewin, Gertrude Weiss (ed.). *Resolving Social Conflicts*. New York: Harper & Brothers, 1948.

Lewin, Kurt. *A Dynamic Theory of Personality*. New York: McGraw-Hill Book Company, Inc., 1935.

——————. *A Conceptual Representation and the Measurement of Psychological Forces*. Durham: Duke University Press, 1938.

——————. "Group Decision and Social Change," in *Readings in Social Psychology*, ed. Theodore M. Newcomb, Eugene L. Hartley, *et al.* New York: Henry Holt & Co., Inc., 1947.

——————. *Principles of Topological Psychology.* New York: McGraw-Hill Book Company, Inc., 1936.

——————, *et al.* "Level of Aspiration," in *Personality and the Behavior Disorders*, ed. J. McV. Hunt. New York: The Ronald Press Company, Inc., 1944.

——————, Ronald Lippitt, and Sibylle K. Escalona. *Studies in Topological and Vector Psychology*, Part I. University of Iowa Studies in Child Welfare, XVI, 3. Iowa City: University of Iowa Press, 1940.

——————, Ronald Lippett, and Ralph K. White. "Patterns of Aggressive Behavior in Experimentally Created 'Social Climates,' " *Journal of Social Psychology*, 10 (May, 1939).

Lindzey, Gardner (ed.). *Assessment of Human Motives.* New York: Holt, Rinehart and Winston, Inc., 1960.

MacKinnon, Donald W. "The Structure of Personality," in *Personality and the Behavior Disorders*, ed. J. McV. Hunt. New York: The Ronald Press Company, 1944.

McGuire, Joseph W. "The Concept of the Firm," *California Management Review* (Summer, 1961).

Parkinson, C. Northcote. "Science in Politics," *Saturday Review*, Vol. 43 (February 27, 1960).

# Chapter 11

# THE CULTURAL APPROACH TO BUSINESS BEHAVIOR

Jean Boddewyn

## Introduction

The story is told of a newly appointed ambassador to Mexico who decided to furnish his home with furniture that was handmade by Indian carpenters who were masters of their craft. Visiting a small shop and finding a chair that was not only comfortable but also reasonably priced, he asked the man to make a dozen for him. The carpenter seemed a little disgruntled at this request and said: "The señor knows, of course, that if I make more than one, I charge more for each chair." "I don't understand," replied the puzzled ambassador. "In my country, it costs less if one buys in quantity. Why do you charge more?" "Because, Señor," replied the man impatiently, "it is much too boring to make twelve chairs exactly alike!"

True or not, this story strikingly contrasts the thinking of two *homines œconomici*. Without having to conjure visions of average cost and revenue curves, the ambassador immediately reasoned in terms of "the more, the better," "the more, the cheaper," "the more alike, the nicer," etc. On the other hand, the Indian carpenter simply thought like a craftsman for whom the "market" came second. The very idea of "maximizing profit" probably never crossed his mind.

Evidently these two men are living in two different economic worlds, and they are the products of two different cultures. The fact is, however, that the economic life of any society is a tissue of such cultural jokes. A large part of economic behavior simply reflects the accepted means and ends of a particular society at a particular time. The cultural approach to business behavior attempts to determine the nature and extent of such cultural influence.

*Purpose and Plan of This Study.* After a brief review of the treatment of the cultural dimension by different schools of economists, this chapter will analyze the concept of culture developed by anthropologists and other social scientists. The cultural approach will then be applied to economic behavior. Since, however, the culture requires some perspective in order to be perceived, economic behavior will be successively analyzed from a cross-cultural, a historico-cultural, and a subcultural point of view. Each one of these three approaches will be described and then applied in an analysis of the notion of profits.

From this survey and these examples it will be possible to appraise the validity of the cultural approach as well as its possible contribution to a general theory of business behavior.

## Beyond Economics

Reality is the ultimate touchstone of all knowledge. The ancient story of Antaeus who lost his strength the moment his feet were off the ground offers a permanent warning to all theorists of things and people. Expounders, detailers, and refiners follow the thinkers until models of men and of societies become dried-out affairs. The study of business is no exception.

*Classical Economists.* At the outset of his analysis of economic activity, Alfred Marshall defined economics as a study of mankind in the ordinary business of life. Unfortunately, the promise of breadth in this definition was never realized by the Cambridge professor—or by any other economist, for that matter.

Most economic studies have obtained data from their present-day environment and have largely ignored the temporal and spatial limitations of these data. Some economists, however, have been concerned with the lack of perspective involved in such a parochial view of economic activity.

*Historians and Institutionalists.* It suffices at this point to mention the efforts of the German historians of the second half of the nineteenth century and those of the American Institutionalists of our day. Both schools have attacked the flat characters and the simple generalizations of traditional economists, and they have proposed to study the economic process in its social environment as well as its evolution.

Such attempts to broaden the field of economics have been received with mixed feelings for being too eclectic or too far removed from the subject at hand.[1] To a large extent, this objection has been about methodology and compartmentalization of human knowledge. As Evans-Pritchard once observed, everything in the world is ultimately related to everything else, but unless we make abstractions we cannot even begin to study phenomena. It has been argued, for that matter, that the strenuous efforts of the classical economists, notably in England, to establish rigid limits for the field were conscious attempts to reverse the historic tendency to merge economics, political philosophy, and moral philosophy into a broad, although somewhat amorphous body of knowledge.[2]

Be it by default or by prudence, most economists have thus refused to venture across traditional borders—either considering other aspects of human behavior as "givens" or dismissing them as essentially noneconomic.[3] This policy left the field wide open for the social scientists.

## Cultural Anthropology

Every human community develops some mode of self-observation to record and ultimately to regulate its own oper-

---

[1] See, for example, Barbara Wootton, *Lament for Economics* (London: George Allen & Unwin, Ltd., 1938), p. 45; or John S. Gambs, *Beyond Supply and Demand* (New York: Columbia University Press, 1946).

[2] C. Addison Hickman and Manford H. Kuhn, *Individuals, Groups and Economic Behavior* (New York: The Dryden Press, 1956), p. ix.

[3] *Ibid.*, p. xiii.

ations.[4] In the poetic metaphor of Clyde Kluckhohn, the social sciences provide such a mirror for man and his societies.

Among the social sciences, *cultural anthropology* takes as its focus those forms and modes of behavior that are the resultants of universal human nature as affected by the accidents of history. Intellectually, the discipline has four unifying factors:

(1) A focus on man in all his variation and similarity.

(2) A consistently comparative point of view.

(3) A stubborn conviction that history, physique, environmental situation, way of life, and language are all related in discoverable patterns.

(4) A premise that the nonrational and irrational aspects of human behavior must be investigated along with the rational.[5]

This last point is particularly important: in contrast to economics, anthropology definitely emphasizes the nonrational (*i.e.*, the customary) as much as the rational.[6] Actually, anthropologists redefine these terms in a cultural way, as will be seen later. Besides, like all social sciences, cultural anthropology is basically inductive in its approach, while economics has traditionally been a deductive or normative discipline.[7]

*The Concept of Culture.* Needless to say, definitions of culture abound. Herskovits' "behavior in the broadest sense of the term—overt acts and their implicit sanctions"[8] catches the flavor of most of them.

---

[4] Daniel Lerner, "Social Sciences: Whence and Whither?" in *The Human Meaning of the Social Sciences*, ed. Daniel Lerner (New York: Meridian Books, 1959), p. 13.

[5] Clyde Kluckhohn, "Common Humanity and Diverse Cultures," *ibid.*, pp. 246-247.

[6] *Ibid.*, p. 246.

[7] Melville J. Herskovits, *Economic Anthropology* (New York: Alfred A. Knopf, Inc., 1952), p. 61. See also Frank H. Knight, "Deduction and Induction in Economics," pp. 508-523 in Appendix to Herskovits, *op. cit.*

[8] *Ibid.*, p. 21.

*Culture and Personality.* The now-prevailing explanation of the effect of culture on the individual emphasizes:[9]

(1) *Primary groups* as transmitters of the norms. Such groups constitute the immediate milieu within which the individual operates—for example, the relatives or the co-workers who help the individual perceive his environment and ascribe meaning to it.

(2) *Language* as the essential vehicle of such social transmission.

(3) *Roles* as prescribed behavior or socially expected plans of action for individuals in various situations.

(4) *Status* as the various positions that constitute the structure of a group—quite apart from the individuals who occupy these positions.

Although the individual possesses an overall awareness of the pattern of his culture and of its socio-economic, regional, sex, age, and occupational differences, he is allowed some latitude in the adoption of the norms. Part of a culture must be learned by everyone, part may be selected from alternative patterns, part applies only to those who perform certain roles. Besides, not all social events are culturally patterned because a certain number of circumstances arise for which no cultural solutions have as yet been devised.[10]

Finally, as Schumpeter remarked:

> Things economic and social move by their own momentum and the ensuing situations compel individuals and groups to behave in certain ways—not indeed by destroying their freedom of choice but by shaping the choosing mentalities and by narrowing the list of possibilities from which to choose.[11]

*Validity of Cultural Anthropology's Findings.* Serious objections have been raised about the methodology of cultural

---

[9] See, for example, Hickman and Kuhn, *op. cit.*, or Richard T. LaPiere, *A Theory of Social Control* (New York: McGraw-Hill Book Company, Inc., 1954). A theory of personality—preferably of the socio-psychological variety—should run parallel to any cultural explanation of behavior since neither the individual nor the culture can be thought to exist without the other.

[10] Clyde Kluckhohn, *Mirror for Man* (Greenwich, Conn.: Fawcett Publications, Inc., 1959), pp. 25-31.

[11] Joseph A. Schumpeter, *Capitalism, Socialism, and Democracy* Third Edition Revised (New York: Harper & Brothers, 1960), p. 129.

anthropology. For example, only recently have anthropologists used sampling methods. How typical then are their descriptions and ensuing interpretations?

Even assuming representativeness, how useful are anthropological generalizations? In the words of Mead:

> Any abstract statement about the cultural character of a people has to be reduced to such a bare skeleton statement that it will have less specific content than a similar statement about a class or region, and less still than a comparable statement about a single individual.[12]

Finally, to paraphrase David Potter's remarks about the American character, to what extent must the behavior of any individual or group of individuals be ascribed to their nationality (*e.g.*, American), their personality (*e.g.*, extrovert), their membership in a social class (*e.g.*, upper-middle), their religion (*e.g.*, Protestant), or their professional affiliation (*e.g.*, businessman)? [13]

## The Cultural Approach to Economic Behavior

Once the pervasiveness of the cultural dimension is recognized, economic activity and business behavior must be perceived as falling under its rule. Where traditional economic theory has concentrated on the individual, the cultural approach recognizes that the economic process takes place within a cultural matrix: economic man is never found in a cultureless state.

This does not mean, however, that a theory of business must go "native." While any approach that is not purely economic in conception or methodology is bound to be anathema to those who like neat little boxes, people with broader tastes must exercise caution lest they fall into the proverbial equal mixture of "one horse-one bird." After all, one can go

---

[12] Margaret Mead, "The Cross-Cultural Approach to the Study of Personality," in *Psychology and Personality*, ed. J. L. McCary (New York: Grove Press, Inc., 1956), p. 216.

[13] David M. Potter, *People of Plenty: Economic Abundance and the American Character* (Chicago: The University of Chicago Press, 1954), p. 19.

all the way from an expansive view of the economic process—or economizing—as including all activity which involves the economy of means quite regardless of the end pursued [14] to an all-cultural approach where everything, *e.g.*, business, is explained in terms of a single referent, namely, culture. Such concepts are probably too extreme for comfort.

One major problem inherent to the cultural approach must be dealt with here. Once it is recognized that business is immersed in the ambient culture, it is to be feared that both its actors and its witnesses will fail to realize to what extent groups, language, roles, and status are culturally determined. Both the contents and the form of business activity are bound, then, to be taken more or less for granted. In such a short-sighted view, "business as usual" is taken literally.

Clearly, some psychological distance is needed to realize the impact of culture on business activity. Such perspective can be gained through approaches which vicariously remove the observer from his own culture. Hence the *cross-cultural* (or comparative) and the *historical* approaches which compare a culture with other cultures removed in space or in time. On the other hand, the *subcultural* approach contrasts various forms of a major culture. All three approaches will be analyzed in the following pages and then applied in an analysis of the concept of profits.

### The Cross-Cultural Approach to Economic Behavior

Strangely enough, few anthropologists have addressed themselves to the systematic task of finding out how other social entities carry out their economic activities. Herskovits presents the major exception to date—although he definitely focuses his attention on nonliterate peoples.[15] From his research, Herskovits concludes that (1) the *scarcity of goods* in the face of the wants of a given people at a given time is a universal fact of human experience; and that (2) on the

---

[14] The name of Frank H. Knight is commonly associated with this view of "economizing."

[15] Herskovits, *op. cit.* The subtitle of this book is *A Study in Comparative Economics*. This is a revised edition of his earlier (1940) book *The Economic Life of Primitive Peoples*.

whole, the individual tends to *maximize his satisfactions in terms of the choices he makes.*[16]

While these generalizations bear striking resemblance to the economists' postulates of scarcity and rationality, Herskovits hastens to qualify his findings by asking: "scarce and rational in terms of what system of thought and behavior?" [17] In other words, while there may well be a universal scarcity factor and a universal rational process, what forms do they assume in different cultures? For example, Europeans and Americans consider as rational to defer the gratification of wants, to accumulate resources, to produce more goods, and to multiply services. Yet, in other societies which display completely different economic behaviors, rational choices not only are made but they are also debated.[18]

Polanyi, however, disagrees with Herskovits about scarcity and rationality on the grounds that for choice to exist there must be given more than one use to the means, as well as graded ends. Since in some societies there is only one culturally defined means and/or end as far as a particular act is concerned, choice is not always possible. Polanyi, consequently, restricts the meaning of the word "economic" to what he calls its *substantive* aspect, *i.e.*, "the interaction of man with his natural and social environment, insofar as this results in supplying him with the means of material want satisfaction." [19] On the other hand, the *formal* "means-end" meaning of the term (1) applies only to market institutions —which Polanyi distinguishes from exchange institutions,[20] (2) requires insufficiency of means, and (3) assumes that choice be induced by this scarcity.[21] Finally, Polanyi deplores the common exclusion from the term "economic" of nonscarce material goods and of nonmaterial scarce goods.[22]

---

[16] *Ibid.*, pp. 17-18.
[17] *Ibid.*, p. 22.
[18] *Ibid.*, p. 24.
[19] Karl Polanyi, "Anthropology and Economic Theory," in *Readings in Anthropology*, Vol. II: *Cultural Anthropology*, ed. Morton H. Fried (New York: Thomas Y. Crowell Company, 1959), p. 162.
[20] *Ibid.*, pp. 181-84.
[21] *Ibid.*, p. 165.
[22] *Ibid.*, p. 163.

To a large extent, this is a matter of defining what constitutes economic activity and what is being maximized. For example, the Kwakiutl of the Pacific Northwest attempted to maintain or attain position and status through giveaway rituals termed potlatches for which they acquired countless blankets and "copper" coins to be given or destroyed in order to impress or shame other Kwakiutl.[23] Codere interprets their behavior as follows:

> In what might be called their "economic life" the Kwakiutl are virtuoso technicians and extravagant producers and storers. It is in their "social life" that they "economize." [24]

In any case, Herskovits' and Polanyi's generalizations about economic activity in a variety of cultures provide a better understanding of what is common and what is proper to different milieus. This viewpoint will presently be applied to an analysis of a particular feature of American economic activity, namely profits.

*A Cross-Cultural Analysis of Profits in American Society.* Because of the threefold process of rapid social change, urbanization, and drastic technological change, few American adults live in the world in which they were reared. Accordingly, interpersonal behavior can be trusted less and less to one's automatic, learned sense of who people are or of what is the right thing to do. Instead of placing another person instantly by caste or class, religion, or occupation, as can be done in slowly changing traditional cultures where dress, speech, and demeanor all provide *clues*, modern American society presents an outward uniformity.[25]

There is, however, a yearning for clues in order to identify people, to make one's behavior intelligible, or to express membership in a particular group. In a symbol-impoverished

---

[23] Ruth Benedict, *Patterns of Culture* (New York: The New American Library, 1959), Ch. VI.

[24] Helen Codere, "Fighting With Property: A Study of Kwakiutl Potlatching and Warfare, 1792-1930," *Monographs of the American Ethnological Society*, XVIII (1950), p. 68. Quoted in Herskovits, *op. cit.*, pp. 19-20.

[25] Mead, *op. cit.*, pp. 244-45.

society such as the United States, money comes closer to being the universal standard of value than anything else.[26] Money provides a common denominator to all ends and means, not because people are greedy or materialistic *per se*, but because money is the main criterion available for ranking people, events, and institutions.[27]

The pursuit of profit represents one phase of this chase of the dollar for rank's sake, and it is quite commonly considered the aim of the institution called business. True to the tenets of cultural anthropology, language is quite revealing here. The very fact that some social units have to be especially tagged as "nonprofit" organizations indicates that they constitute an exception to a behavior considered customary. Other institutions are judged in terms of income, independently of any rationalization in terms of reward for performance or necessity for survival and growth.

The following discussion, however, will show that such a conception of profit is now undergoing change.

## The Historico-Cultural Approach to Economic Behavior

In the introduction of his essay on the American character,[28] David Potter points out that although behavioral scientists may use the culture to explain human behavior, they must rely upon history to explain the culture—unless a somewhat circular explanation *à la* White [29] is adopted. This is particularly true in the case of a society in a state of fairly rapid change. Such society and the behavior of its members cannot be explained except in terms of the process of change —and the concept of culture provides no means for such an explanation without the aid of history.

---

[26] Kluckhohn, *op. cit.*, p. 185.

[27] Erich Fromm, *The Sane Society* (New York: Rinehart & Company, Inc., 1955), pp. 114-18. Fromm discusses this phenomenon under the title "Quantification, Abstractification." George Santayana also has addressed himself to this subject.

[28] Potter, *op. cit.*, p. xxi.

[29] Leslie A. White, *The Science of Culture* (New York: Grove Press, Inc., 1949), Ch. VI. White maintains that culture must be explained in terms of culture and not in terms of people (p. 141). Other authors mostly disagree with such a view; see LaPiere, *op. cit.*, pp. 30-31.

The historical approach thus provides a dynamic view of a culture by showing its evolution and the forces that brought about such transformations. It records the norms, the ideas, and the institutions that used to prevail and those that displaced them, while attempting to describe the nature of the social change that took place.[30]

Besides explaining the changes, the historical approach provides some grounds for hypothesizing about future cultural developments. But, "this is another story," as Kipling used to say, and any argument about the predictive value of history might as well be left to professional jostlers in the field.

*A Historico-Cultural Analysis of Profits in American Society.* A score of economists, sociologists, and historians[31] have linked capitalism—the dominant form of business activity in the Western world—with Protestantism, and particularly with Calvinism and its notion of the "calling."

According to the Calvinistic doctrine of predestination, only a few will be saved. Meanwhile, the "elect" will be recognized by their success here on earth—especially in economic affairs. However, to be a legitimate proof of their election, success must be pursued and obtained continually and methodically, and it must not be enjoyed *per se.*

A later secular version of this sacred pursuit epitomizes the rational pursuit of profit in an American society known for its ability to make and to earn but not to enjoy the fruits of hard, methodical work—at least, not so far as males are concerned.

The formula, however, is now endangered by its very success. A society that prides itself on its productive talents and on its abundance can hardly keep denying itself full and happy consumption (or is there a rationale here for foreign aid?) Hence, the progressive discarding of old ideals and

---

[30] Potter, *op. cit.,* p. xvii.
[31] See, for example, Max Weber, *The Protestant Ethic and the Spirit of Capitalism* (New York: Charles Scribner's Sons, 1958), and R. H. Tawney, *Religion and the Rise of Capitalism* (New York: Harcourt, Brace & Company, 1926).

justifications and their replacement by new visions of man as a consumer (Fromm, Riesman), of industry as a provider of employment and income rather than as a manufacturer of goods (Galbraith), and of organizations as cooperative associations rather than as formal hierarchies (W. H. Whyte, Jr.).

In this new society, the traditional emphasis on profit maximization appears somewhat ludicrous. Besides, as Schumpeter remarked, the recognition of profit as reward for risk-taking and innovating may well seem *passé* in a society conditioned for change:

> It is much easier now than it has been in the past to do things that lie outside familiar routine—innovation itself is being reduced to routine. Technological progress is increasingly becoming the business of teams of trained specialists who turn out what is required and make it work in predictable ways. The romance of earlier commercial adventure is rapidly wearing away, because so many more things can be strictly calculated that had to be visualized in a flash of genius. On the other hand, personality and will power count for less in environments which have become accustomed to economic change . . . and which, instead of resisting, accept it as a matter of course.[32]

Society, then, is holding business to a new role in which profits still play a part, but only a subsidiary and diminishing one, other goals and other yardsticks, such as the dimly perceived "social responsibilities of business," being progressively applied to this institution.

### The Subcultural Approach to Economic Behavior

A third way to gain perspective in cultural matters is to distinguish and compare the various groups found in a culture. Mead prefers to consider such parts as "versions" of a major culture,[33] but other social scientists recognize them as "subcultures" with "cultural patterns which are real and

---

[32] Schumpeter, *op. cit.*, p. 132. Compare this quotation with some of the comments made by corporation trainees in William H. Whyte, Jr.'s *The Organization Man* (New York: Simon and Schuster, Inc., 1956).

[33] Mead, *op. cit.*, p. 209.

compelling only for special individuals or groups of individuals." [34] As a matter of fact, most people belong to several of these groups:

> The conduct of any actual American is only in part a reflection of his basic culture and is in far larger measure a reflection of the various and quite varying subcultures into which he has been socialized. [35]

Business—as an art and/or a profession—is such a subculture with its own primary groups, roles, status, and language. [36] A large part of this business subculture is indistinguishable from the general culture within which it operates. In other segments, however, conflict or at least disparity with society prevails—to the delight of moralists and novelists. [37]

This subculture itself is a mosaic of sub-subcultures which take different forms depending on how the "genus" business —like the proverbial bologna—is sliced into "species."

Numerous are the scholars who have discerned such varieties of businesses and business behaviors, from Max Weber and his trilogy of traditional capitalist, entrepreneurial capitalist, and pariah (or speculative) capitalist, [38] to Whyte's contrast of the organization man with the small businessman. [39] Not only are there small businesses, large corporations, lone speculators, and rentiers, but there are also species such as department stores and discount houses, railroad companies and pharmaceutical firms. In each case, there appear distinct patterns in matters such as the form of organization,

---

[34] Edward Sapir, *Culture, Language and Personality* (Berkeley: University of California Press, 1958), p. 155.

[35] LaPiere, *op. cit.*, p. 41.

[36] See, for example, the "businese" jargon described by William H. Whyte, Jr., in *Is Anybody Listening?* (New York: Simon and Schuster, Inc., 1952).

[37] There is a good illustration of this conflict in Thomas C. Cochran, *The American Business System; A Historical Perspective: 1900-1955* (Cambridge: Harvard University Press, 1957), pp. 198-199; or Kluckhohn, *op. cit.*, pp. 178-183.

[38] Weber, *op. cit.*, pp. 59-69, 166, 271.

[39] William H. Whyte, Jr., *The Organization Man, op. cit.*, p. 19, and *passim*.

the type of men who make the grade, or the choice of facts on which decisions are made.[40]

Subcultures, however, change as industries rise and fall. Individual companies themselves, besides playing endless variations on these industrial themes, display different behaviors during different phases of the business cycles.[41]

As can be seen, the subcultural approach ultimately leads to the atomization of business behavior, until finally only the behavior of a particular company, or group of companies, can be explained or predicted. This, however, is the essence of the cultural approach.

*A Subcultural Analysis of Profits in American Society.* An illustration of the subcultural approach is given by Bernstein in an article where he proposes to replace the traditional discussion of different *kinds* of profits by an analysis of different *makers* of profits (whose profits?). In the following quotations, he contrasts the distinct approaches to profit making that prevail in three industries: [42]

> In the chemical and pharmaceutical industries, for example, Schumpeter's theory [of innovation] seems to be especially appropriate. The pace of technological progress is very rapid, but the industry is also highly competitive. Huge profits are earned, for a relatively brief period of time, from the introduction of new products, but the competition soon cuts these profits down to nominal levels, and the maintenance of high earnings in the company depends upon the development of another new product. As a result of this process, these industries are probably the most daring and dynamic areas of the American economy today.

On the other hand,

> In the steel industry, monopoly (or, more properly oligopoly) is the basic determinant of profit. The dominant posi-

---

[40] Herbert A. Simon, "The Role of Expectations in an Adaptive or Behavioristic Model," in *Expectations, Uncertainty and Business Behavior*, ed. Mary Jean Bowman (New York: Social Science Research Council, 1955), pp. 53-55.

[41] John K. Galbraith, *American Capitalism* (Boston: Houghton Mifflin Company, 1952), p. 135.

[42] Peter L. Bernstein, "Profit Theory—Where Do We Go From Here?" *The Quarterly Journal of Economics* (August, 1953), pp. 412-13.

tion of a very few companies combined with the barrier to the entry of new firms, caused by the enormous amounts of fixed capital needed to set up a steel plant, definitely tend to keep earnings higher than they would be in a more fully competitive environment. The absence of competitive pressures and the fact that more profit accrues by shunning risks than by taking them makes the steel industry one of the least daring and dynamic in our economy.

## In retail distribution,

> Certain elements of monopolistic competition—particularly merchandising and spatial monopolies—are important . . . but a study of profits in the industry suggests that the influence of windfalls resulting from price changes may be the primary factor in setting the level of earnings.

Such different circumstances—themselves the products of past and present social forces—definitely shape different traditions or fit different temperaments.

## Conclusion

This inquiry into the nature and application of the cultural approach to economic and business behavior corroborates Dewey's observation that simple questions do not beget simple answers! In any case, the following conclusions can reasonably be drawn:

(1) The cultural approach and its cross-cultural, historico-cultural, and subcultural versions offer a multidimensional picture of the economic "genus" in place, time, and species. As such, it helps one to perceive the broadness and diversity of economic behavior above and beyond the simplified models of economic theory.

(2) Yet, the cultural approach is insufficient by itself. Not only does it require a socio-psychological theory to explain the interaction of individuals and their culture, but it cannot even claim to interpret satisfactorily all economic phenomena. Other theories are needed to refine gross cultural concept or to explain culture itself.

(3) Graver still: are cultural explanations too amorphous or atomized to be of any use? The search for a general theory of business attempts to replace simple economic models by something more substantial—yet of general application. The fact is, however, that—beyond recognizing the universality of the scarcity factor and of the rational process—the cultural approach proposes instead a variety of explanations to fit particular times, places, and circumstances.

But, is that bad?

It may well be that a realization of the diversity of economic and business behavior is exactly what is needed before business theory gets into "simplified" models of its own!

## BIBLIOGRAPHY

Benedict, Ruth. *Patterns of Culture*. New York: The New American Library of World Literature, Inc., 1959.

Bernstein, Peter L. "Profit Theory—Where Do We Go From Here?" *The Quarterly Journal of Economics* (August, 1953), pp. 407-422.

Bowman, Mary Jean (ed.). *Expectations, Uncertainty, and Business Behavior*. New York: Social Science Research Council, 1955.

Cochran, Thomas C. *The American Business System; A Historical Perspective: 1900-1955*. Cambridge: Harvard University Press, 1957.

Codere, Helen. "Fighting with Property: A Study of Kwakiutl Potlatching and Warfare, 1792-1930," *Monographs of the American Ethnological Society*, XVIII, 1950.

Fromm, Erich. *The Sane Society*. New York: Rinehart and Company, Inc., 1955.

Galbraith, John K. *The Affluent Society*. Boston: Houghton Mifflin Co., 1958.

—————. *American Capitalism*. Boston: Houghton Mifflin Co., 1952.

Gambs, John S. *Beyond Supply and Demand*. New York: Columbia University Press, 1946.

Harbison, Frederick, and Charles A. Myers. *Management in the Industrial World: An International Analysis*. New York: McGraw-Hill Book Company, Inc., 1959.

Herskovits, Melville J. *Economic Anthropology*, Second Edition. New York: Alfred A. Knopf, Inc., 1952.

Hickman, C. Addison, and Manford H. Kuhn. *Individuals, Groups and Economic Behavior*. New York: The Dryden Press, 1956.

Jordan, Elijah. *Business Be Damned*. New York: Henry Schuman, 1952.

Kluckhohn, Clyde. *Mirror for Man*. Greenwich: Fawcett Publications, Inc., 1959.

——————. "Common Humanity and Diverse Cultures," in *The Human Meaning of the Social Sciences*, ed. Daniel Lerner. New York: Meridian Books, The World Publishing Company, 1959.

Knight, Frank H. "Deduction and Induction in Economics," in *Economic Anthropology*, Second Edition. New York: Alfred A. Knopf, Inc., 1952.

LaPiere, Richard T. *A Theory of Social Control*. New York: McGraw-Hill Book Company, Inc., 1954.

Lerner, Daniel (ed.). *The Human Meaning of the Social Sciences*. New York: Meridian Books, The World Publishing Company, 1959.

McCary, J. L. (ed.). *Psychology and Personality*. New York: Grove Press, Inc., 1956.

Mead, Margaret. "The Cross-Cultural Approach to the Study of Personality," in *Psychology and Personality*, ed. J. L. McCary. New York: Grove Press, Inc., 1956.

Polanyi, Karl. "Anthropology and Economic Theory," in *Readings in Anthropology*. Vol. II, *Cultural Anthropology*, ed. Morton H. Fried. New York: Thomas Y. Crowell Company, 1959.

Potter, David M. *People of Plenty: Economic Abundance and the American Character*. Chicago: University of Chicago Press, 1954.

Riesman, David, *et al.* *The Lonely Crowd.* Garden City: Doubleday and Company, Inc., 1954.

Sapir, Edward. *Culture, Language and Personality.* Berkeley: University of California Press, 1958.

Schumpeter, Joseph A. *Capitalism, Socialism, and Democracy,* Third Edition Revised. New York: Harper & Brothers, 1950.

Simon, Herbert A. "The Role of Expectations in an Adaptive or Behavioristic Model," in *Expectations, Uncertainty and Business Behavior,* ed. Mary Jean Bowman. New York: Social Science Research Council, 1955.

Tawney, R. H. *Religion and the Rise of Capitalism.* New York: Harcourt, Brace & Company, 1926.

Veblen, Thorstein. *The Theory of Business Enterprise.* New York: The New American Library of World Literature, Inc., 1958.

Weber, Max. *The Protestant Ethic and the Spirit of Capitalism.* New York: Charles Scribner's Sons, 1958.

White, Leslie A. *The Science of Culture.* New York: Grove Press, Inc., 1949.

Whyte, William H., Jr. *Is Anybody Listening?* New York: Simon and Schuster, Inc., 1952.

—————. *The Organization Man.* New York: Simon and Schuster, 1956.

Wootton, Barbara. *Lament for Economics.* London: George Allen & Unwin, Ltd., 1938.

# Chapter 12

# HOW SHOULD BUSINESS BEHAVE?

Richard Robinson

---

## Introduction

In volumes of testimony before Congressional committees, in popular novels, in movies, in textbooks, in television presentations, and in reams of newspaper copy, business has been seen as evil and has been attacked. And the emphasis of these attacks has been on its morality. "Capitalism is being attacked not because it is inefficient or misgoverned, but because it is cynical." [1] Glover enlarges on this point by saying, "Of the three planes of criticism of big business, it is this one concerned with ethical and moral values, this one which expresses ethical and moral convictions and assumptions, which is the most basic." [2]

These charges have caused great concern about the morality of business. Symptoms of this concern are to be found everywhere. A tremendous number of articles and books have been written on this topic. Practically every issue of the *Harvard Business Review* for the past few years has had at least one article on the ethical problems of business. Evidence of this concern is also shown by the growing recognition of morality in management creeds and business philosophies.[3] Indeed, "one of the most heartening signs of our times is the

---

[1] P. Drucker as quoted by O. A. Ohmann, "Search for a Managerial Philosophy," *Harvard Business Review*, Vol. 35, No. 5 (September-October, 1957), p. 43.

[2] J. D. Glover, *The Attack on Big Business* (Boston: Harvard University Press, 1954), p. 210.

[3] Francis Sutton, Seymour Harris, Carl Kaysen, and James Tobin, *The American Business Creed* (Cambridge: Harvard University Press, 1956); Steward Thompson, "Management Creeds and Philosophies," and Carl Stover, "Changing Patterns in the Philosophy of Management." *The Executive*, Vol. II, No. 4 (September, 1958).

growing concern of businessmen with the ethical implications of their work." [4] The same concern is held by the National Council of Churches, which is conducting a study on Christian ethics and economic life.[5]

*Reasons for Concern.* Certainly these attacks on business morality are nothing new. Indeed, business has always been blamed for one thing or another. Consequently, the business executive should be confident in himself and capitalism. "On the contrary, we see on every hand doubt, insecurity, uncertainty." [6] Why should this be? Why should the businessman be concerned now?

Though there are many probable answers to these questions, a better understanding of business morality may be had by examining some of the reasons for this uneasiness. One view is that these attacks have pressured business into introspection.[7] It is argued that the public has condemned business as a whole. Therefore, the truth about individual businessmen is disregarded. Unfavorable incidents, such as bribery of government officials and collusion with union officers, have intensified the public charges against business. Unable to stem these outcries, the reaction of business has been a questioning of its moral values.

Another possible explanation for this present concern is society's suspicion of power. "People believe that success begets power, and that power is too likely to be used for evil purposes." [8] This feeling is also shared by businessmen. "It may be that we shall find that it is the very possession of power that causes the fear and confusion which besets us." [9]

[4] Benjamin Selekman, "Cynicism and Managerial Morality," *Harvard Business Review*, Vol. 36, No. 5 (September-October, 1958), p. 61.

[5] John Bennett, Howard Bowen, William Brown, and G. Bromley Oxnam, *Christian Values and Economic Life* (New York: Harper & Brothers, 1954), p. vii.

[6] Marquis Childs and Douglas Cater, *Ethics in a Business Society* (New York: The New American Library, 1954), p. 6.

[7] E. Learned, A. Dooley, and R. Katz, "Personal Values and Business Decisions," *Harvard Business Review*, Vol. 37, No. 2 (March-April, 1959), p. 111.

[8] Robert Dunlop, "A Perspective for Business Leadership," *The Executive*, Vol. I, No. 1 (June, 1957), p. 28.

[9] Sylvia Selekman and Benjamin Selekman, *Power and Morality in a Business Society* (New York: McGraw-Hill Book Company, Inc., 1956), p. 16.

In this perplexing position, business has been seeking other values to resolve its anxiety over power.

Of course, it is highly probable that the trend toward a greater interest in morality is just another characteristic of our period. This is "a time that has lent itself to the 'luxuries of conscience.' " [10] Now that success has been achieved, the businessman has the opportunity to concern himself with other values.

A symptom of our age is the swift and irresistible pace of events. Some express fear that this has made man surrender his destiny to forces beyond his control.[11] Rather than be overwhelmed, man has been looking for something, spiritual values, to enable him to live in this maelstrom of history. "The evidences of modern man's search for his soul are all about us." [12]

Another reason for the concern for moral values is business's great accumulation of wealth. The effect of the public's attacks has caused businessmen to doubt, to lose confidence in themselves and capitalism. Consequently, they have a guilt complex about their successes. They wonder if what they do is right, and seek a moral basis for their actions. In the words of one group of writers, "all manifestations of interest in ultimate values (particularly those which have been associated with outstandingly successful business careers) are an attempt to 'buy respectability.' " [13]

It is also entirely possible that this concern is the natural result of the businessman's search for himself. An executive is no different from any other man. He wants a clear definition of life. "As a man, he shares the universal trait of wanting to be certain that his life has meaning and purpose." [14] Perhaps, then, the executive has just begun to realize that he can't live "by bread alone."

---

[10] Learned, Dooley, and Katz, *op. cit.*, p. 112.
[11] Childs and Cater, *op. cit.*, p. 63.
[12] O. A. Ohmann, "Skyhooks," *Harvard Business Review*, Vol. 33, No. 3 (May-June, 1955), p. 34.
[13] Learned, Dooley, and Katz, *op. cit.*, p. 111.
[14] *Ibid.*, p. 112.

There is probably an element of truth in each of these various views on the concern of business with its moral values. Nevertheless, regardless of the specific reason, it is evident that businessmen do desire a moral basis for their actions. They want to know the ethical principles which can be applied to business behavior.

In this chapter, several moral concepts which endeavor to provide ethical standards for business decisions and actions will be explored. In making this examination, the confusion which exists in this area should become evident. Instead of one clear-cut code for business to follow, there are many. It is contended that this condition is the fault of society, not of business.

## Ethics and Business Morality

Through the timeless ages, rules of social conduct have grown and evolved into what we call ethics or moral responsibility. Since the study of ethics is concerned with the proper patterns of human behavior, its standards are constantly changing with man and his culture. Consequently, it is difficult to properly define this changing moral responsibility. To avoid a senseless discussion on this point and to provide a guide for our thinking, ethics will be defined as: "The art or science of man's efforts to live in a proper harmonious relationship with other men, groups, or institutions; and the study of his moral responsibility to discern the rightness or wrongness of his actions." [15]

This definition has some implications which are important to this study. First, the individual has a basic responsibility for making ethical decisions. Even though society sets up proper standards of conduct and controls conduct through fear of expulsion, the individual must decide the propriety of his own actions within himself. Second, ethics include what should be, as well as what is. These implications create many conflicts within the individual and the society, and between the individual and society.

---

[15] J. Whitney Bunting, (ed.), *Ethics for Modern Business Practice* (New York: Prentice-Hall, Inc., 1953), p. 5.

*Religion and Ethics.* In discussing this concept of ethical responsibility, some individuals feel that ethics must be based on religious or legal codes. Since the Christian doctrine has been concerned with the proper manner of living, religion has endeavored to build a code of ethical principles to govern daily conduct. However, in addition to this, Christian doctrine decides the proper course for moral action. For example, the Golden Rule indicates not only what is morally right but what the individual should do. Thus, for the most part, the individual is removed from the necessity of making the moral decision. At the same time, religion acts as a control force for the acceptance of moral codes. With this in mind, the individual must decide for himself whether or not his ethical code should be based on religious concepts.

*Law and Ethics.* Society has also developed, over the years, legal codes for governing human behavior. Unfortunately, these regulations do not entirely solve the moral problems of the community. Moral dilemmas appear only in the mind of each individual. Consequently, in order to control the innumerable cases that might occur from these perceptions, the public would have to pass an infinite number of regulations. For this reason, society should not forget that it is practically impossible to govern the ethical behavior of people or institutions by legislation.

*Moral Concepts.* Although this is a study of the ethical behavior of business, general theories of moral thought are pertinent to this subject. Unfortunately, there are far too many and varied interpretations of ethical theory for separate consideration. For simplification, the philosophies of idealism and materialism will be emphasized. It is recognized that the possible danger here is over-simplification. Nevertheless, this is not an arbitrary classification. "Since the fifth century before Christ, (these) two great tendencies in philosophy have ever opposed and reacted upon each other." [16]

---

[16] Lewis Haney, *History of Economic Thought,* Fourth and Enlarged Edition (New York: The Macmillan Company, 1949), p. 8.

In a strict sense, idealism is based on the philosophy in which the objects of perception are actually ideas of the perceiving mind, so that it is impossible to know whether reality exists apart from the mind.[17] As applied to ethics, this doctrine has come to regard "man, not as a creature of material environment, but as a more or less independent force, capable of adapting or conquering nature."[18] It is in this role that man has the definite responsibility of loving God and his neighbors as himself. Idealists, then, are guided in moral actions by spiritual values and social responsibility.

The materialist believes that the individual is dominated by his environment. "The materialistic tendency not only regards matter as existing independently of mind, but may go so far as to deny the existence of anything but matter."[19] Practically speaking, the materialist, then, is more concerned with material matters and his well-being than with spiritual values. Control of moral actions is therefore vested with the individual. "We find the thorough-going materialist formulating his doctrine of right and wrong with an eye to the problems of adjustment to material environment, advocating that men do unto one another such things as will enable them to survive, and finding in 'survival' the test to right."[20]

Idealism and materialism should not be regarded as complete dichotomies. They are not entirely unrelated and independent of one another. "These two philosophical tendencies represent two sides of human social life, and they constantly react upon one another."[21] It should also be noted that each concept is composed of many different degrees of thinking. Thus, it is sometimes difficult to label or differentiate moral concepts as being completely either idealistic or materialistic.

## Present Theories of Business Morality

These two ethical philosophies, idealism and materialism, may be used to provide an understanding of the moral be-

---

[17] *Ibid.*, p. 9.
[18] Albert Avey, *Handbook in the History of Philosophy* (New York: Barnes and Noble, Inc., 1954), p. 287.
[19] Haney, *op. cit.*, p. 10.
[20] *Ibid.*, p. 12.
[21] *Ibid.*, p. 18.

havior of business. In making this application, idealists have taken the stand that our industrial civilization is not good because its values are of the wrong order. Business has been concerned only with material gain. "Economic expediency is taken to be the sole criterion of decision." [22] Therefore, according to idealists, business is evil.

The absolute materialist, on the other hand, believes that economic expediency is a just standard for business decisions. By maximizing its project objectives, business will gratify its personal desires and, at the same time, satisfy the needs of society. As a result, business should not have any responsibility beyond obeying certain legal codes in achieving its goals.

Based to some extent on these thoughts, present theories of business morality develop conflicting recommendations to correct these supposed evils.

*Idealistic Views.* There are a number of idealists—Tawney, Jordan, Marx, *et al.*—who support the position that business is evil because of its materialistic desires. Since these theorists all, more or less, suggest the same remedial action for this immorality, Tawney has been arbitrarily selected to symbolize their viewpoint. He first remarks, "Compromise is impossible between the Church of Christ and the idolatry of wealth, which is the practical religion of capitalist societies, as it was between the Church and the State idolatry of the Roman Empire." [23] Continuing in this vein, he feels that the obsession with material gain or the idolatry of wealth is a poison. Accordingly, he states:

> Society will not solve the particular problems of industry which conflict it until that poison is expelled and it has learned to see industry itself in the right perspective. If it is to do that, it must rearrange its scale of values. It must regard economic interests as one element of life, not as the whole of life.[24]

---

[22] Glover, *op. cit.*, p. 229.
[23] R. H. Tawney, *Religion and the Rise of Capitalism* (New York: The New American Library, 1926), p. 235.
[24] R. H. Tawney, *The Acquisitive Society* (New York: Harcourt, Brace & Company, 1920), p. 184.

Tawney believed that business would not rearrange its scale of values, for he further indicated that business should be controlled by the community.[25] Business would then be governed by those who are responsible to the people. Hence, because of the immorality of business standards, these philosophies would advocate a socialistic change in our industrial society.

In rebuttal, Knight makes a plea for understanding our own business system before taking any modifying action. He warns that a free democratic society cannot exist in the atmosphere advocated by these idealists.[26]

*Social Responsibility.* There are other idealists who disagree with Tawney. While they also deplore the *laissez faire* pursuit of individual self-interest, their concept centers around the possibilities of businessmen being controlled by a conscience which prompts them to consider their responsibilities to the welfare of society. These idealists do not contemplate a change in the economic system.

In recent years there has been much soul-searching about the social role of business. "The social and moral responsibilities of industry have become a major concern of the American businessmen during the past quarter of a century." [27] This point is further illustrated by a recent study of the social responsibilities of businessmen.[28] In this latter work, Bowen emphasizes that the degree of influence and power that the businessman exercises over the lives of others places upon him a moral responsibility to recognize the social implications of his decisions and to consider their social interest, with their private interest, in making his decisions. Social responsibility is, however, not definable. "My reluctance to attempt definitive formulations of the social responsibilities of businessmen has been based on a belief that the way to greater responsiveness of businessmen toward their social

---

[25] *Ibid.*, pp. 6-7.
[26] Frank Knight, *Economic Freedom and Social Responsibility* (University Center, Georgia: Emory University Press, 1952), p. 2.
[27] Selekman and Selekman, *op. cit.*, p. vii.
[28] Howard R. Bowen, *Social Responsibilities of Businessmen* (New York: Harper & Brothers, 1952).

obligations lies in the processes of broadly based discussion and individual soul-searching on the part of actual participants—not in the spelling out of 'answers' by outside observers." [29]

There are some businessmen who support this thesis of social responsibility. For example, Charles Percy, president of Bell and Howell Company, believes that the responsibility of business goes beyond making products for a profit. "Businessmen are also obliged to serve society," [30] says Percy.

There are several other reasons for the emphasis on social responsibilities. For example, some writers feel that responsibility is necessary to justify the existence of business to society. It is the businessman's social obligation for his freedom to exercise the right of private property. Others believe that responsibility is based on the Christian doctrine of the welfare of society. These philosophers feel that social responsibility is the chosen path to be followed by business if it seeks to attain a moral basis for its actions. Business would then become a contributor to social welfare rather than a parasite preying upon it.[31]

*Materialistic Views.* There is another group of writers, such as Levitt, who tend to take an individualistic view of business morality in opposition to the philosophy of social responsibility. "Business has only two responsibilities—to obey the elementary canons of everyday, face-to-face civility (honesty, good faith, and so on) and to seek material gain." [32] He continues his attack by saying, "Welfare and society are not the corporation's business. Its business is making money." [33] Business, therefore, can be of the greatest service to society by maximizing its profits. If business once begins to serve the public, it will never be able to serve enough. Levitt regards this moral conflict as a life-and-death struggle

[29] *Ibid.*, p. xi.
[30] *Time*, Vol. LXXIII, No. 19 (May 11, 1959), p. 93.
[31] John Clark, *The Ethical Basis of Economic Freedom* (Westport, Conn.: The Calvin K. Kazanjian Economics Foundation, Inc., 1955), p. 26.
[32] T. Levitt, "The Dangers of Social Responsibility," *Harvard Business Review*, Vol. 36, No. 5 (September-October, 1958), p. 49.
[33] *Ibid.*, p. 47.

between the business's interests and society's welfare. "Business must fight as if it were at war. And, like a good war, it should be fought gallantly, daringly, and above all, not morally." [35] This is Levitt's view on the morality of business.

There are others who tend to agree with this theory. One of these writers, Selekman, states his views as follows:

> Would it not serve the public interest best to restore the businessman to his traditional role as a creator of wealth, to respect him as such, to pay (but not overpay) him what he is worth in terms of relative service to the community, and to encourage him to go forward with the greatest possible speed in the job we entrust to him—the creation of as strong a material foundation as possible for our society? [35]

Even so, there is more an implied moral basis here for the businessman than under Levitt's philosophy.

> Finally, we hold strongly to a sense of community, of fellowship, indeed of communion. We aspire to a moral climate in which the community and communion are interchangeable, in which we all share the glory as well as the pain, the gains as well as the sacrifices of a democratic, Judaeo-Christian nation.[36]

Before passing on, one may certainly wonder how Selekman would reconcile his divergent thoughts. Where would he draw the line between the individual's interests and the welfare of society?

In comparing these theories, the various arguments resolve once again into the age-old differences between idealism and materialism. At this period of our culture, is the individual and his interests or society and its welfare more important? To resolve this philosophical issue, there is another theory, pragmatism, which is worth considering.

*Pragmatic Views.* Followers of this concept subscribe to the thought that the test of truth of a belief is in the way

---

[34] *Ibid.*, p. 50.
[35] Benjamin Selekman, "Sin Bravely: The Danger of Perfectionism," *Harvard Business Review*, Vol. 37, No. 1 (January-February, 1959), p. 118.
[36] Benjamin Selekman, "Is Management Creating a Class Society?" *Harvard Business Review*, Vol. 36, No. 1 (January-February, 1958), p. 39.

in which it works. This test is left to the judgment of the believer in the idea. This is best interpreted by Childs and Cater in *Ethics in a Business Society.*[37]

These writers agree with Bowen in the importance of social responsibility. Nevertheless, the businessman's first responsibility is to keep his business solvent.[38] A bankrupt business will not serve him, his family, or society. They contend that the individual is the one who must resolve this conflict between his interests and society's desires.

> Man alone is capable of asking what he will do with his life; with the little span of time allotted to him. And likewise he can help to shape the society of which he is a part for good or ill. It is this God-given choice that sets man apart and enables him in the face of an infinite universe to call his soul his own.[39]

At the same time, they bluntly state that the businessman should not depend on a policy of *laissez faire.* If he did so, he would find little to guide him when confronted with a moral issue. This view, of course, doesn't resolve the dilemma of what values will guide the individual in making his decision on the relative importance of the responsibilities.

## The Religious Approach to Business Morality

There are many who advocate that religion can provide the necessary moral basis for business behavior. Since religion endeavors to provide a meaning for life and to aid man in meeting his crises in life, it can exert a powerful influence in man's conduct.[40]

In the past, religion has had a tremendous impact on the morality of business. Unfortunately, religious concepts have lost some of their relevance. In referring to the difficulties of applying these concepts to modern-day problems, one author says, "The situations posed have become unreal, the dilemmas

---

[37] Childs and Cater, *op. cit.*
[38] *Ibid.,* p. 179.
[39] *Ibid.*
[40] Francis Merrill and H. Wentworth Eldredge, *Culture and Society* (New York: Prentice-Hall, Inc., 1952), p. 477.

have become unimportant, and the proposed solutions help us not at all in the way of life into which we are forced by conditions of our time." [41] This condition has led to a separation of business morality from religion which can best be seen from a consideration of the concept of self-interest, under which the businessman has no responsibility to anyone but himself.

The divorce between religion and business has created a morality vacuum which has led to an increasing awareness of the need for a modern application of religious thought to business behavior.[42] Worthy, in discussing religion and business, indicates that we are badly in need of a more adequate frame of reference for business; we need to define the relationship of man, his faith, and business, and we need to establish Christian principles to guide businessmen.[43]

Before this can be done, there are those who say that religion must endeavor to understand business. Since there are some religious leaders who still have the attitudes of the past, this indeed poses a problem. Even Pope John XXIII regards business as being materialistic.[44] In so doing, he and others tend to support Tawney's position. However, the situation isn't hopeless. Writing in the *Harvard Business Review*, Campbell concludes that religion can provide a framework of principles and values for business. "Given a sense of confidence in the harmonious relationship between religion and our capitalistic system, each businessman can proceed to work out his own code and operating philosophy for his own situation." [45] And, it is interesting to note, some religious leaders are conducting studies to determine these relevant principles.[46]

---

[41] Rexford Tugwell (ed.), *The Trend of Economics* (New York: F. J. Crofts and Co., 1930), p. 382.

[42] Wayne Broehl, "Looking Around: Do Religion and Business Mix?" *Harvard Business Review*, Vol. 36, No. 2 (March-April, 1958).

[43] James Worthy, "Religion and Its Role in the World of Business," *The Journal of Business*, Vol. XXXI, No. 4 (October, 1958).

[44] Associated Press dispatch, April 23, 1959.

[45] Thomas Campbell, "Capitalism and Christianity," *Harvard Business Review*, Vol. 35, No. 4 (July-August, 1957), p. 44.

[46] Bennett, Bowen, Brown, and Oxnam, *op. cit.*

## Conclusion

In presenting these moral concepts for consideration, there is no attempt to indicate the preferable moral philosophy for business. There are far too many writers who are doing this at the present time. Instead, this decision is left for the businessman to make for himself.

Nevertheless, the businessman has the responsibility to be concerned with the morality of his decisions and actions. To fulfill this obligation, he must judge the propriety of his own behavior. And in so doing, the businessman must follow those ethical values which are consistent with those of his society.

Here, then, is the problem which plagues business: What are these ethical standards? Society has partially answered this question by formulating many codes of behavior. Unfortunately, when applied to business situations, they are often in conflict with each other. Even though there is the desire to do right, what is right?

For not knowing the answer to this question, business shouldn't be condemned as being immoral. If so, then there are other segments of our society, such as labor unions, governmental institutions, sports organizations, entertainment activities, etc., which should also be similarly judged. This problem of moral decay is not the sole responsibility of business organizations. Instead, this should be regarded as a problem of society.

Society determines the customs of its members. The behavior of business is merely a reflection of society's mores. Consequently, failure to maintain the proper standards of conduct is partly the failure of society to provide the necessary codes. Instead of indicating a morality of right or wrong, society has presented business with a profusion of vague and conflicting rules. The result has been chaos for the businessman. Thus, before attacking business for being immoral, or amoral, society must first establish definitive, applicable ethical codes for business behavior.

However, in spite of society's failure to determine these standards, it is hopeful to realize that businessmen are becoming concerned, are recognizing that these moral problems do exist, and are seeking answers to these problems.

## BIBLIOGRAPHY

Angell, Robert. "Free Society and Moral Crises," *The Executive*, 2, 6 (November, 1958), pp. 9-11.

Aristotle. *On Man in the Universe*. New York: Classics Club, 1943.

Avey, Albert. *Handbook in the History of Philosophy*. New York: Barnes & Noble, Inc., 1954.

Barnard, Chester. *Elementary Conditions of Business Morals*. Committee on the Barbara Weinstock Lectures. Berkeley, Calif.: University of California Press, 1958.

Bennett, John, Howard R. Bowen, William Brown, and G. Bromley Oxnam. *Christian Values and Economic Life*. New York: Harper & Brothers, 1954.

Boulding, Kenneth. "The Image," *The Executive*, 1, 4 (September, 1957), pp. 8-9.

———————. "Religious Foundations of Economic Progress," *Harvard Business Review*, 30, 3 (May-June, 1952), pp. 33-40.

Bowen, Howard R. *Social Responsibilities of Businessmen*. New York: Harper & Brothers, 1953.

Broehl, Wayne. "Ethics and the Executive: The Small Decisions that Count," *Dun's Review and Modern Industry*, 69, 7 (May, 1957), pp. 45, 122-124.

———————. "Looking Around: Do Business and Religion Mix?" *Harvard Business Review*, 36, 4 (March-April, 1958), pp. 139-146, 151-152.

Bunting, J. Whitney (ed.). *Ethics for Modern Business Practice*. New York: Prentice-Hall, Inc., 1953.

Campbell, Thomas. "Capitalism and Christianity," *Harvard Business Review*, 35, 4 (July-August, 1957), pp. 37-44.

Childs, Marquis, and Douglas Cater. *Ethics in a Business Society*. New York: The New American Library of World Literature, Inc., 1954.

Clark, John. *The Ethical Basis of Economic Freedom*. Westport, Conn.: The Calvin K. Kazanjian Economics Foundation, Inc., 1955.

Cleveland, Harlan. "Dinosaurs and Personal Freedom," *The Executive*, 2, 11 (April, 1959), pp. 14-15.

Cole, A. "Transcendental Aspects of Business," *Harvard Business Review*, 36, 5 (September-October, 1958), pp. 51-60.

Collier, A. "Faith in a Creative Society," *Harvard Business Review*, 35, 3 (May-June, 1957), pp. 35-41.

Colwell, David. "Toward More Effective Community Action," *The Executive*, 2, 11 (April, 1959), pp. 17-18.

Dampier, Sir William. *A History of Science and Its Relations with Philosophy and Religion*, Fourth Edition. Cambridge, England: Cambridge University Press, 1952.

De Rougemont, Denis. "The World Role of Western Values," *The Executive*, 1, 4 (February, 1958), pp. 31-32.

Dimock, Marshall. "A Philosophy of Administration: Toward Creative Growth," *The Executive*, 2, 7 (December, 1958), pp. 5-9.

Dunlop, Robert. "A Perspective for Business Leadership," *The Executive*, 1, 1 (June, 1957), pp. 28-29.

Ericson, R. "Should Management Be Idealistic?" *Harvard Business Review*, 36, 5 (September-October, 1958), pp. 144-156.

Finn, D. "Struggle for Ethics in Public Relations," *Harvard Business Review*, 37, 1 (January-February, 1959), pp. 49-58.

Fisher, Burton, and Stephen Withey. *Big Business as the People See It*. Ann Arbor: University of Michigan Press, 1951.

Galbraith, John. *The Affluent Society*. Boston: Houghton Mifflin Co., 1958.

Glover, J. D. *The Attack on Big Business*. Boston: Harvard University Press, 1954.

Gossett, William. "The Role of the Corporate Conscience," *The Executive*, 1, 2 (July, 1957), p. 10.

Greenwalt, Crawford. "The Culture of the Businessman," *The Executive*, 1, 3 (August, 1957), pp. 18-19.

——————. "The Uncommon Man," *The Executive*, 2, 11 (April, 1959), pp. 12-13.

Haney, Lewis. *History of Economic Thought*, Fourth and Enlarged Edition. New York: The Macmillan Company, 1949.

Harris, Abram. *Economics and Social Reform*. New York: Harper & Brothers, 1958.

Heermance, E. L. *The Ethics of Business*. New York: Harper & Brothers, 1926.

Higgins, George. "Social Aspects of Automation," *The Executive*, 2, 7 (December, 1958), pp. 9-10.

Hollingum, Jack, Moses Parker, and A. Falden. "The Church and Automation," *The Executive*, 1, 2 (July, 1957), pp. 15-16.

Houser, Theodore V. "Big Business and Human Values," *The Executive*, 1, 9 (February, 1958), pp. 4-5.

Johnson, Harold. "An Evaluation of the Social Responsibility of Businessmen Concept," *The Executive*, 1, 2 (July, 1957), pp. 21-22.

Jordan, Elijah. *Business Be Damned*. New York: Henry Schuman, Inc., 1952.

Kelso, L., and M. Adler. *The Capitalist Manifesto*. New York: Random House, 1958.

Knight, Frank. *Economic Freedom and Social Responsibility*. University Center, Georgia: Emory University Press, 1952.

Learned, E., A. Dooley, and R. Katz. "Personal Values and Business Decisions," *Harvard Business Review*, 37, 2 (March-April, 1959), pp. 111-120.

Levitt, T. "The Dangers of Social Responsibility," *Harvard Business Review*, 36, 5 (September-October, 1958), pp. 41-50.

Lewis, W. Arthur. *The Theory of Economic Growth.* Home-wood, Ill.: Richard D. Irwin Company, Inc., 1955.

Lippmann, Walter. *A Preface to Morals.* New York: The Macmillan Company, 1929.

Littlejohn, Edward. "The Heirs of the Robber Barons," *The Executive,* 2, 1 (June, 1958), pp. 25-27.

MacPhee, E. D. "The Conscience of Business," *The Executive,* 1, 2 (July, 1957), pp. 17-18.

Merrill, Francis, and H. Wentworth Eldredge. *Culture and Society.* New York: Prentice-Hall, Inc., 1952.

Nordling, Rolf. "Social Responsibilities of Today's Industrial Leaders," *Advanced Management,* XXII, 4 (April, 1957), pp. 18-22.

Ohmann, O. A. "Search for a Managerial Philosophy," *Harvard Business Review,* 35, 5 (September-October, 1957), pp. 41-51.

——————. "Skyhooks," *Harvard Business Review,* 33, 3 (May-June, 1955), pp. 33-41.

Parsons, Talcott. *The Structure of Social Action.* Glencoe, Ill.: The Free Press, 1949.

Potter, David. "People's Capitalism," *The Executive,* 1, 3 (August, 1957), pp. 6-7.

Randall, J. H. *The Making of the Modern Mind.* New York: Houghton Mifflin Company, 1942.

Robinson, Daniel. *The Principles of Conduct.* New York: Appleton-Century-Crofts, Inc., 1948.

Roll, Eric. *A History of Economic Thought,* Revised Edition. New York: Prentice-Hall, Inc., 1942.

Samuelson, Paul, Robert Bishop, and John Coleman (eds.). *Readings in Economics,* Second Edition. New York: McGraw-Hill Book Company, Inc., 1955.

Selekman, Benjamin. "Cynicism and Managerial Morality," *Harvard Business Review,* 36, 5 (September-October, 1958), pp. 61-71.

——————. "Is Management Creating a Class Society?" *Harvard Business Review,* 36, 1 (January-February, 1958), pp. 37-46.

————. "Sin Bravely: The Danger of Perfectionism," *Harvard Business Review*, 37, 1 (January-February, 1959), pp. 105-118.

Selekman, Sylvia, and Benjamin Selekman. *Power and Morality in a Business Society*. New York: McGraw-Hill Book Company, Inc., 1955.

Sharp, Frank, and Philip Fox. *Business Ethics*. New York: Appleton-Century-Crofts, Inc., 1948.

Spencer, Daniel. "Dare We Renege? The Social Responsibility of Business in the World Scene," *Business Horizons*, 1, 4 (1958), pp. 38-47.

Stover, Carl. "Changing Patterns in the Philosophy of Management," *The Executive*, 2, 4 (September, 1958), pp. 9-10.

Sutton, Francis, Seymour Harris, Carl Kaysen, and James Tobin. *The American Business Creed*. Cambridge: Harvard University Press, 1956.

Taeusch, C. F. *Policy and Ethics in Business*. New York: McGraw-Hill Book Company, Inc., 1931.

Tawney, R. H. *The Acquisitive Society*. New York: Harcourt, Brace & Co., 1920.

————. *Religion and the Rise of Capitalism*. New York: The New American Library of World Literature, Inc., 1926.

Thompson, Steward. "Management Creeds and Philosophies," *The Executive*, 2, 4 (September, 1958), pp. 25-26.

Tugwell, Rexford (ed.). *The Trend of Economics*. New York: F. J. Crofts and Company, 1930.

Urwick, Lyndall. "The Pattern of Management," *The Executive*, 1, 1 (June, 1957), pp. 9-10.

Whyte, William H. *The Organization Man*. New York: Simon and Schuster, Inc., 1956.

Wilbur, John. "The Dignity of the Individual in the Twentieth Century," *The Executive*, 2, 1 (June, 1958), pp. 21-22.

Worthy, James. "Freedom within American Enterprise," *Advanced Management*, XIX, 6 (June, 1954), pp. 5-8.

————. "Religion and Its Role in the World of Business," *The Journal of Business*, XXXI, 4 (October, 1958), pp. 293-303.

# Chapter 13

# A BEHAVIORAL APPROACH TO THE THEORY OF BUSINESS

David L. Huff

## Introduction

This chapter suggests the lines along which an effort might be made to formulate the kind of systematic strategy necessary for deriving generalizations and principles about business behavior.

The core of the analysis involves an examination of human decision making as the primary causal force affecting business behavior. Since some of the most important decisions from a social and economic viewpoint are made in business firms, the study will focus its attention on individual decision making within the firm.

Unlike the traditional economic theory of the firm, which also has decision making as its basis, the present study does not assume that business decisions are largely determined by variables related to the external environment of the firm, e.g., the market. Rather, it assumes that the behavior of the firm is primarily a function of endogenous variables related to individual decision makers. The primary objective of this investigation, then, is to attempt: (1) to ascertain the significant variables that affect the decisions of individuals within the business firm; (2) to integrate these variables into a logical framework that could serve as a foundation for the subsequent development of a unified theory of individual business decision making, which in turn would provide the basis for a general theory of business behavior. An effort has been made to formulate this theoretical framework in such a manner that it possesses sufficient generality to be applied in principle to any process of individual business decision making in any given environment.

## Significance of This Chapter

The *general* approach which is being taken in this study does not claim to be unique. Certainly a large number of writers have recognized, at least implicitly, the possible value of using decision making as the core for a general theory of business behavior. The sizeable body of literature that has emerged in recent years concerning the process of business decision making testifies to the preceding statement.[1] However, most of these works have approached decision making from a single perspective, *e.g.*, economic, psychological, sociological, etc. The heuristic value of each of these works is not to be denied, but taken together, they still do not possess the "mosaic" necessary to encompass, as a whole, the cultural, economic, psychological, and social determinants of human action within the business setting. Furthermore, it seems reasonable to assert that without an organized and systematized theoretical framework to first give overall direction to the design, testing, analysis, and synthesis of research efforts in business decision making, accumulation of still more material will not necessarily fulfill this objective either. Therefore, if the approach taken in this study can provide the degree of generality necessary to supply the foundation for a comprehensive explanation of business decision making, it does have grounds for making the claim that it has made a contribution toward a greater theoretical understanding of business behavior. Its real relevance, however, will have to be determined subsequently on how capable it is as compared to the traditional economic theory of the firm in terms of explaining actual empirical business behavior.

Immediately following this introductory discussion, a review is presented of current theoretical concepts pertaining

---

[1] Paul Wasserman and Fred S. Silander, *Decision-Making: An Annotated Bibliography*, Graduate School of Business and Public Administration (Ithaca, N. Y.: Cornell University Press, 1958).

to human decision making. Such a review is designed to assist in providing the insights necessary for formulating and evaluating the broader theoretical frame of reference which follows.

## Behavioral Frames of Reference

Basically, three primary behavioral frames of reference have been employed to analyze and explain human decision making, or more broadly, human behavior: (1) psychoanalytical, (2) psychological, and (3) social and cultural.

*Psychoanalytical.* Psychoanalysis is basically a biological theory of personality. Its theoretical foundation is based, for the most part, on the concepts and methods advanced by Sigmund Freud. Various manifestations of human behavior are regarded as originating from neurological and physiological functions of man. That is, the structure of the central nervous system of man influences various specific and fixed reactions patterns, and the physiological factor affects various biological needs or drives such as sex, hunger, sleep, thirst, etc. Human behavior, as viewed from this frame of reference, is fundamentally self-interested. Man is interested primarily in satisfying his given biological drives. The relationships of man to others in his society as viewed from this theoretical perspective is well stated by Erich Fromm:

> These relations as Freud sees them are similar to the economic relations to others which are characteristic of the individual in a capitalistic society. Each person works for himself, individualistically at his own risk, and not primarily in cooperation with others. But he is not a Robinson Crusoe; he needs others as customers, as employees, or as employers. He must buy and sell, give and take. The market, whether it is the commodity or the labour market, regulates these relations. Thus the individual, primarily alone and self-sufficient, enters into economic relations with others as means to one end: to sell and to buy. Freud's concept of human relations is essentially the same: the individual appears fully equipped with biologically given drives, which need to be satisfied. In order to satisfy them, the individual enters into relations with other "objects." Other individuals thus are always a means to one's

end, the satisfaction of strivings which in themselves originate in the individual before he enters into contact with others. The field of human relations in Freud's sense is similar to the market—it is an exchange of satisfaction of biologically given needs, in which the relationship to the other individual is always a means to an end, but never an end in itself.[2]

*Psychological.* In general, the psychological frame of reference maintains that an individual's personality is a function of a set of responses to life based on past conditioning. The neurological factor is recognized as being important in terms of its impact on the temperament and intelligence of individuals, but the deep-rooted aspects of human behavior are attributed to an individual's interpretation of his early life experiences. The core of an individual's personality is asserted as being set in his infancy and early childhood based on attitudes which have been developed through the mediation of the family. These attitudes thus become structuralized into the individual and become the basis with which he will react toward other individuals under various circumstances during his life span. Such overt characteristics as timidness, outgoingness, cautiousness, aggressiveness, submissiveness, etc., that are observed in different people are maintained to be a function of differences in upbringing. This personality core is claimed to be very rigid in nature and extremely difficult, if not impossible, to change.

*Social and Cultural.* Cultural theory contends that the behavior of individuals is affected by the historically transmitted types of patterns of behavior which are learned by individuals but which are not derived directly from the individuals themselves or from the situations as such. This enculturalization process begins at birth, and as an individual grows and matures, he is equipped with language, customs, beliefs, etc., all of which condition the form and content of his behavior. Such a cultural environment is transmitted, shared, and internalized in the personalities of individuals

---

[2] Erich Fromm, *Escape From Freedom*, pp. 11-12, copyright 1941 by Erich Fromm. Reprinted by permission of *Holt, Rinehart and Winston, Inc.*, New York.

constituting various social systems. It is readily admitted by the culturalists that culture has its source from human beings, for without them there would be no culture, and furthermore, that the general character of culture is an expression of the biological properties of the human specie. But, when it comes to an explanation of any particular culture or to an explanation of the process of culture change in general, a consideration of the human organism is irrelevant. For example, Leslie White claims:

> We cannot explain the culture trait or process of enameling nails in terms of innate desire, will, or caprice. We can, however, explain the behavior of such an individual in terms of the culture that embraces him. The individual, the average, typical individual of a group, may be regarded as a constant so far as *human*, symbolic behavior is concerned.[3]

Such behavior patterns represent systems of ideas or beliefs, systems of expressive symbols, and systems of value orientation, all of which are being continually influenced by the attitudes and behavior of those individuals comprising various culture groups. Such social control tends to induce conformity to the norms of that group by operating on the individual's desire for social recognition and status. The striving for such status is claimed to be one of the dominant motives of human behavior.

A somewhat broader conceptual framework advanced by Lawrence Frank permits recognition of the many dimensions of human behavior as observed in the cultural-social environment.[4] Such a dimensional analysis focuses attention on the developmental processes of the individual organism in relation to other human beings within a cultural-social field. This approach treats the systematic relationships of human conduct as transactional processes occurring between and among persons. All the varied patterns, rituals, institutional prac-

---

[3] Leslie A. White, *The Science of Culture*, p. 165, copyright 1949 by Leslie A. White. Used by permission of *Farrar, Straus & Cudahy, Inc.*

[4] Lawrence K. Frank, "Social Systems and Culture," *Toward A Unified Theory of Human Behavior*, ed. Roy R. Grinker (New York: Basic Books, Inc., 1956), pp. 203-205.

tices and symbols of group life are viewed as different modes of communication in and through which each individual can approach, negotiate, and seek consummation. In this way, the economic, political, legal, and social patterns and transactions are viewed as prescribed modes of human behavior which each member of the group must utilize if he is to communicate with others. It does not look upon the various components of the cultural system as coercing the individual to always act in accordance with accepted beliefs as does the traditional cultural approach. Rather each individual is thought of as being a unique organism with idiosyncratic feelings constantly engaged in goal-seeking, purposive striving. Such an individual attempts to bring about the kinds of situations and relations in and through which he can pursue his goal and attain symbolic consummations. He relies upon socially sanctioned modes of communication or codes and translates his messages in such a way that they will be recognized, accepted, and responded to by the individual or group to whom they are addressed. The adequacy and effectiveness of modes of communication by the individual are governed by words as well as the use of more or less standardized ceremonies and rituals which have been established for the different transactional processes and by the complex patterns which are referred to as roles. These roles can be considered codified patterns for communication since each role serves to focus and guide the activities of the individual in such a way as to facilitate their recognition by others and to evoke from them a readiness to receive and respond. These roles serve not only to reduce the ambiguity of most human communications but they also serve to direct human activities into the recurrent patterns and regularities through which the social order is maintained. Each individual, then, exists as an organism in a geographical environment and is exposed to all the impacts to which an organism is subject in a natural setting, but he is also exposed to all the approaches from other individuals in his social-cultural environment. Culture, as viewed from this perspective, has a very intimate connection with communication. If an individual is to be understood, he has to observe the conventions of the language. This applies to all forms of symbolic communication. The boundaries of culture, then, exist in terms of those individuals who recognize the same norms. To some extent, the cultural elements of one society may be shared by individuals in another society. But, even though the same cultural elements are found in a plurality of societies, each of these social systems will be found to have a distinctive cultural basis which differentiates it from others.

## A Holistic Approach to Decision Making

A major contribution was made through the cooperative efforts of four psychologists, three sociologists, and two anthropologists who worked together at Harvard University for a period of time in an attempt to set up, clarify, and interrelate the theoretical and philosophical aspects of the various social science disciplines into one general theoretical framework.[5] The basic objective of these noted social scientists was to formulate a theory which would apply in principle to any process of human action relative to a given environment. The formulation of this general theory was based on a convergence of personality, economic theory, and the study of modern social structure. The basic assumption of the theory is that an actor strives to achieve goals, i.e., purposive behavior. In his goal-seeking, the actor is oriented to objects, and the orientation is assumed to be in three modes: cognitive, cathetic, and evaluative. These modes are the basic principles by which activity is conceptualized as action. Objects of orientation are assumed to be relevant in the situation because they afford alternative possibilities and impose limitations on the ways of gratifying the needs and achieving the goals of the actor. Orientation of action toward these objects hence entails selection. Since actors, objects, and modes of orientation (principles relating actors to objects) represent the basic conceptual material of personality, culture, and social sys-

---

[5] Talcott Parsons and Edward A. Shils (eds.), *Toward a General Theory of Action* (Cambridge, Massachusetts: Harvard University Press, 1954).

tems, the authors contend that it should be possible to provide a unified basis for the development of these latter three categories in terms of the basic conceptual material. A very complicated classification and cross-classification of modes, objects, and alternative possibilities of selection among them is developed which crosscuts and intermingles with the concepts of personality, culture, and social systems and allows the categorization of a variety of different kinds of action. The theory is all embracing, and the possibilities it has in providing the basic theoretical framework for a general theory of business decision making are favorable, provided one can give factual meaning to the categories of the theory in terms of operations, and provided one can derive from these categories relationships subject to empirical test.

## A Behavioral Model of Individual Business Decision Making

The descriptive nature of the behavioral facets of decision making that have been presented up to this point provide valuable insight concerning some of the factors as well as the process of individual decision making.

The purpose of this section is to present a schematic outline of business decision making. It incorporates many of the ideas presented in the preceding material as well as additional ones which seem particularly pertinent.

The outline which has been formulated to reveal the structural properties of this theoretical framework is organized among three sets of variables: (1) a dependent variable which represents the behavior that is to be identified and defined in terms of the ways an individual in business tends to respond to a given decision-making situation; (2) an independent variable which is the initiating cause of the individual's action; and (3) intervening variables which represent postulated explanatory entities that are functions of the independent variable as well as the dependent variable.

A relatively simple diagram was first constructed to assist in thinking through the basic factors and relationships as well as to aid in the preparation of a logical write-up of the structural properties. This diagram is shown in Figure 1.

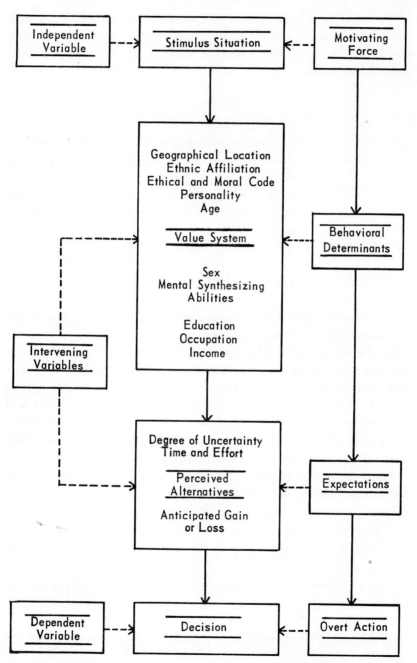

Figure 1:  Individual Business Decision-Making Diagram

After preparing the diagram, a conventional equation was written to describe the relationships of these variables to one another. The symbolic notation summarizing these relationships is as follows:

$$D = f_1 [S (V, P)] \qquad (1)$$
$$D = f_2 [V, P (S)] \qquad (2)$$

where: $D$ = the dependent variable, business decisions;

$S$ = an independent variable representing a given stimulus situation;

$V$ = an intervening variable representing the value system of the individual decision maker; and

$P$ = an intervening variable representing the perceived alternatives available to the decision maker.

It can be seen from these two equations that the relationships among these variables have been varied. The purpose of such variations would be to: (1) hold the value system and the associated perceptive aspects constant while the stimulus situation is varied to determine the nature of an individual's decisions in terms of varying stimulus situations, and (2) hold the stimulus situation constant to observe the effect of an individual's value system and his perceptive characteristics in a given decision-making situation.

A description of each of these variables (except for the dependent variable) is given below.

*Stimulus Situation.* The stimulus situation consists of physical, social, and cultural objects and processes that initiate the decision-making process. These environmental entities in business consist of various governmental, consumer, supplier, labor, and competitive actions that bring about a resultant readiness on the part of an individual, that is effected by one or more of them, to perceive and respond. The degree of readiness will depend on the intensity of the stimulus situation.

*Value System.* The manner in which an individual will react to a particular stimulus situation will depend on his beliefs and values. The elements comprising an individual's "value system" include such factors as his ethical and moral code, ethnic affiliation, geographical location, income, sex, personality, occupation, age, education, and mental synthesizing abilities. The value system is perhaps the most important force in conditioning the perceptions and resultant actions of an individual decision maker in business. However, it is not inconceivable to imagine that if a given stimulus situation is strong enough, it might override an individual's value system with regard to a particular decision-making situation. For example, if an individual in business is faced with a stimulus situation involving certain demands by an organized labor group in his employ, he may feel very hostile toward complying with their requests but is forced to do so because of the unfavorable consequences.

*Perceived Alternatives.* Once an individual in business is forced to make a decision as a consequence of some stimulus situation, he perceives in time and space various courses of action. All other things being equal, he will eliminate those which are not compatible with his beliefs and values. Those alternatives remaining will tend to be evaluated in terms of such factors as the degree of uncertainty, the anticipated gain and/or loss, and the time and effort associated with each. In most cases, the course of action that will be chosen will be that one which possesses the best combination of comprehension and positive reward and which involves a minimal amount of time and effort.

## Conclusions

The theoretical formulation that has just been presented provides a scheme for explaining observed behavior related to various decision-making situations in business. It is not intended, in its present state, to be interpreted as a predictive tool. It is designed merely to point out *why* differences in decision making should prevail and *what* elements or factors are felt responsible in affecting such behavior. However, it is felt that one of the major advantages of this formulation is that it provides a target for empirical investigation. That is, it permits the formulation and testing of hypotheses which specify the distinctive features of the variables specified in the model with respect to individuals of various types as well as varying decision-making situations. The results of such future empirical evidence, of course, will also determine whether or not the elements of the model and their structural relations provide accurate explanations of observed behavior. However, since the model is empirically oriented it can be modified and improved whenever empirical evidence necessitates such changes.

The weight of each variable will naturally vary among individuals of various sorts as well as under varying behavioral conditions. Therefore, individual predictability may not be possible. However, it may be possible to group individuals in business according to various similarities which they possess such as income, ethnic group, age, sex, occupation, etc., to determine what empirical regularities exist under various decision-making situations.

## BIBLIOGRAPHY

Alderson, Wroe. *Marketing Behavior and Executive Action.* Homewood, Ill.: Richard D. Irwin, Inc., 1957.

Ashby, Ross W. "The Effect of Experience on a Determinate Dynamic System." *Behavioral Science*, 1, 1 (January, 1956), pp. 35-42.

Barnett, H. G. *Innovation.* New York: McGraw-Hill Book Company, Inc., 1953.

Bayton, James A. "Motivation, Cognition, Learning—Basic Factors in Consumer Behavior," *Journal of Marketing*, XXII, 3 (January, 1958), pp. 282-289.

Benedict, Ruth. *Patterns of Culture.* New York: The New American Library of World Literature, Inc., 1934.

Brennan, Michael J. "Economics and the Theory of Social Systems," *The American Journal of Economics and Sociology*, 17, 2 (January, 1958), pp. 113-122.

Brown, J. A. C. *The Social Psychology of Industry*. Baltimore: Penquin Books, Ltd., 1954.

Campbell, Donald T. "Adaptive Behavior from Random Response," *Behavioral Science*, 1, 2 (April, 1956), pp. 105-110.

Dixon, Russell A., and E. Kingman Eberhart. *Economics and Cultural Change*. New York: McGraw-Hill Book Company, Inc., 1938.

Dodd, Stuart C. *Systematic Social Science*. Social Science Series No. 16. Beirut, Lebanon: American University of Beirut, 1947.

——————. "Conditions for Motivating Men: Comprehensive and Testable Models for Predicting Behavior," *Journal of Personality*, 25, 4 (June, 1957), pp. 489-504.

Frank, Lawrence K. "Social Systems and Culture," in *Toward a Unified Theory of Human Behavior*, Roy R. Grinker, ed. New York: Basic Books, Inc., 1956.

Fromm, Erich. *Escape from Freedom*. New York: Rinehart and Company, Inc., 1941.

Gerard, R. W., Clyde Kluckhohn, and Anatol Rapoport. "Biological and Cultural Evolution: Some Analogies and Explorations," *Behavioral Science*, 1, 1 (January, 1956), pp. 6-33.

Grinker, Roy R. (ed.). *Toward a Unified Theory of Human Behavior*. New York: Basic Books, Inc., 1956.

Haley, Bernard F. (ed.). *A Survey of Contemporary Economics*. Homewood, Ill.: Richard D. Irwin, Inc., 1952.

Harring, Douglas G. *Personal Character and Social Milieu*. Syracuse: Syracuse University Press, 1956.

Herbst, P. G. "Situation Dynamics and Theory of Behavior Systems," *Behavioral Science*, 2, 1 (January, 1957), pp. 13-29.

Herrick, C. Judson. *The Evolution of Human Nature*. Austin: University of Texas Press, 1956.

Hill, W. C. Osman. *Man As an Animal*. London: Hutchinson University Library, 1957.

Kluckhohn, Clyde. *Mirror for Man*. New York: Fawcett Publications, Inc., 1959.

Kochen, Manfred, and Marion J. Levy. "The Logical Nature of an Action Scheme," *Behavioral Science*, 1, 4 (October, 1956), pp. 265-289.

LaPiere, Richard T. *A Theory of Social Control*. New York: McGraw-Hill Book Company, Inc., 1954.

McCary, J. L. (ed.). *Psychology of Personality*. New York: Grove Press, Inc., 1956.

Meier, Richard L. "Communications and Social Change," *Behavioral Science*, 1, 1 (January, 1956), pp. 43-58.

Merrill, Francis E., and H. Wentworth Eldredge. *Culture and Society*. New York: Prentice-Hall, Inc., 1952.

Osgood, Charles E. "Behavior Theory and the Social Sciences," *Behavioral Science*, 1, 3 (July, 1956), pp. 167-185.

Parsons, Talcott, and Edward A. Shils (eds.). *Toward a General Theory of Action*. Cambridge: Harvard University Press, 1954.

——————, and Neil J. Smelser. *Economy and Society*. Glencoe, Ill.: The Free Press, 1956.

Simon, Herbert A. *Models of Man*. New York: John Wiley & Sons, Inc., 1957.

Tead, Ordway. "Toward the Knowledge of Man," *Yearbook of the Society for General Systems Research*, 3, (1958), pp. 248-259.

Wasserman, Paul, and Fred S. Silander. *Decision Making: An Annotated Bibliography*. Ithaca: Cornell University Press, 1958.

Weiner, Norbert. *The Human Use of Human Beings*. New York: Doubleday & Company, Inc., 1954.

White, Leslie A. *The Science of Culture*. New York: Farrar, Straus and Cudahy, Inc., 1949.

Yeager, L. B. "Measurement as Scientific Method in Economics," *The American Journal of Economics and Sociology*, 16, 4 (July, 1957), pp. 337-346.

# INDEX OF REFERENCES

# INDEX OF TOPICS

endpoint in, 75; matrices and relationship to linear, 77; mathematical numbers of points and lines, 79; path and length of path of, 73; planar, 86; root, 76; subgraph, 76; tree, 76; type of, 77; vertices, knots, or points, 71

Graph theory, 9, 70; an application of, 80; basic concepts of, 70; history of, 71

## H

Historico-cultural approach, 195

Hodology, 174

Homeostasis, in theory of the firm, 8, 28, 36, 44, 49

## I

Ideal level, 180

Idealism, 211, 213

Income equilibrium, 179

Inner-personal region, in topology, 175

Institutionalists, in economics, 191

Insurance, in dealing with risk, 110

## K

Keynesian view of probability, 107

Knowledge, as obstacle to progress, 171, 191

## L

Language, cultural anthropology and, 192; dilemmas of, 172; social norms, 193, 198

Law, ethics and, 211; of large numbers, 39, 103, 106, 110, 111

Leisure, as motive, 24

Life space, 175

Linear programming, 117; an application of, 118; characteristics of, 123; compared to marginal analysis, 125; effect of linearity,

124; limitations, 121, 123; simplicfications required in, 122; theorem, 120

Liquidity, as goal, 20

Locomotion, in field theory, 177

## M

Map, "gambler indifference," 113

Marginal analysis, 5, 10, 28, 117; compared with mathematical programming, 125

Marginal cost, defined, 5

Materialism, 211, 213, 215

Mathematical programming, 9, 117, 124; linear, 10, 117

Matrix, 77, 93; game, 136

Measurement of social space, 174

Morality, 12, 210; current theories of business and, 212; idealistic views of, 213; materialistic views of, 215; pragmatic views of, 216; religious approach, 217; social responsibility and, 214

Motivation, 152, 158; animal theories, 166; aspiration level concept, 163; business, types of, 18, 161, 165; complexity and multiplicity of, 162; control, 26; criticisms, 166; definition of "motive," 159; determination of, 179; effects of, 11; "inner," 159; liquidity, 20; nonprofit, 18, 42; "outer," 160; personal, 22; problems in ascertaining, 165; profit maximization, 158; role theory in relation to, 161

Motor perceptual region, in topology, 175

## N

Nonlinear programming, 127; see also Linear programming

Nonprofit motives, 18

Nonprofit organizations, 198

Nonsufficient reason, principle of, 105